Organizing the World's Money

THE POLITICAL ECONOMY OF
INTERNATIONAL RELATIONS SERIES
Edited by Benjamin J. Cohen

POWER AND WEALTH
The Political Economy of International Power
Klaus Knorr

THE CHARITY OF NATIONS
The Political Economy of Foreign Aid
David Wall

THE QUESTION OF IMPERIALISM
The Political Economy of Dominance and Dependence
Benjamin J. Cohen

U.S. POWER AND THE MULTINATIONAL CORPORATION
The Political Economy of Foreign Direct Investment
Robert G. Gilpin

INTERNATIONAL TRADE UNDER COMMUNISM:
POLITICS AND ECONOMICS
Franklyn D. Holzman

ORGANIZING THE WORLD'S MONEY
The Political Economy of International Monetary Relations
Benjamin J. Cohen

ORGANIZING THE WORLD'S MONEY *The Political Economy of International Monetary Relations*

BENJAMIN J. COHEN

Basic Books, Inc., Publishers   *New York*

Library of Congress Cataloging in Publication Data

Cohen, Benjamin J.
   Organizing the world's money.

   (The Political economy of international relations
series)
   Includes index.
   I. International finance.   II. Title.
HG3881.C587   332.4'5   77-75240
ISBN: 0-465-05327-0

For

the

MEATBALL

(A.K.A. Ch. C.V.R.)

Contents

PART I
The Analytical Groundwork

PART II

Alternative Organizing Principles

Acknowledgments

This book was written between June 1975 and August 1976, while I was on academic leave from the Fletcher School of Law and Diplomacy, Tufts University. Final revisions of the manuscript were completed in October 1976.

The book was written at the Atlantic Institute for International Affairs (Paris), at the invitation of the chairman of the Institute's Board of Governors, Jonkheer John H. Loudon, and the Institute's Director-General (now retired), Mr. John W. Tuthill. (The present Director-General is Dr. Martin Hillenbrand.) The Institute provided an exceptionally stimulating environment for reflection and writing. With a well-stocked specialized library, a congenial and supportive staff, and a location in close proximity to OECD headquarters in Paris, the Institute is highly conducive to productive research on international economic policy issues. I consider myself extraordinarily fortunate to have had the opportunity to spend fifteen months there.

Principal financial support for this book was provided by the Rockefeller Foundation, in the form of a generous fellowship under the Foundation's Program on Conflict in International Relations. The Atlantic Institute provided supplementary resources, including financial and logistical support for interview trips to Belgium, Germany, Greece, Italy, the Netherlands, Sweden, Turkey, the United Kingdom, and the United States. I am, of course, deeply grateful for the assistance of both organizations.

I am also deeply grateful to a number of colleagues and friends who offered me the benefit of their thoughtful comments and criticisms while this book was in preparation. These include Robert

Aliber, Vittorio Barattieri, Fabio Basagni, Victoria Chick, Marcello
de Cecco, Sven Grassman, John Karlik, Peter Kenen, Charles
Kindleberger, John Nash, Joseph Nye, Luigi Spaventa, John Spraos,
Susan Strange, Robert Triffin, Judith Trunzo, Pierre Uri, and John
Williamson. Needless to say, none of these individuals bears the
slightest responsibility for any errors or omissions remaining in the
book.

Finally, I wish to express my appreciation to four individuals
who played indispensable roles in the preparation of this book.
These are Fabio Basagni, research associate of the Atlantic Institute,
for his efficient and faithful assistance; Olivia Freeman, former li-
brarian of the Atlantic Institute, for her patient and resourceful support; Madeleine Mair, who typed the first draft of the manuscript;
and Cecily Barthelemy, who typed the final revisions. My special
thanks to them all.

B. J. C.

November 1976

Organizing the World's Money

Introduction

This book is about international monetary relations. Specifically, it is about the international monetary *order*—the framework of rules, regulations, conventions, and norms governing the foreign financial conduct of nations. The focus of the book is on the problem of how to *organize* the international monetary order.

Analytically, the international monetary *order* should be distinguished from the international monetary *system*.[1] A system is "an aggregation of diverse entities united by regular interaction according to some form of control."[2] In the context of international monetary relations, this definition applies to the aggregation of individuals, commercial and financial enterprises, and governmental agencies that are involved, either directly or indirectly, in the transfer of purchasing power between countries. The international monetary system exists because, like the levying of taxes and the raising of armies, the creation of money is widely acknowledged as one of the fundamental attributes of political sovereignty. Virtually every state issues its own currency; within the national frontiers, no currency but the local currency is generally accepted to serve the three traditional functions of money—medium of exchange, unit of account, and store of value. Consequently, across national frontiers some integrative mechanism must exist to facilitate interchanges between local money systems. That mechanism is the international monetary system.

The international monetary order, by contrast, is the legal and conventional framework within which this mechanism of interchange operates—the set of governing procedures to which the system is subject, either explicitly or implicitly. Control is exerted through policies implemented at the national level and interacting at the international level. Formally or informally, the monetary order specifies which instruments of national policy may be used and which targets of policy may be regarded as legitimate. It thereby establishes the setting of the monetary system and an understanding of that environment by all participants. As Robert Mundell says: "A monetary order is to a monetary system somewhat like a constitution is to a political or electoral system. We can think of the monetary system as the *modus operandi* of the monetary order."[3]

The argument for a well-organized international monetary order is essentially the same as that for a well-organized global economy. The ultimate raison d'être of both is to maximize the economic welfare benefits of foreign trade and investment (economic welfare being defined as the sum total of goods and services available for final use). An autarkic world would not need to worry about organizing its international monetary relations—there would not be any. But strategies of economic isolation have been rejected by all nations, even the very largest, as costly and self-defeating. No country is so well endowed in physical or human resources that it can afford to "go it alone" economically. All countries appreciate the enormous gains to be realized from even limited participation in the global economy: the availability of goods and services that either cannot be produced at home or can be produced only at relatively high cost; the access to foreign markets, capital, and investment opportunities; and the spread of technological and scientific knowledge. Without relations of trade and investment, nations would be unable to sustain a very high level of prosperity.[4] And without a well-organized international monetary order, nations would be unable to sustain a very high level of trade and investment.

The monetary order is fundamentally instrumental in nature. On its own, it does not add significantly to the welfare gains of the global economy. Rather, what it does is to enable other, more fundamental economic processes of production and distribution to operate smoothly and efficiently. As Robert Aliber has written, the monetary order is like a fine-tuning device on an automobile engine: "the device may enable the engine to operate at greater efficiency and produce more power, but it cannot cause a two-cycle, two-cylinder engine to become the equivalent of a V-8"[5] Harry Johnson was right when he said that "we are therefore discussing the marginal, and not the central, determinants of economic welfare."[6] But as Johnson himself went on to add, "the subject is no less interesting on that account."[7] For in this as in so many other instances, the margin can in fact be crucial to the whole. Even if a well-organized monetary order cannot add significantly to the world's welfare gains, a poorly organized monetary order can certainly subtract from them, by disrupting other economic activities. Adam Smith called the international monetary order the "Great Wheel." As Sidney Rolfe and James Burtle have written:

> As long as the wheel is turning effortlessly, the goods of the world can flow profitably, enriching and gratifying men and nations in the process. Like a well-ordered inheritance, it works quietly in the background, making possible the fuller economic life. . . . But when the wheel stops or goes awry, the consequences can be serious, even disastrous.[8]

In recent years, the Great Wheel clearly has not been turning effortlessly (see below, Chapters 3 and 4). During the 1960s the monetary order was in an almost continual state of flux. In August 1971 the Great Wheel almost stopped altogether. And since 1971 the rules and conventions that were called the "Bretton Woods system" have mostly passed into history. Moreover, although repeated efforts have been made to reform the structural framework of monetary relations— that is, to rewrite the rules and regulations governing the financial conduct of nations—the international community so far has failed to arrive at anything like a new constitution for the monetary system. As I suggest in Chapter 4, major outstanding issues of reform have been largely suppressed rather than resolved.

Why is it that monetary reform has proved so difficult to achieve? What are the obstacles, in practice and in principle, to putting the Great Wheel right again? And what organizing principles can properly ensure that, once it is put right again, the Wheel will continue to turn effortlessly in the future? These are the questions with which this book is concerned. The object of the book is to contribute to an understanding of both the potentialities and the limits of global monetary reform.

Few subjects have attracted as much attention recently among specialists in international relations as the problem of monetary reform. A list of scholarly publications on the subject written just since 1971 would easily run into the hundreds; a complete list of contributions since the Bretton Woods system first came into existence (1944) would require literally thousands of entries. The coverage of this literature has been extensive, touching on every conceivable issue of reform. Yet for all the intellectual energy expended in these efforts, most discussions have been seriously deficient in at least one fundamental respect. They have failed to integrate satisfactorily the economic and political aspects of the problem into a single analytical framework. With few exceptions, economists and political scientists have each relied on their separate disciplinary approaches to design parallel analyses of the same set of issues. In the words of Susan Strange: "It is as if the economist and the political scientist were standing back to back, and describing and analyzing the two systems—the international political system and the international economic and monetary system—as though each operated in a totally different and quite separate world, and not with the same cast of players at all."[9] The result has been a vain sort of dialogue of the deaf.[10]

Economists traditionally concern themselves almost exclusively with considerations of technical efficiency and economic welfare— that is, with the goal of maximizing production of goods and services for final use—and normally rely for the bulk of their analysis on the tools of the conventional "neoclassical" economic paradigm. The major strengths of the neoclassical paradigm are its high degree of refinement and its capacity for dealing effectively with causal relationships of a quantifiable kind. Its principal weaknesses are a bias toward mechanistic analysis and a tendency toward political naïveté. Political problems are treated superficially, without benefit of systematic theory or logical rigor. Political considerations are introduced merely as a constraint on economic activity, with the existing political structure or pattern of power relationships among states being taken more or less for granted. As has often been pointed out, the neo-classical paradigm is "better suited to comparative statics than to explaining social dynamics."[11] Orthodox economics is singularly unable to address questions concerning how rules or conventions are established or how they support or undermine different configurations of economic activity through time.

Such questions are the meat and drink of political scientists, for whom patterns or structures of interstate relations and the conscious use of resources to influence behavior have traditionally been fundamental concerns. But political scientists too have been deficient in their writings on international economic relations. Most go to the opposite extreme and underplay the importance of economic values in political processes. As Robert Keohane and Joseph Nye (themselves political scientists) have noted:

> Political scientists are even more guilty of disciplinary tunnel-vision. Most professional students of international politics know relatively little about international economics. Generally, like neophytes at three-dimensional tic-tac-toe, political analysts take formal cognizance of economic planes of power, but in fact succumb to the habit of playing the game on the familiar military-diplomatic plane.[12]

The truth of the matter, of course, is that both economics and politics are inextricably intermingled in international economic relations—particularly so in a problem like world monetary reform. "International monetary matters have always been and will continue to be a complex blend of economic and political considerations."[13] Therefore, both considerations must be combined into a single analytical framework if a genuinely complete understanding is to be gained of the potentialities and limits of reform. The approach must be one not merely of economics alone, or of political science, but rather one that integrates the two disciplines—the approach of *political economy*.

Political economy means a methodology. It is a way of evaluating problems of economic relations, either within or between states, that takes into account not only the traditional concerns of orthodox economic analysis (i.e., technical efficiency and economic welfare) but also those values most stressed by conventional political science (e.g., the distribution of economic welfare, prestige, autonomy of decision making, and power). Political economy is an integrated approach to the analysis of interactions between economic and political processes. That is the approach employed in this book.

In the pages that follow, interactions between economic and political processes in international monetary relations are explicitly examined. Economic and political values alike are assumed to play a role both in the establishment of an international monetary order and in its subsequent development. In game theory terms, international monetary relations are viewed informally as a mixed-motive game incorporating elements of both cooperation and competition. The element of cooperation stems from the common policy interest that all countries have in promoting the highest possible level of technical efficiency and economic welfare; the element of competition stems from the divergent policy interests that all countries have in influencing the distribution of economic welfare, political prestige, and the burden or privilege of decision making. Every international monetary order is therefore assumed to be partly consensual and partly conflictual. The problem of organizing the international monetary order is regarded as a problem of finding some structural framework of relations—some constitution for the monetary system— that will accommodate and balance these two elements. The structure must support some minimum level of economic efficiency; this may be called *efficiency objective*. It must also ensure some minimum degree of consistency among national policies; this may be called the *consistency objective*.

What organizing principles can properly satisfy both these objectives? At one extreme there is the alternative of *autarky*. A world with no international monetary relations would, by definition, avoid inconsistency of national policies. But such a regime may be rejected because, as already suggested, it would undoubtedly do so only at an intolerably high cost in terms of economic inefficiency. At the other extreme there is the alternative of *anarchy* (i.e., no rules or conventions at all)—what Richard Cooper calls a "free-for-all regime."[14]

Such a world conceivably could achieve a fairly high degree of efficiency through reliance on private market decisions. But such a regime may also be rejected, for it would undoubtedly do so only at an intolerably high cost in terms of policy inconsistency. As Cooper says:

> A free-for-all regime does not commend itself. It would allow large nations to exploit their power at the expense of smaller nations. It would give rise to attempts by individual nations to pursue objectives that were not consistent with one another (e.g., inconsistent aims with regard to a single exchange rate between two currencies), with resulting disorganization of markets. Even if things finally settled down, the pattern would very likely be far from optimal from the viewpoint of all the participants.[15]

Between these extremes only four possible organizing principles do in fact commend themselves. These are:

(1) *Automaticity*—a self-disciplining regime of rules and conventions binding for all nations.

(2) *Supranationality*—a regime founded on collective adherence to the decisions of some autonomous international organization.

(3) *Hegemony*—a regime organized around a single country with acknowledged responsibilities (and privileges) as leader.

(4) *Negotiation*—a regime of shared responsibility and decision-making.

Each of these four principles represents a theoretical limiting case in organizing monetary relations. Any international monetary order must be based on one of the four, or on some combination of them. Part II of this book is devoted to a detailed evaluation of alternative monetary orders based on one or more of these principles.

Part I lays the analytical groundwork for this evaluation by examining in greater detail the efficiency and consistency objectives, and by reviewing the modern history of international monetary relations and the major issues and actors in monetary relations today. These initial chapters provide the necessary analytical tools for the discussion in Part II.

Chapter 1 examines the efficiency objective. (Most of this material will be quite familiar to readers trained in international economics.) The chapter emphasizes that at the technical level there are really just two central issues in organizing any international monetary order. One concerns the mechanism for balance-of-payments adjustment, the other the mechanism for creating international liquidity. These two issues provide the practical focus for the discussion in subsequent chapters.

Chapter 2 concentrates on the consistency objective and examines the potential sources of policy conflict between states. The chapter illustrates how conflict can arise from either the mechanism of payments adjustment or the mechanism of liquidity creation. This in turn emphasizes the key role of power in international monetary relations.

Chapter 3 provides a brief review of the history of international monetary relations, with particular stress on the evolutionary changes that have occurred in the monetary order over the last century. The discussion demonstrates the close connection between economic and political processes in monetary relations, and shows how the two processes interact both in establishing rules and conventions for the monetary system and in reshaping the structural framework of relations through time.

Chapter 4 provides a brief review of the major issues and actors in international monetary relations today. The focal point of this survey is the series of efforts that have been made since 1971 to re-write the rules and regulations governing the financial conduct of nations. The chapter concludes that the monetary order at present more closely resembles a free-for-all regime than it does any of the four alternative organizing principles for international monetary relations.

These four alternative principles are evaluated in Chapters 5 through 8. The structures of each of the four chapters are quite similar. Each chapter first states the case for the pure principle under consideration and then outlines the main criticisms that may be made of the case. Analysis then turns to possible compromise arrangements based on an optimizing approach to the efficiency and consistency objectives. The discussion makes clear that while no one of the four principles is on its own a viable policy option, neither are they, when disaggregated, mutually exclusive. Compatible elements are found in each that in combination can provide an effective and efficacious reform package. Each principle is seen to contribute an ingredient essential to a well-organized monetary order.

Chapter 5 looks at the principle of automaticity and evaluates the case for either a reconstructed gold standard or a regime of absolutely flexible exchange rates. Comparative analysis demonstrates that neither case is very convincing. In practice, what is needed in this regard is some compromise between the two extremes that would achieve an optimal degree of exchange-rate flexibility. The preferred alternative, the chapter concludes, would be a regime of managed floating based on a "code of good conduct" fulfilling four key conditions. This would be one ingredient of a well-organized monetary order.

Chapter 6 looks at the principle of supranationality and evaluates the case for a world central bank. The analysis here suggests that what is needed is an optimal degree of supranationality in monetary affairs. This, the chapter concludes, could be achieved by preserving the International Monetary Fund in its central position in monetary affairs and by redefining its traditional functions of regulation, finance, and consultation. This would be a second ingredient of a well-organized monetary order.

Chapter 7 looks at the principle of hegemony and evaluates the case for a pure dollar standard. The analysis here suggests a need for an optimal degree of accommodation to asymmetry in international monetary relations. The chapter concludes that this calls for a multiple-reserve-currency standard featuring certain special currencies and based on its own "code of good conduct"—a third ingredient of a well-organized monetary order.

Chapter 8 looks at the principle of negotiation and evaluates the case for a monetary order based exclusively on an ad hoc process of multilateral bargaining. The analysis here suggests a need for optimization of the bargaining process along lines outlined in the chapter. This would be a fourth ingredient of a well-organized monetary order.

The four ingredients are then brought together in Chapter 9, which concludes the book with a brief summary of the main lines of argument of the previous chapters.

PART I

The Analytical Groundwork

Chapter 1

The Efficiency Objective

Efficiency concerns the effectiveness with which the world's resources are used to increase global economic welfare. In conventional economic theory, the concept of efficiency is normally regarded as having two broad, multivariate dimensions: a *macroeconomic* dimension, involving the overall level of employment of resources and the attainment of price stability; and a *microeconomic* dimension, involving the allocation of scarce resources among alternative ends in production and consumption. The structure of any international monetary order necessarily affects both of these dimensions. The purpose of this chapter is to examine the relationship between the monetary order and global economic efficiency.

Four Key Concepts

To begin with, we must take a brief look at four key economic concepts that are of particular importance to an understanding of this relationship. These are (1) money, (2) the foreign-exchange market, (3) the balance of payments, and (4) the process of payments adjustment.

Money

What is money? That is not so simple a question as might appear. In fact, money can only be defined in terms of the functions it performs—that is, by the needs it fulfils. As Sir Ralph Hawtrey once noted, "money is one of those concepts which, like a teaspoon or an umbrella, but unlike an earthquake or a buttercup, are definable primarily by the use or purpose which they serve."[1] Money is anything, regardless of its physical or legal characteristics, that customarily and principally performs certain functions.

Three such functions are usually specified, corresponding to the three basic needs served by money—the need for a *medium of exchange*, the need for a *unit of account*, and the need for a *store of value*. Most familiar is the first, the function of a medium of exchange, whereby goods and services are paid for and contractual obligations discharged. In performing this role the key attribute of money is general acceptability in the settlement of debt. The second function of money, that of a unit of account, is to provide a medium of information—a common denominator or *numeraire* in which goods and services may be valued and debts expressed. In performing this role, money is said to be a "standard of value" or "measure of value" in valuing goods and services and a "standard of deferred payment" in expressing debts. The third function of money, that of a store of value, is to provide a means of holding wealth.

The development of money was one of the most important steps in the evolution of human society, comparable, in the words of one writer, "with the domestication of animals, the cultivation of the land, and the harnessing of power."[2] Before money there was only barter, the archetypical economic transaction, which required an inverse double coincidence of wants in order for exchange to occur. The two parties to any transaction each had to desire what the other was prepared to offer. This was an obviously inefficient system of exchange, since large amounts of time had to be devoted to the necessary process of search and bargaining. Under even the most elemental circumstances, barter was unlikely to exhaust all opportunities for advantageous trade:

Bartering is costly in ways too numerous to discuss. Among others, bartering requires an expenditure of time and the use of specialized skills necessary for judging the commodities that are being exchanged. The more advanced the specialization in production and the more complex the economy, the costlier it will be to undertake all the transactions necessary to make any given good reach its ultimate user by using barter.[3]

The introduction of generalized exchange intermediaries cut the Gordian knot of barter by decomposing the single transaction of barter into separate transactions of sale and purchase, thereby obviating the need for a double coincidence of wants. This served to facilitate multilateral exchange; with costs of transactions reduced, exchange ratios could more efficiently equate the demand and supply of goods and services. Consequently, specialization in production was promoted and the advantages of economic division of labor became attainable—all because of the development of money.

The usefulness of money is inversely proportional to the number of currencies in circulation. The greater the number of currencies, the less is any single money able to perform efficiently as a lubricant to improve resource allocation and reduce transactions costs. Diseconomies remain because of the need for multiple price quotations (diminishing the information savings derived from money's role as unit of account) and for frequent currency conversions (diminishing the stability and predictability of purchasing power derived from money's roles as medium of exchange and store of value). In all national societies, there has been a clear historical tendency to limit the number of currencies, and eventually to standardize the domestic money system on just a single currency issued and managed by the national authorities. The result has been a minimization of total transactions costs within nation-states.

Between nation-states, however, costs of transactions remain relatively high, because the number of currencies remains high. Does this suggest that global efficiency would be maximized if the number of currencies in the world were minimized? Is this the optimal organizing principle for international monetary relations? Not necessarily. It is true that total transactions costs, other things being equal, could be minimized by standardizing on just a single global money. "On the basis of the criterion of maximizing the usefulness of money, we should have a single world currency."[4] But there are other criteria of judgment as well; economic efficiency, as I have indicated, is a multi-variate concept. And we shall soon see that the costs of a single world currency or its equivalent, taking full account of both the microeconomic and macroeconomic dimensions of efficiency, could easily outweigh the single microeconomic benefit of lower transactions costs. As Charles Kindleberger has written: "The case for international money is the general case for money. [But] it may well be that the costs of an international money are so great that the world cannot afford it."[5]

The Foreign-Exchange Market

I have said that the international monetary system exists because of the need for some integrative mechanism to facilitate interchanges between local money systems. In practical terms, this function is performed by the foreign-exchange market, which is the medium through which different national moneys are bought and sold. The basic role of the foreign-exchange market is to transfer purchasing power between countries—that is, to expedite exchanges between a local currency and foreign currencies ("foreign exchange").

The foreign-exchange market is not an organized exchange like a stock or commodity exchange. It has no centralized meeting place, nor is it limited to any one country. It is best thought of as a mechanism whereby buyers and sellers of foreign exchange are brought together. Essentially it consists of a number of banks actively engaged in the trading of currencies. The banks "make" the foreign-exchange market: each maintains an inventory of foreign currencies to which it adds or subtracts in the course of doing business with its regular customers. Clearings are effected through foreign-exchange brokers, who function as middlemen for the banks. The banks, in turn, function as currency wholesalers for foreign traders and investors in general, who are the ultimate participants in the market.[6]

The foreign-exchange market comes as close to the perfectly competitive model of conventional economic theory as any market can. The product is homogeneous, in that foreign currency purchased from one seller is the same as foreign currency purchased from another. Participants in the market have nearly perfect knowledge, since it is easy to obtain exchange-rate quotations from alternative sources in a short period of time. And there are large numbers of buyers and sellers.

As in any competitive market, therefore, the key question is one of price—the rate at which local money is bought and sold for foreign money (the "foreign-exchange rate" or "rate of exchange"). If the price of each national money were unalterably fixed in terms of every other national money, there would be no need at all for the foreign-exchange market. Despite the formal existence of separate national moneys, there would effectively be one single global currency. Traders and investors could use any national currency to value and settle debts and hold wealth. *Ex hypothesi*, there would be no difficulty at all in transferring purchasing power between countries. In practice, however, exchange rates are not unalterably fixed; foreign-exchange prices may either rise or fall for a variety of reasons. Hence, traders and investors cannot be indifferent to their choice of money for denominating or discharging obligations. Because of the risk of exchange-rate changes, difficulties may indeed arise in transferring purchasing power between countries, and a foreign-exchange market is therefore needed.

Broadly speaking, foreign-exchange rates are (again, as in any market) a function of demand and supply. In any given country, the demand for foreign exchange represents the sum of the demands of domestic importers, investors, and the like, all of whom must usually purchase foreign currencies in order to consummate their intended transactions abroad. Correspondingly, since foreign transactors must generally sell their own currencies for local currency in order to effect local payments, the supply of foreign exchange represents the sum of demands by foreigners for domestic goods, services, and assets. Demand and supply may be conceived in terms of schedules, relating effective demand and supply of foreign ex-

change at the current exchange rate and at alternative, hypothetical
rates. Like any other price, the price of foreign exchange is the
product of the interaction of the demand and supply schedules.

When demand and supply schedules intersect at the current price,
the foreign-exchange market is said to be in *equilibrium*: there is no
pressure on the exchange rate to change. If demand and supply always intersected at the current price, the market always being in
equilibrium, there would never be a risk of exchange-rate change,
and accordingly there would never be any difficulty in transferring
purchasing power between countries. Again, this would be the equivalent of one single global currency. Difficulties arise only when demand and supply do not intersect at the current price—that is, when
the foreign-exchange market is in *disequilibrium*. Then, either the
exchange rate must eventually be brought to a new equilibrium level,
or some alternative actions must be taken or tolerated to remove or
suppress the disequilibrium. Technically, the problem of organizing
international monetary relations is the task of designing rules and
conventions for dealing with situations of disequilibrium in the
foreign-exchange market. This is otherwise known as the problem of
balance-of-payments adjustment.

The Balance of Payments

The term "balance of payments" is an ambiguous one that can be
used either in an *ex post* sense (to describe events after the fact) or
in an *ex ante* sense (to describe potential or intended events). In its
ex post sense, the term refers to an *accounting balance*—a balance of
credits and debits. In its *ex ante* sense, it is used most often to refer
to a *market balance*—a balance of supply and demand.[7]

The *accounting balance of payments* is a systematic statistical
record of all economic transactions between the residents of a
country and the rest of the world. It is constructed according to the
principles of double-entry bookkeeping, every transaction being assumed to have two equal sides, a debit and a credit. Any transaction
giving rise to a receipt from the rest of the world, increasing net
claims on foreigners, is recorded as a credit. The receipt itself may
take the form of a rise in residents' foreign assets or balances of

foreign currencies, or it may take the form of a decline in foreign liabilities or foreign-owned balances of local currency. Whatever its form, the receipt is recorded as a debit. Conversely, any transaction giving rise to a payment to the rest of the world, increasing net liabilities to foreigners, is recorded in the accounting balance as a debit; the payment is recorded as a credit.

Debits and credits divide the accounting balance vertically. Horizontally, the balance is divided into two alternative categories, according to the broad nature of the transactions concerned and their relationship to the national economy. These categories are the *current account*, which comprises all transactions relating to the country's current national income and current expenditure; and the *capital account*, which comprises all transactions affecting the country's international investment position. *Current-account transactions* include imports and exports of goods (merchandise trade) and services ("invisibles"), as well as so-called unilateral transfers,[8] all of which give rise to or are a use of current national income. *Capital-account transactions* directly affect wealth and debt (hence national income) in future periods, but not national income produced or consumed currently. They include direct investments (transactions involving a permanent equity interest), long-term or short-term portfolio investments (transactions in financial assets and liabilities, including currency balances), and transactions in official reserve assets (governmental holdings of gold, convertible foreign currencies, and Special Drawing Rights, as well as net reserve positions in the International Monetary Fund).[9]

Apart from statistical discrepancies, the current account must always equal the capital account (with sign reversed), since the balance of payments is constructed as an accounting identity. With each transaction recorded twice, the sum total of debits and credits must be equal. The balance of payments must balance in an accounting sense. In an economic sense, this means that if increases in claims on foreigners are to exceed increases in liabilities to foreigners by any amount—that is, if the country is to be able to invest abroad— exports must be made to exceed imports.[10] There must be a credit on current account to match the debit on capital account. Conversely, a country may borrow abroad only to the extent that it can promote a net inward movement of real goods and services. For a net "financial" transfer to occur, a "real" transfer must occur.

How, then, do we measure "balance" or "imbalance" in the balance of payments? The fact that the balance of payments always balances in an accounting sense does not mean that a country never experiences payments difficulties. Quite the opposite. An overall payments balance requires equality not of the sum total of debits and credits but of certain categories of debits and credits. Surpluses and deficits are defined in terms of certain groupings of items that are segregated from the main body of the balance of payments in order to reflect net movements of financial assets and liabilities having a sufficient degree of liquidity to be regarded as means of international payment—that is, in order to reflect changes in the *net foreign liquidity* of a country.

To identify such changes, it is convenient once again to distinguish analytically between two types of transactions in the balance of payments: this time, between *autonomous transactions*, which are undertaken for their own sake, for the profit they entail or the satisfaction they yield; and *accommodating transactions*, which are not undertaken for their own sake, but rather have their source in other (autonomous) transactions elsewhere in the balance of payments. Autonomous transactions arise from the fundamental differences between countries in prices, incomes, interest rates, tastes, and so forth. Accommodating transactions are the residual money flows (including flows of official reserves) that occur to fill any gaps left by autonomous transactions.[11] Accommodating transactions reflect increases or decreases of the net foreign liquidity of a country. They are, therefore, the best measure of surplus or deficit in the balance of payments.

A deficit appears in the balance of payments when autonomous transactions requiring money payments exceed autonomous transactions involving money receipts. The deficit means that the country is losing net liquidity to others: it is running down its liquid foreign assets (including official reserve assets) and/or accumulating liquid foreign liabilities. Conversely, a surplus exists when autonomous money receipts exceed autonomous money payments.

It follows that surpluses and deficits could be easily identified if we could simply place all autonomous transactions inside the main body of the balance of payments ("above the line") and all accommodating transactions outside it ("below the line"). But the process of measuring "balance"—of drawing the "line"—is not nearly so simple. The empirical difficulties associated with it are enormous. There is no unique, "right" statistical measure of balance. There are only observed measures that more or less closely approximate the precise analytical distinction between autonomous and accommodating transactions.

Different countries use different measures of balance. Most may be classified into two broad categories that shade into one another. One category is the *basic balance*, which places only current-account transactions and long-term capital movements "above the line"; these are supposed to comprise the autonomous transactions that determine the basic course of the balance of payments. The other category is the *official settlements balance*, which places everything "above the line" but official reserve transactions; these, reflecting official intervention in the foreign-exchange market, are alone assumed to represent accommodating flows. Unfortunately, neither of these categories is free of defects; as approximations of the analytical distinction between autonomous and accommodating transactions, both are artificial constructs.[12] For this reason, the accounting balance of payments is, by itself, not really a sufficient information base for formulating and conducting governmental policy.

The accounting balance can be a rather powerful instrument for *ex post* description of events. But it is not a very strong instrument for *ex ante* analysis of events. Being essentially a classificatory device, the accounting balance can do little more than indicate, in an approximate fashion, the extent of balance or imbalance of past transactions. But what governments most need to know for policy purposes, and in as precise a fashion as possible, is the extent of balance or imbalance of present and future transactions—that is, the extent of equilibrium or disequilibrium of autonomous, *intended* transactions. For these purposes, the accounting balance is inconvenient and cumbersome. Of much more interest is the main alternative concept of the balance of payments—the market balance.

The *market balance of payments* can best be understood as a model of a given situation in the foreign-exchange market, characterized by the effective demand and supply of foreign exchange at the current exchange rate and at alternative, hypothetical rates. By definition, it is an *ex ante* concept, comparing autonomous spending and receipts given present and expected future incomes, prices, interest rates, tastes, and so forth. The market balance describes currently, as the accounting balance describes historically, the balance of autonomous international transactions.[13] In effect, it is the signal of current international payments equilibrium or disequilibrium.

We thus return to the interaction of demand and supply in the foreign-exchange market. In fact, the interaction of demand and supply in the foreign-exchange market is what the balance of payments is all about. When demand for foreign exchange is just equal to supply at a given exchange rate, the implication is that autonomous transactions requiring foreign money payments are just equal to autonomous transactions involving foreign money receipts. The balance of payments is in equilibrium, and no problem of adjustment arises. On the other hand, when demand and supply are not equal, the implication is that autonomous money payments and receipts must be out of line, and the balance of payments is in disequilibrium. At that point, a problem of adjustment arises. The essence of the problem of adjustment is to reconcile any such differences between autonomous demand and supply of foreign exchange at some rate of exchange.

The Process of Payments Adjustment

There are in principle two "pure" mechanisms of adjustment to a disequilibrium in the balance of payments. Assume an excess of demand over supply in the foreign-exchange market (an excess of autonomous money payments over money receipts). If the exchange rate is free to move (rates are "floating" or "flexible"), the price of foreign currencies will immediately be bid up and domestic money will decline in value. In the domestic economy, prices of tradable goods, services, and assets will rise relative to prices of nontradables, and the gap between autonomous demand and supply of foreign exchange will be closed by movements along the existing schedules to the point where they intersect. Alternatively, if the exchange rate is not free to move (rates are "fixed" or "pegged"), the deficit in the balance of payments gradually will reduce the net foreign liquidity of the country, siphoning off internal purchasing power as domestic money is sold for foreign currencies. The money will be withdrawn from circulation, and domestic incomes and prices will decline, eventually contracting the country's autonomous demand for foreign exchange and possibly also expanding the supply. The gap between the two schedules will be closed as both of them shift until they intersect at the prevailing rate of exchange.[14]

These two mechanisms of adjustment are both automatic. They describe how the private market will respond to a payments disequilibrium in the absence of overt official intervention (other than intervention to keep the exchange rate from moving). Income and price changes, generated either directly (when rates are fixed) or indirectly (via exchange-rate changes when rates are flexible), will compel a reallocation of resources,[15] leading to shifts in the volume and direction of current-account transactions and autonomous international investments. This is what distinguishes the adjustment process. Balance-of-payments adjustment may be defined as a *marginal reallocation of productive resources (and hence of exchanges of real goods, services, and investments) under the influence of changes of relative incomes, prices, and/or exchange rates*. The precise form that the process of adjustment will take, in any given situation, will depend on the policies formulated and carried out by national governments.

When confronted by a balance-of-payments disequilibrium, governments basically have two policy options. Either they may *finance* the disequilibrium or they may *adjust* to it. Financing implies that the authorities prefer to avoid any marginal reallocation of resources and exchanges. Instead, in the case of deficit (surplus), they seek to sell (buy) foreign exchange or to intervene in the financial and exchange markets to induce inward (outward) movements of private short-term capital. Financing also implies that the authorities are prepared to counteract ("sterilize") any impact of the consequent change of the country's net foreign liquidity on internal purchasing power by conducting domestic open-market operations in government securities or by adjusting private bank reserve requirements or liquidity ratios. Incomes and prices, the existing demand and supply schedules of foreign exchange, and the prevailing exchange rate are all meant to remain as before. The payments gap is to be closed simply by accommodating flows of public and/or private funds. Financing requires that governments have access to some kind of stockpile of internationally acceptable liquid assets. That is the reason why every national government traditionally holds a certain quantity of official monetary reserves. Finally, financing requires an adequately large pool of government securities for domestic open-market operations or sufficient latitude for adjusting private bank reserve requirements or liquidity ratios for the complementary policy of sterilization to be practicable.

Adjustment, by contrast, implies that the authorities are prepared to accept a marginal reallocation of resources and exchanges, either by actively reinforcing the automatic market response to a payments disequilibrium (or at least allowing that response to operate by reacting passively) or by promoting an alternative market response. Governments have a wide range of balance-of-payments adjustment policies at their disposal. In fact, their range of choice is virtually as wide as that for national economic policy in general, since nearly all instruments of national economic policy are capable of influencing the balance of payments in some degree, great or small. Payments adjustment policies may be classified under two headings, *expenditure-changing policies* and *expenditure-switching policies*, depending on whether they rely primarily on income changes or on price changes.

Expenditure-changing policies rely primarily on income changes, and aim to adjust to a deficit (surplus) by means of deflationary (expansionary) monetary and fiscal policies. *Monetary policy* involves the use of variations in the quantity of money to decrease or increase aggregate demand. *Fiscal policy* involves the use of taxation and expenditure policies by the government sector to decrease or increase aggregate demand. (Monetary and fiscal policy together often are designated as financial policy.) The objective of expenditure-changing policies is to reinforce, actively or passively, the automatic market response to payments disequilibrium when exchange rates are fixed.

Expenditure-switching policies, by contrast, rely primarily on price changes, and aim to adjust to a disequilibrium by altering not the level of aggregate demand but rather the allocation of total spending between tradable and nontradable goods, services, and assets. The objective is to alter the ratio of prices between tradables and nontradables. In case of deficit, for instance, the idea is to raise the relative price of tradables in order to induce a switch of expenditures by residents toward nontradables (thereby reducing imports and/or releasing tradable-goods production for export).[16]

One way to do this is by facilitating, actively or passively, a formal movement of the exchange rate, in order to reinforce the automatic market response when rates are flexible. The authorities may change the rate themselves, by devaluing (revaluing) the home currency in case of deficit (surplus); or they may simply allow the currency to depreciate (appreciate) on its own, in accord with market forces. Another way to do this is by introducing or removing restrictions (tariffs, quotas, etc.) or subsidies on current-account or capital-account transactions, in order to promote a preferred alternative to the automatic market response. And a third way to do it is by suspending the free market in foreign exchange and resorting instead to exchange control. With convertibility of the home currency into foreign currencies suspended, the authorities can ration foreign exchange to domestic residents under terms of their own choosing. In the short term, exchange control leaves incomes, prices, and the exchange rate unaffected. But over the longer term, rationing of foreign exchange inevitably causes expenditure switches, leading to shifts of resources and exchanges at the margin. Policies using restrictions, subsidies, and exchange control all induce payments adjustment through selective price changes: they are like an informal, partial movement of the exchange rate. A policy of formally moving the exchange rate differs in principle from these other expenditure-switching devices only in that the consequent change of relative prices is generalized to all goods, services, and assets.[17]

What determines a government's choice from among this wide array of policy options? When will a government choose to finance an external imbalance, and when it will adjust to it? When will it choose to use expenditure-changing policies, and when it will use expenditure-switching policies? At the technical level, these are precisely the questions with which the legal and conventional framework of international monetary relations is concerned. The efficiency of the monetary order will depend directly on how these questions are answered.

A Triad of Problems

The efficiency objective of the monetary order has of course been the traditional concern of economists. In their analytical discussions, economists have distinguished three separate (though interrelated) structural problems of international monetary relations: (1) adjustment, (2) liquidity, and (3) confidence.[18] Every international monetary order is challenged to find solutions to this crucial triad of problems, which together condition the financial conduct of nations. The adjustment problem is essentially concerned with the choices that governments make between alternative expenditure-changing and expenditure-switching policies. The liquidity and confidence problems are mainly concerned with the choices that governments make between adjustment and financing. The role of the international monetary order, as the constitution for the monetary system, is to develop rules and conventions to govern these policy choices.

The Adjustment Problem

The adjustment problem relates to the capacity of countries to maintain or restore equilibrium in their international payments. The essence of the problem is that every policy of adjustment generates economic costs; moreover, some adjustment policies (or combinations of policies) may be a good deal more costly to the world economy than others. The challenge to the monetary order, insofar as the efficiency objective is concerned, is to minimize these economic costs (in other words, to "optimize" the adjustment process).

Two different types of economic costs of adjustment may be distinguished—a "continuing" cost and a "transitional" cost.[19] The difference between the two is one of time. The continuing cost of adjustment is an open-ended phenomenon: the continuing real burden associated with the new international equilibrium prevailing after all change has occurred. The transitional cost of adjustment is a once-for-all phenomenon: the cost of the change itself, the temporary real burden associated with making the transition to the new international payments equilibrium.

The continuing cost of adjustment reflects the loss of the benefit of disequilibrium. It is not really an economic cost in the sense of a loss of global welfare; rather, it is an economic cost only to some countries, offset by equivalent gains to others. When a country is in deficit it is, in a sense, "living beyond its means." It is spending more for goods, services, and assets abroad than it can currently earn at prevailing price levels and exchange rates; in technical terms, its real domestic absorption is in excess of its real national output (national income).[20] This is the benefit of disequilibrium. Conversely, when a country is forced to eliminate its external deficit, it must somehow once again learn to live within its means. Normally, this requires that the country reduce its real domestic absorption relative to its current real income (though there may be important exceptions to this, as we shall see in Chapter 2). This is the continuing cost of adjustment.

The transitional cost of adjustment, by contrast, is a genuine economic cost. It reflects the loss of real global output that occurs during and on account of the process of payments adjustment. This cost, like the concept of efficiency itself, potentially has both a macroeconomic and a microeconomic dimension.

At the macroeconomic level, there may potentially be a decline in the overall level of employment of resources, and/or there may be an increase in the rate of price inflation. Idle resources are clearly a real burden in terms of production forgone; so too are accelerated price increases, insofar as they disrupt social expectations and thereby create incentives for diverting investment capital from normal productive channels into such speculative activities as transactions in real estate and on the stock and commodity exchanges. At the microeconomic level, there may potentially be a decline in the overall productivity of resources because of distortions introduced into the pattern of resource allocation. In addition, there will certainly be frictional costs of the sort that always occur whenever resources are reallocated. In the case of labor, these frictional "changeover" costs involve temporary unemployment between jobs and the costs of information gathering and decision making associated with adjusting to new economic realities (job search, relocation, retraining, etc.); analogous costs can be inferred for real capital as well. Frictional costs are genuine costs because by definition they divert available resources away from production for final use. Furthermore, if recent theoretical developments are correct in suggesting that economic welfare is a function not only of the level but also of the stability of earnings, there is an additional frictional cost insofar as resource reallocation temporarily adds to the instability of individual income streams.

Since the continuing cost of adjustment mainly involves the distribution of welfare gains from international economic activities, and not the overall level of those gains, this cost will not be further considered here (though we shall necessarily return to it in Chapter 2). In analyzing the global efficiency of the international adjustment process, our direct concern is with the transitional cost of adjustment. All of the policy options that are available to governments for adjusting to payments disequilibrium potentially may generate transitional costs. As indicated above, the challenge to the monetary order, insofar as the efficiency objective is concerned, is to minimize these costs by developing rules and conventions to indicate which policies (or combinations of policies) may or should be used, and when. The problem for the monetary order is that the costs of these alternative policies are neither certain nor easily predictable: they may be either great or small, depending on the circumstances. Optimal rules and conventions, therefore, are not easy to design. The challenge is a tough one.[21]

The cost of expenditure-changing policies, for example, will vary considerably depending on the state of the domestic economy. Expenditure-changing policies mainly generate costs at the macroeconomic level, since they rely primarily on income changes. These costs may be quite high if a payments deficit (surplus) happens to coincide with domestic unemployment (inflation); deflationary (expansionary) monetary and fiscal policies will then simply aggravate the domestic macroeconomic problem. Such conjunctures are called dilemma situations because governments cannot use financial policy to approach the targets of internal balance (full employment and reasonable price stability) and external balance simultaneously. Converse conditions (deficit coinciding with inflation, surplus with unemployment) are labeled nondilemma situations because governments then can use financial policy to approach both targets simultaneously. In such situations, expenditure-changing policies may actually reduce the level of unemployment or rate of price increase; in a sense, they may be said to generate *negative* costs (i.e., welfare gains rather than losses) at the macroeconomic level. Clearly, an efficient monetary order would not discourage the use of expenditure-changing policies in nondilemma situations. It would not, conversely, promote their use in dilemma situations.

The cost of selective switching devices too will vary considerably depending on existing economic relationships. Restrictions, subsidies, and exchange control mainly generate costs at the microeconomic level, since they rely on selective price changes that can distort the pattern of resource allocation.[22] Traditional economic theory assumed that these costs, in the form of reduced resource productivity, would necessarily be quite high. However, more recent theoretical developments tend to suggest that such selective distortions may actually improve economic welfare if they offset other distortions attributable to governmental or other interferences in the marketplace. These developments are summarized in what has become known as the theory of the second-best (or theory of distortions).[23] The general theorem for the second-best optimum states that if there is even a single distortion in the environment to prevent attainment of a global welfare maximum, then there is no longer any a priori presumption against the introduction of further distortions. Economic welfare should be maximized if no distortions at all are present (the first-best optimum). But in a second-best world, attainment of the second-best optimum may actually require that governments add to existing distortions in the environment. As Tibor Scitovsky has pointed out in this connection:

> In a world in which the flow of a large segment of international transactions is slowed by import duties and quantitative restrictions, it is by no means certain that the imposition of similar restraints also on the remaining segment would lower the efficiency of resource allocation.[24]

Like expenditure-changing policies, therefore, selective switching devices can actually generate welfare gains rather than losses. This will certainly be true if the theory of the second-best obtains in the particular situation; it will also be true if adjustment takes the form of removal of existing restrictions, subsidies, or exchange control by surplus countries when first-best conditions obtain. An efficient monetary order consequently would not altogether discourage the use of selective switching devices, though again their use would be promoted only in certain circumstances.

Finally, consider a policy of formally moving the exchange rate. In certain circumstances, a general price adjustment through the foreign-exchange market will be far less costly than either expenditure-changing policies or more selective switching devices. For instance, in dilemma situations a formal change of the exchange rate will enable the authorities to approach both internal and external balance simultaneously without aggravating the domestic macroeconomic problem: in case of deficit (surplus), a devaluation (revaluation) or depreciation (appreciation) will improve the balance of payments while also reducing domestic unemployment (inflation). Likewise, in situations where the theory of the second-best does not obtain, a general price adjustment would avoid introducing undesirable distortions into the pattern of global resource allocation. It is for these reasons that I suggested earlier that a single world currency (or its equivalent) would not necessarily be the optimal organizing principle for international monetary relations. Unalterably fixed exchange rates do reduce transactions costs to a minimum. But in circumstances such as these, that particular benefit may be far outweighed by the economic cost of inapposite adjustment policies. An efficient monetary order could not entirely forgo the advantages of exchange-rate flexibility.

But neither could an efficient monetary order rely exclusively on exchange-rate flexibility.[25] The economic cost of this option may also be quite high at times—for instance, in nondilemma situations where a downward (upward) movement of the exchange rate in case of deficit (surplus) will add to domestic inflation (unemployment). Furthermore, when exchange rates are free to move there is always the risk that their movements, at least temporarily, will be exaggerated (excessive amplitude or frequency) or even occasionally perverse (in the wrong direction). Any time an exchange rate moves, it creates an incentive for a marginal reallocation of resources; the more exchange rates move, the greater will be the reallocations that occur; and if many exchange-rate movements turn out in the end to have been exaggerated or perverse, many of the resource reallocations that were induced by them will turn out to have been unnecessary. Since every resource reallocation not only generates frictional changeover costs, but also adds to the temporary instability of individual income streams, the total transitional cost of adjustment incurred through relying on exchange-rate flexibility alone could turn out to be quite substantial.

In any event, it is well known that even if governments are able to *approach* both internal and external balance by means of a single adjustment policy, only rarely will they be able simultaneously to *achieve* both targets in this way. The general theory of economic policy teaches that for governments to achieve multiple independent targets with a variety of effective policy instruments, the number of instruments must be at least as large as the number of targets.[26] In our context, this means that the authorities responsible for domestic and international equilibrium must in general make use of at least two policy variables at all times.[27] Reliance on exchange-rate flexibility alone will not suffice; the system would be "underdetermined." Efficiency calls for varying combinations of policies to deal with different sorts of adjustment dilemmas.

The Liquidity Problem

Efficiency also calls for a certain quantity of official reserves in the system, to act as a kind of universal solvent in the adjustment process. Like money in the domestic economy (see above), reserves in the international economy perform as a lubricant to reduce economic costs. Not all payments disequilibria actually require real adjustment. Some simply call for financing by accommodating flows of public and/or private funds. And indeed, even in those cases where real adjustment is required, the availability of financing can potentially reduce the total cost of the adjustment process. A second challenge to the monetary order, therefore, is to ensure a supply (and rate of growth) of reserves that is optimal for financing purposes. This is the liquidity problem.

Official monetary reserves are held, as indicated earlier, because financing requires that governments have access to some kind of stockpile of internationally acceptable liquid assets. In principle, such a stockpile need not be fully owned by each individual country. National governments could simply rely on induced movements of private short-term capital or on conditional access to public external credit facilities to finance payments imbalances. In practice, however, such sources have always been regarded as inferior, mainly for political reasons (see Chapter 2). Governments traditionally prefer to put their faith in reserves that they themselves own. Reserves are generally defined to include total governmental holdings of gold, convertible foreign currencies, Special Drawing Rights, and net reserve positions in the International Monetary Fund. The common synonym for official reserves is *international liquidity*.[28]

Reserve assets play any or all of three different monetary roles. They may be used as a medium of intervention in the foreign-exchange market (the *intervention role*, corresponding to the medium-of-exchange function of money); as a common denominator for expressing currency values (the *numeraire role*, corresponding to the unit-of-account function of money); or as a means of holding wealth (the *reserve role*, corresponding to the store-of-value function of money).[29] Historically, few reserve assets have ever monopolized all three of these roles of international liquidity for any significant length of time. More generally, each role tends to be shared, to a greater or lesser extent, by a variety of reserve assets.

The importance of international liquidity in the monetary order is twofold: first, it determines the ability of governments to finance disequilibria rather than to adjust; and second, it affects the choices that are made between alternative policy options when real adjustment is undertaken. In both respects, liquidity influences the efficiency of the adjustment process. Indeed, in a real sense the problem of liquidity may simply be regarded as the other side of the coin labeled "problem of adjustment." The problem of liquidity is the task of designing rules and conventions to govern the supply (and rate of growth) of monetary reserves. Insofar as the efficiency objective is concerned, this is simply another way of describing the challenge to the monetary order to minimize total costs of adjustment in the event of payments disequilibria.

All payments disequilibria may be classified as either *stochastic* or *nonstochastic*. Stochastic disequilibria include reversible seasonal or cyclical variations of the balance of payments, as well as imbalances arising from simple random disturbances in the economic environment—that is, from such temporary and nonrepetitive upsets as natural catastrophes, civil disturbances, or "honest policy mistakes." (In technical terms, stochastic disturbances are said to have a long-run average value of zero.) Nonstochastic disequilibria are those arising from disturbances of a more lasting nature, such as persistent monetary inflation or deflation in individual countries (*monetary disturbances*), or permanent changes in demand and supply schedules for particular goods, services, and assets in the world economy (*structural disturbances*). (In technical terms, such disequilibria have a nonzero expected value.)

In cases of nonstochastic disequilibria, real adjustment is clearly called for. Financing in such circumstances merely postpones the inevitable—and worse, actually tends to increase the total cost of the real adjustments that will eventually be required. The longer a disequilibrium persists, the more it tends to distort patterns of capital investment in individual economies and, consequently, the more it tends to add to the stock of plant and equipment (and human capital invested in skills) that, becoming redundant, will ultimately have to be written off. Stochastic disequilibria, on the other hand, clearly do not require a reallocation of real resources. The gap between demand and supply in the foreign-exchange market is by definition temporary and nonrepetitive. To force real adjustment in such circumstances is to impose unnecessary transitional adjustment costs on the world economy. Global economic welfare will actually benefit to the extent that such disequilibria are handled simply by a policy of financing.

Where stochastic disequilibria are concerned, therefore, financing is a substitute for adjustment. This is the first of the two respects in which liquidity is important to the monetary order. If reserves are too scarce, countries will be compelled to adjust needlessly; by the same token, if reserves are too abundant, they will be tempted to postpone adjustment needlessly. Either way, adjustment costs will be greater than the minimum which constitutes the efficiency objective.

At the same time, as Peter Kenen has rightly stressed, for nonstochastic disequilibria "financing and adjustment should be considered as complements rather than rivals."[30] This is the second of the two respects in which liquidity is important to the monetary order. The ability to finance determines a government's effective range of choice among adjustment alternatives. Some adjustment policies work much more rapidly than others, and frequently a slower-working policy will be the preferred alternative on welfare grounds. A fast-working reaction to payments imbalance is not always the most efficient reaction. Yet it is impossible for governments to opt for a slower policy if their reserves are inadequate. Governments can choose from the full range of real adjustment policies only to the extent that sufficient international liquidity is available to them.

The optimal supply (and rate of growth) of reserves, therefore, may be defined as the one that ensures the most efficient mix of financing and adjustment in both of these respects—the one, in short, that optimizes the global adjustment process. Unhappily, there is no easy way to go about actually identifying such a reserve optimum.[31] Partly this is because of the uncertainty and unpredictability of adjustment costs already referred to. Partly, as well, it is due to the inherent practical difficulty of trying to distinguish between stochastic and nonstochastic disequilibria among real-world payments disturbances. Rules and conventions to deal with the liquidity problem are no easier to design than those for dealing with the adjustment problem. This is an equally tough challenge to the monetary order.

The Confidence Problem

The third major challenge to the monetary order relates to the composition of official reserves. This is the confidence problem. When several different kinds of international monetary assets co-exist simultaneously, there is always a possibility of destabilizing shifts among them. Not only can such shifts discourage a significant amount of autonomous trade and investment, but they may also detract from the efficiency of the adjustment process, by forcing governments to alter the optimal mix of financing and adjustment. The confidence problem refers to the need to design rules and conventions to cope with such international shifts of confidence or disturbing attempts to alter the composition of asset holdings.

Essentially, the structural instability inherent in the confidence problem is the same as that described by the old formula of Gresham's Law: "Bad money drives out good."[32] Given the simultaneous coexistence of two or more monetary assets in mutual price relationships that are not unalterably fixed, asset holders are continuously tempted to buy those assets that are most likely to rise in value, and to sell those whose prices are more likely to fall. In the context of international monetary relations, there are actually two aspects of this problem—an *official* confidence problem, arising from the use of several different kinds of assets in official monetary reserves; and a *private* confidence problem, arising from speculative shifts of funds by private individuals and institutions. In principle, however, any volume of speculative shifts by private investors, no matter how massive, can be compensated by counteracting shifts among central banks. So long as central banks are willing to "recycle" such funds, private liquid capital movements may disrupt individual markets but cannot threaten the stability of the monetary system as a whole. Consequently, it is really only with the official aspect of the confidence problem that we must be directly occupied here. Insofar as the efficiency objective of the monetary order is concerned, the challenge is to minimize the danger of destabilizing attempts by national governments to alter the composition of their official reserve holdings.

Broadly speaking, there are three alternative ways to cope with a Gresham's Law problem. One is to adjust the relative supplies of the several monetary assets to correspond to the asset preference of holders. The second is to adjust the asset preferences of holders by altering various attributes of the several assets (the most important of these attributes being interest income, convertibility risk, and exchange risk). The third is to reduce the total number of assets to a single-money system. Only the third is a foolproof solution; neither of the other two approaches can completely eliminate the practical risk of shifts of confidence among assets. Yet in modern international monetary relations there has never once been a system based entirely on a single reserve asset. This suggests that here too there is no easy way to design optimal rules and conventions.[33] The confidence problem also is a tough challenge to the monetary order.

Conclusions

It is obvious that the relationship between the monetary order and global economic efficiency is complex. Few clear-cut conclusions emerge from our discussion. We can see that total transactions costs in the international economy would be minimized by standardizing on a single world money. We can also see that the confidence problem would be resolved, in a world of multiple national moneys, by standardizing on a single asset for official reserves. But neither of these alternatives necessarily represents an optimal organizing principle for international monetary relations. A single world money (or its equivalent) would not necessarily maximize the efficiency of the payments adjustment process. A single official reserve asset would not necessarily ensure the most efficient mix of financing and adjustment. Rules and conventions to govern the financial conduct of nations, regrettably, cannot be designed quite so simply as that.

What does emerge clearly from the discussion is that, at the technical level, there are really just two central issues in organizing any international monetary order. One concerns the mechanism of balance-of-payments adjustment. The other concerns the mechanism for creating international liquidity (since it is obvious that arrangements concerning the supplies and attributes of separate reserve assets are really quite inseparable from structures determining the overall quantity and rate of growth of reserves). These two issues define the critical elements of the structural framework of monetary relations. They will provide the practical focus for the remainder of the discussion in this book.

Chapter 2

The Consistency Objective

The efficiency objective reflects the common policy interest that all countries have in promoting the highest possible level of global economic welfare. From this stems the strong element of cooperation that exists in international monetary relations. However, maximization of technical efficiency is not the only policy interest that countries have. Governments are also concerned to influence the *distribution* of economic welfare, both internationally and intranationally, as well as of national prestige and decision-making authority in monetary affairs. These concerns introduce a second element into international monetary relations—an element of competition—that can lead to serious policy conflict among governments if not subject to some form of control. The structure of the international monetary order must also ensure some minimum degree of consistency among the policies of nations. The purpose of this chapter is to examine the relationship between the monetary order and this element of competition in monetary relations.

The Role of the State

To begin with, we must take a closer look at the role of the state in international monetary relations. The operation and stability of the monetary order are profoundly affected by the existence and behavior of politically sovereign states.

The Importance of the State

The role of the state in international relations has of course been the traditional concern of political scientists. Economists, preoccupied with the efficiency objective, tend to downplay the importance of political sovereignty in their discussions. Indeed, in the dominant neoclassical paradigm of conventional economic theory, the state is not even taken seriously. Attention is principally focused on the competitive actions and reactions of large numbers of single, atomistic individuals and enterprises who, as it happens, can be classified into roughly homogeneous subgroups by their nationality. The state itself is given little significance beyond the fact that some of the participants in international trade and finance live and work there, obey its laws, and use its currency. Economics is the "only game in town," with political considerations intruding into the analysis only as a constraint on private behavior. Any *systemic* determinants or consequences of governmental action are either ignored or conveniently forgotten.

That such a de-emphasis of the state's importance is inappropriate should be manifest. Political sovereignty obviously plays an important role in world monetary affairs. As a former Managing Director of the IMF (who should know) has written, "there is no field where governments at present attach so much importance to sovereignty as the monetary field."[1] An eminent British economist has noted that "by ignoring the crucial intermediary position of States in the international relations of 'productive units' or other economic agents, the analysis has become characterized by a sort of monetary perfect competition, so that the reactions of these units to the policies of others can be disregarded. In fact, international monetary affairs are dominated by oligopoly between States . . . and by the sort of oligopolistic struggle that this may entail."[2]

The very existence of the international monetary system is attributable to the fact of political sovereignty; both the nature of the system and the control to which it is subject are clearly influenced by the pattern of interstate relationships. Governmental actions must be assumed to have both systemic determinants and consequences. In the words of Lawrence Krause and Joseph Nye: "An international economic order presupposes a political structure or pattern of relations among states. . . . [The state] must be considered endogenous in the model and cannot be assumed away."[3]

Why, then, is conventional economics so indifferent to the role of the state? Partly, of course, because of the traditions of disciplinary division of labor: politics is what political scientists worry about, not economists. But even more importantly, conventional economic theory just does not lend itself very easily to the analysis of governmental behavior.

Conventional economic theory always begins with the assumption of scarcity; the best things in life (Tin Pan Alley notwithstanding) are not all free. Choices therefore are necessary. The task for economic decision makers (assuming they are rational) is to do the best they can to maximize some value or other—or several values simultaneously—under the constraint of scarcity. Policy is viewed as a problem of "maximization under constraint," and attention is concentrated on three sets of interrelated variables: (1) *independent variables*, which are the instruments available to decision makers; (2) *dependent variables*, which are the targets of decision makers; and (3) *parameters*, which are the constraints on decision makers. For analytical purposes these three sets of variables are, implicitly or explicitly, combined together to form "models," in which the dependent variables are assumed to be functionally related to the independent variables, and the nature of each functional relationship (in mathematical terms, the magnitude and sign of each partial derivative) is assumed to be determined by the parametric constraints. For any given problem, specification of a model (implicit or explicit) enables the economist to analyze how available instruments may be used, subject to the constraints imposed by objective circumstances, to maximize a certain target. When the model incorporates multiple targets the problem becomes one of joint maximization of values, with analysis focusing on the "trade-offs" at the margin among the several targets.

This mode of analysis has always lent itself quite readily to explanation and prediction of the behavior of private economic units. Economic theory speaks of the producing enterprise, for example, rationally maximizing the target of profit by making use of the instruments at its disposal—principally, its price and quantity of output—subject to such constraints as input costs, demand for output, and the prices of related goods. Or theory speaks of the consuming individual, rationally maximizing the target of personal utility by varying purchases subject to the constraints of income and tastes. Analysis of this sort has proved to be both highly relevant and rich in practical insights. It is also relatively straightforward: first, because in dealing with private economic units, discussion can usually proceed in terms of a single dependent variable; and second, because the specified targets of private economic units can normally, though not always, be quantified.

On the other hand, when it comes to explanation and prediction of the behavior of public (i.e., governmental) economic units, analysis of this sort becomes a great deal more complex. In the first place, governmental decision makers usually have multiple rather than single policy targets. Specifically, political variables enter alongside economic variables as separate and independent objectives of action, which means that public economic policy must be viewed realistically as a problem of *joint* maximization, with much of the focus of analysis thus being trained directly on the marginal trade-offs among values. Furthermore, since political variables cannot usually be easily quantified, analysis also must necessarily be rather more qualitative than quantitative in nature. And the problem becomes even more complex when we move from domestic economic policymaking to external economic policy, where foreign political targets must be added to the already crowded array of economic and domestic political variables.

For these reasons, conventional economics has usually tended to eschew "positive" (i.e., descriptive or predictive) analysis of governmental behavior in such arenas as the international monetary system. Consideration of the role of the state has instead been largely limited to "normative" (i.e., prescriptive) judgments of public economic policy (the sole standard of judgment being economic welfare). The state is acknowledged to be capable of manipulating the parametric constraints on private decision makers; indeed, that is what the theory of economic policy is all about (see Chapter 1). But at the same time, two key assumptions about governmental behavior are implicitly or explicitly made: (1) state action cannot be explained or predicted by the structure or operation of the economic system; and (2) state action cannot fundamentally alter the structure or operation of the economic system. In other words, the state is entirely exogenous rather than endogenous to the economic system, and the existing pattern of interstate relationships may be taken simply as a datum. The advantage of these two key assumptions is that they enormously simplify the task of technical economic analysis. The disadvantage, as should be obvious, is that they also tend to distort and misrepresent reality. As Robert Keohane and Joseph Nye have written: "The problem with this has been that often the economists have not addressed the political questions, or recognized that the processes they studied were fundamentally affected by the political framework."[4]

The State as Actor

In political science, the state has always been regarded as an endogenous and purposive actor in world affairs. The state is a social collectivity organized within a particular constitutional order prevailing over some specific geographical terrain. In a world of innumerable and overlapping organizations, these communities are the focal point of political power. All of them claim the right to exercise complete sovereignty over their own internal affairs. This is their most fundamental and enduring characteristic. Consequently, no one of them can exercise anything even approximating complete sovereignty except within its own borders. The most a state can hope to do is *influence* its external environment, using whatever instruments are at the command of its national government. All such actions intended to affect situations beyond the national jurisdiction represent together the foreign policies of the state. It is in this sense of governmental foreign policy that the state is spoken of as an actor.

Two caveats, however, are in order. First, in speaking of state action in this sense, I do not mean to imply that the state is a *unitary* actor. Much of international political theory, unfortunately, has traditionally tended to regard the state in this way.[5] Governmental foreign policy has been treated as if it were the reasoned, coherent product of farsighted and creative leadership—concerted, purposive action arising out of a rational perception of the fundamental interests of the state. In fact, nothing could be further from reality; the political processes out of which external policies normally spring are just not that simple. The state is not the proverbial "black box" but a complex social collectivity, a society of groups of all kinds, many with extensive foreign as well as domestic interests, and each with its provisional conception of the overall national interest related ideologically to its own special interest. To the extent that interests are institutionalized, particular interests express themselves with political power, and out of governmental processes of tension and conflict the foreign policies of the state emerge—a consensus of purposes and actions that are essentially the end products of a system of domestic power relationships.

One interesting implication of this system of domestic power relationships is that foreign policies of states are almost certain to serve the interests of the world community less well than they do those of the national community. It is an inherent tendency of any collectivity of diverse interests to reconcile conflicts among their separate ambitions, as much as possible, at the expense of outsiders. Foreigners don't vote, after all—but citizens do. We shall soon see that this fact has much significance for our discussion of the consistency objective in international monetary relations.

Among political scientists, Marxist and radical theorists have always shown the keenest awareness of the domestic background of foreign policy. Indeed, the very idea is inherent in the traditional

Marxist theory of class, which takes for granted that the purposes and actions of the state abroad will reflect directly the system of power relationships at home. The only difference is that in the Marxist scheme of things the power system is monopolized by a monolithic capitalist class, with the result that foreign policy equates the conception of overall national interest with the particular interest of the bourgeoisie. The weaknesses of this extreme view are well known.[6] In advanced capitalist countries at least, political rule in practice has been a good deal more pluralistic than the traditional theory of class would have us believe. Governmental processes have operated to reconcile the conflicting interests of all groups with bargaining power within the system. Consequently, state action abroad usually turns out to be far less monolithic than Marxists and radicals generally allege.[7] Often, in fact, state action abroad seems to be random, haphazard, or even irrational. Foreign policy frequently takes the form of uneasy compromise as a result of deadlocked domestic judgments. At times, governments may even adopt no policy at all; instead, owing to indecision or unwillingness or inability to act, they merely drift with the force of events. Such outcomes, which are certainly quite distant from any simple, naïve image of the state as a rational unitary actor, can only be explained in terms of the dynamics and complexities of domestic power relationships.[8]

The second caveat in speaking of state action is that states are not the *only* actors in international relations. Unfortunately, much of international political theory has traditionally tended to regard the state in this way; as late as 1972, two political scientists could write that "a state-centric view of world affairs prevails."[9] But this view, too, is very far from reality; world affairs are really much more complex than the state-centric paradigm of traditional political science implies. This is precisely where the value of the neoclassical paradigm of conventional economic theory may be most appreciated. Private individuals, enterprises, and other nongovernmental organizations also engage in international relations, and these are clearly not all the same thing even when they are all part of the same state. Interactions across state boundaries involving nongovernmental actors are characterized in political science as *transnational relations*. As some younger political scientists have recently emphasized, the importance of transnational relations in such arenas as the international monetary system should not be underemphasized:

> Outcomes in an issue-area such as international monetary policy, for instance, cannot be understood solely as the result of state action and interaction: the behavior of multinational enterprises and multinational banks, as well as the activities of international civil servants and the effects on national policies of institutionalized forums for discussion, must also be taken into account.[10]

However, neither should the importance of such behavior be overemphasized. Analysts could be tempted to focus on nongovernmental actors alone, treating state action simply as an exogenous constraint. But that would just replicate the error of conventional economic theory. The point is that governments and nongovernmental actors alike must be included in a truly comprehensive analysis: both must be treated as endogenous, and the significance of both must be stressed. If in discussing the international monetary order we speak most of state action, it is only because the legal and conventional framework of monetary relations is most directly concerned with governmental behavior. But in considering alternative organizing principles for the world monetary order, the systemic determinants and consequences of nongovernmental action can hardly be ignored or forgotten. The state must be treated as an actor in monetary affairs—but by no means as the only actor.

The Risk of Policy Conflict

As actors in world monetary affairs, states almost inevitably find themselves involved, to some degree, in policy conflict. Richard Cooper has identified five separate potential sources of disagreement among states on international monetary issues: (1) different preferences concerning the distributional implications of alternative policy decisions; (2) different weights attached to alternative policy targets when compromises (trade-offs) must be made among values; (3) different national economic circumstances, even when policy preferences are similar; (4) disagreement over the practical effectiveness of alternative instruments to achieve agreed policy objectives; and (5) uncertainty about the trustworthiness of other states.[11]

Of these five problems, three—the second, fourth, and fifth—involve considerations that are really much more subjective than objective. Agreements on the different weights to attach to alternative policy targets, for instance, involve explicit *value judgments* regarding necessary trade-offs at the margin (e.g., between employment and efficiency when a country's balance of payments is in deficit). Honest men may honestly disagree on the most desirable lines of compromise when a multiplicity of goals exists. Likewise, agreements on the best means to achieve commonly accepted objectives require explicit technical judgments of the effectiveness of alternative instruments with respect to these ends (e.g., the effectiveness of alternative expenditure-changing or expenditure-switching devices to influence trade and payments flows). Usually, even technicians themselves are unsure about the precise nature of the functional relationships between dependent and independent variables; as indicated in the previous chapter, these relationships are neither certain nor easily predictable. And as for the trustworthiness of other states, this clearly demands explicit *political judgments* which may vary from individual to individual. Who can be absolutely certain how various governments will behave under different circumstances, and how faithfully they will tend to honor their international commitments?

The remaining two potential sources of conflict listed by Cooper—the first and third—involve more objective considerations. Alternative policy decisions generate varying distributions of gains and losses both between countries and within countries. States can clearly disagree on what should be the proper allocation of values; and these disagreements in turn will certainly be influenced by the different environmental circumstances of each individual country. As Cooper writes:

> A small, high-income country may be highly dependent on foreign trade for its welfare and hence be reluctant to sanction any measures that restrict trade.... A large, relatively closed economy, in contrast, will desire to maintain the maximum freedom of domestic monetary management and thus will oppose a system that restrains its freedom on domestic economic policy.[12]

In fact, although Cooper does not explicitly acknowledge this, these two problems really collapse into just one—the problem of how to parcel out the benefits and costs of maintaining order in international monetary relations (when one of the determinants of the allocation of values is the existing variance of national economic circumstances). This problem of distribution is undoubtedly the most fundamental source of controversy in world monetary affairs.

The problem of distribution is by no means easy to resolve. Although all states have a common interest in maintaining order in international monetary relations, they also are inclined, like most individuals, to prefer more of all values to less. Consequently, they are all prepared, at times, to contest the allocation of values even at the risk of reducing the sum total of values to be allocated. In the language of the economic theory of public goods, states are prepared to sacrifice the public good (international order) for the sake of the private good (national distributive share). The theory of collective goods teaches that, in practice, there is an almost inevitable tendency toward underproduction of public goods because of this potential for controversy regarding the allocation of values. This is as true in domestic economic relations as it is in international economic relations.

In international economic relations, the problem is further complicated by the fact that among the values to be allocated are noneconomic as well as economic objectives. This means that even with respect to the problem of distribution there are some subjective considerations. The economic objective of course is welfare. This value is normally assumed to be objectively measurable. The noneconomic objectives include, at a minimum, the two key values of *prestige* and *autonomy*. Prestige refers to a state's political status in the international community; autonomy refers to the degree of external constraint in governmental decision making. Both derive directly from the fact of political sovereignty; each has traditionally been regarded by political scientists as having importance in the policies of individual states. Neither value, however, can be easily quantified. As a result, conflict over the problem of distribution in an issue-area such as international monetary relations almost inevitably erupts, to some degree, and can have serious consequences for the operation and

stability of the monetary order. Not only are states likely to be confronted with larger and more frequent external disturbances than if
they were all agreed on distributional issues, but more crucially, they
may all find themselves worse off in absolute terms than they need be.

The problem may be characterized in game-theoretic terms. The
theory of games was originally created by mathematician John von
Neumann and economist Oskar Morgenstern to provide a new approach to analysis of economic problems.[13] Relations within an
economic system can be viewed as a sort of "game"—a strategical,
competitive interaction between two or more "players." The behavior (strategy) of each player is based upon an expectation concerning the behavior (strategy) of all the others, with the final outcome ultimately determined by the actions of all the players taken
together. Some games are "zero-sum"; that is, the sum of winnings is
always zero (a loss being a negative win). What one player gains is
what another player loses. In such games the interests of the players
are diametrically opposed and utterly irreconcilable. Other games are
"nonzero-sum" ("general games"). The sum of winnings may be
greater than (or less than) zero, and all players may gain (or lose)
simultaneously, though not necessarily always in the same proportions. In such games the interests of the players are neither completely
irreconcilable nor entirely harmonious. Such games are characterized, simultaneously, by elements of both competition and cooperation, conflict and consent, and the players' motives are inevitably
mixed. As von Neumann and Morgenstern put it, "the advantage of
one group of players need not be synonymous with the disadvantage
of the others. In such a game moves—or rather changes in strategy—
may exist which are advantageous to both groups."[14]

International monetary relations are a clear example of a mixed-
motive, nonzero-sum game.[15] States share certain interests in common even as they compete against each other. Their principal common
interest is that the sum of winnings should turn out to be positive
rather than negative—in other words, that the pie (the welfare benefits of the monetary order) should, in absolute terms, be as large as
possible. What they compete over is the question of relative shares:
how the welfare pie will be sliced and how national prestige and

decision-making authority will be distributed. The crucial danger is that the competition over the question of relative shares can become so severe that it reduces the size of the pie for all. It is a basic tenet of game theory (characterized as the "prisoner's dilemma") that in many nonzero-sum games a competitive outcome may well turn out to be inferior for all players as compared with some cooperative solution. As Krause and Nye have noted:

> There are two dimensions . . . joint gain and the distribution of gain. The joint gain may be reaped almost entirely by one party, or it may be shared more evenly between the parties. Where there is strong disagreement over distribution, the ensuing conflict can sometimes destroy the potential for joint gain, leaving one or both parties worse off.[16]

In game-theoretic terms a mixed-motive, nonzero-sum game may be described by a so-called "payoff matrix" specifying the net winnings of each player arising from alternative choices of strategy. Consider, for example, two states (*A* and *B*) choosing between two alternative policy decisions (*I* and *II*), as shown in Figure 2-1. Each of the four cells of the payoff matrix represents a choice of policy by each state; the two numbers in each cell represent the hypothetical

FIGURE 2-1
Hypothetical Payoffs for Two Alternative Policy Decisions

A \ B	I	II
I	3 *(B)* 3 *(A)*	2 *(B)* 6 *(A)*
II	6 *(B)* 2 *(A)*	4 *(B)* 8 *(A)*

net gain ("payoff") for each state, defined arbitrarily to include net gains of prestige and autonomy as well as welfare. (For example, the northeast cell represents the choice of policy *I* by state *A* and policy *II* by state *B*, with *A* gaining 6 and *B* gaining 2.) As the payoff matrix is constructed, joint gain is maximized when both states choose policy *II* (the southeast cell). Two-thirds of the joint gain, however, will then be reaped by state *A* alone. Consequently, state *B* may well prefer to shift to policy *I* (the southwest cell), in order to carve out a greater slice of the collective pie for itself. But then state *A* may well prefer to shift to policy *I* as well, in order to recover a piece of the pie. Eventually the two are likely to find themselves in the northwest cell, sharing the joint gain evenly. However, as a result of their conflict, both will unfortunately be worse off than before in absolute terms, and the size of their collective pie will be reduced by half.

Other outcomes, of course, are also possible, depending *inter alia* on the payoffs associated with alternative policy decisions and on the severity of the competition for shares. In principle, negative-sum outcomes can always be avoided if states are prepared to cooperate and are sufficiently well informed about the net rewards implied by different choices of strategy. In practice, however, a formal quantitative application of game theory to international monetary relations is virtually impossible, since there is no known way to construct the necessary payoff matrix. Such a matrix would have to allow for the very large number of possible alternative policy decisions in international monetary relations, as well as for the very large number of countries that are involved. It would also have to allow for the divergent interests of nongovernmental actors, which may form coalitions and alliances across state boundaries; and for the uncertainties in payoffs owing to the several subjective considerations that have been mentioned (the necessary value, technical, and political judgments, and the nonquantifiable prestige and autonomy objectives). As Cooper argues, "in the present state of knowledge, it simply cannot be done."[17] This does not mean that game theory offers no useful insight into the problem of organizing international monetary relations. Quite the opposite. It means only that the analysis must necessarily remain of a more informal and qualitative sort.

In fact, the insight of game theory is extremely useful to a discussion of the international monetary order. It highlights the element of competition in monetary relations that tends to be obscured by analyses focusing exclusively on efficiency and welfare considerations. The risk of policy conflict is high, because how the welfare pie is sliced and how national prestige and decision-making authority are distributed matter at least as much to governments as the absolute size of the pie. Game theory clearly demonstrates the serious implication of this risk: the danger that if governments are sufficiently dissatisfied about the distribution of benefits in the system, they may act in such a way as to destroy completely all the potential for joint gain.

Power in International Monetary Relations

The insight of game theory is also useful in one other respect: it highlights as well the key role of *power* in international monetary relations. In any game situation a crucial requirement is a rational strategy for behavior. Each player must develop a strategy based on his perception of his own bargaining strength within the overall system of interrelationships, since the outcome of the game as a whole (the size of the welfare pie, as well as the question of shares) will ultimately be determined by the relative bargaining strength of all the players taken together—in other words, by their relative power. Power sets the limits to the individual player's choice of strategy. Where the risk of conflict is high, all players have an incentive to accumulate power to the extent possible, in order to maximize their range of available strategies.[18] This is as true in international monetary relations as it is in any other game situation.

Political scientists have long acknowledged "the innate tendencies of virtually all states to try to use their power to seize an increased share of the benefits of any order."[19] Among economists, however, the role of power in international monetary relations, like all other aspects of state action, has long been neglected.[20] This is largely because of the singular difficulty of defining precisely what is meant by the concept of state power.[21]

In the abstract, state power may be defined as the ability to control, or at least influence, the behavior of others or the outcome of events. This ability need not actually be exercised; it need only be acknowledged by others to be effective. It also need not be exercised with conscious intent; the behavior of others or the outcome of events can be controlled or influenced simply as a by-product of "powerful" acts (or potential acts). State power derives from the entire range of a country's resources, and in particular from those resources that have been or could be placed at the disposal of the national government. Foremost among these resources, of course, is the military establishment: the organizational and physical entity that wages war. But state power is more than just "forces in being." It is a function of all of the country's other resources as well—its industries, population, geographic location and terrain, natural resources, scientific, managerial, financial, and diplomatic skills, and so on. In addition, it is a function of the resources available to the country's principal rivals, for power is potent only insofar as it balances or outweighs power elsewhere. What truly matters is not so much influence in absolute terms as influence in relation to that of others.

Taking all these resources into account necessarily means that state power must remain an imprecise concept. With such diverse sources, power can hardly be analyzed as if it were a simple, homogeneous phenomenon, and no one has yet been able to develop satisfactory criteria for measuring its various components and ranking them. Nevertheless, the concept is obviously relevant to state action and can hardly be ignored. Each state must—and in practice does—form an approximate idea of its own power and that of its principal rivals. Even though the risk of miscalculation is considerable, such estimates are indispensable. They are the necessary raw material from which the choice of policy strategy is fashioned.

One way to bring some degree of unity to the analysis of state power is, as Keohane and Nye have suggested, "to regard power as deriving from patterns of asymmetrical interdependence between actors in the issue-areas in which they are involved with one another."[22] States are mutually involved in all sorts of issue-areas, economic and otherwise. The international system, indeed, is a vast network of interrelationships in which, to a greater or lesser extent, every state is dependent on all the others. Asymmetrical interdependence in any given issue-area gives less dependent states the ability manipulate the relationship as a source of power, either within the issue-area itself or in some other issue-area. The power consists of the state's control or influence over that for which others are dependent on it. As Albert Hirschman wrote nearly a third of a century ago, "the power to interrupt . . . relations with any country, considered as an attribute of national sovereignty, is the root cause of the influence or power position which a country acquires in other countries."[23]

Keohane and Nye suggest that interdependence between states has two important dimensions: *sensitivity* and *vulnerability*.[24] Sensitivity interdependence involves the responsiveness of interrelationships—the degree to which the conditions in one state are affected in a positive or negative way by events occurring elsewhere. Vulnerability interdependence involves the reversibility of interrelationships—the degree to which (in other words, the cost at which) a state is capable of overriding the effects of events occurring elsewhere. A state is "sensitive" if it is unable to avoid being influenced by outside occurrences. It is "vulnerable" if it is unable to reverse the influence of outside occurrences except at very high cost to itself. Less dependent states are not so sensitive to events elsewhere and can alter or terminate outside relationships at relatively low cost to themselves.

These two dimensions of interdependence are closely related to the two levels of analysis stressed by Keohane and Nye, the *process-level* and the *structure-level*:

[We] distinguish between two levels of analysis, a "process-level," dealing with short-term allocative behavior (i.e., holding institutions, fundamental assumptions, and expectations constant), and a "structure-level," having to do with long-term political and economic determinants of the incentives and constraints within which actors operate. At the structural level, we are interested in how the institutions, fundamental assumptions, and "rules of the game" of political systems support or undermine different patterns of allocation for economic activity, as well as in the converse—how the nature of economic activity affects the political structure.[25]

Sensitivity interdependence is particularly relevant for the analysis of state action at the process level, where the structural framework of relations is well established and generally accepted. It focuses attention mainly on the effects of marginal changes within a given set of rules and conventions. Vulnerability interdependence, by contrast, is more relevant for analysis at the structure level—for analysis of such questions as how rules and conventions are established and how they may be altered through time. At the process level one asks: who is best able to manipulate the allocation of values in the short term? At the structure level one asks: who is best able to determine the underlying shape of incentives and constraints over the longer term? At both levels, the answers identify the states with power.

State power, then, like the concept of interdependence from which it derives, has two dimensions corresponding to the two levels of analysis of relations. One dimension is that of process, the other of structure. Power at the process level involves the ability to extract advantage within the existing interaction situation (in game-theoretic terms, the ability to select a preferred outcome within the existing payoff matrix). Power at the structure level means the ability to extract advantage by favorably modifying the interaction situation (that is, the ability to favorably restructure the payoff matrix). Put differently, process power is the ability to gain under the prevailing rules of the game, while structure power is the ability to gain by rewriting the rules of the game.

How much power any given state may have at either of these levels will vary from one issue-area to another, and also between geographic regions. A country may be more dependent in some issue-areas or regions and less dependent in others, depending on the direction of asymmetries in specific interrelationships. Moreover, a state may have much greater power at one level than at the other. A high degree of rule-making capacity does not necessarily imply control over every process occurring within those rules. An ability to manipulate the allocation of values in the short term does not necessarily imply control of the underlying shape of incentives and constraints over the longer term.

In international monetary relations, these two dimensions of power (process and structure) apply to both of the critical systemic issues identified at the conclusion of the previous chapter: the mechanisms for balance-of-payments adjustment and for creating international liquidity. International monetary power consists of an ability either to *utilize* the existing adjustment mechanism or the liquidity-creation mechanism to advantage (process power) or to *modify* either mechanism to advantage (structure power). There are thus really four forms of international monetary power; states may have none, some, or all at their command. Whenever controversy over the problem of distribution in monetary affairs leads to serious policy conflict, states have an incentive to use whatever forms of international monetary power are at their disposal to favorably affect how the welfare pie will be sliced and how national prestige and decision-making authority will be distributed. Such uses of power can profoundly influence the operation and stability of the monetary order. *In extremis*, the implied danger, as indicated, is that states may end up by destroying completely all of the potential for joint gain.

The Issues of Policy Conflict

The consistency objective reflects the destructive potential of competition in international monetary relations. Every international monetary order is challenged to ensure some minimum degree of consistency among national policies. Rules and conventions governing policy choices must not only aim to increase as much as possible the total of economic welfare (the efficiency objective). If the potential for joint gain is to be preserved, they must also aim to decrease as much as possible controversy over the distribution of economic welfare, as well as of national prestige and decision-making authority (the consistency objective). This applies both to the mechanism of payments adjustment and to the mechanism of liquidity creation.

The Mechanism of Payments Adjustment

The previous chapter indicated that the essence of the adjustment problem is that every policy of adjustment generates economic costs. Insofar as the efficiency objective is concerned, the challenge to the monetary order is to minimize these economic costs (to optimize the adjustment process). Insofar as the consistency objective is concerned, the principal challenge is to minimize conflict over the distribution of these economic costs; a related challenge is to minimize conflict over the burden or privilege of taking action to initiate the adjustment process. If the former challenge is a tough one, these latter two are even tougher.

These latter two challenges are not identical. Taking action to initiate the adjustment process is not the same as bearing the costs of adjustment.[26] The "responsibility" for taking action may or may not be freely chosen; it may be imposed by circumstances—say, if a deficit country is running out of reserves. But whether freely chosen or not, it need not always impose real economic costs on a country. Initiating the adjustment process is clearly a burden in dilemma situations (deficit coinciding with unemployment, surplus with inflation) if only expenditure-changing policies are available. Then, if the deficit country acts first to eliminate the payments disequilibrium by tightening monetary and fiscal policy, it will necessarily suffer an even greater rate of unemployment; if it is the surplus country that acts first by loosening monetary and fiscal policy, it will necessarily suffer an even greater rate of inflation. But if expenditure-switching policies are available in such situations, the responsibility for taking action may actually turn out to be a privilege, e.g., if states use the option of exchange-rate change, which is by definition a substitute for a more direct realignment of domestic incomes and prices. Currency devaluation (depreciation) or revaluation (appreciation) can actually serve to transfer much of the economic costs of adjustment to other countries. An upward movement of the exchange rate by the surplus country, for instance, could enable it to avoid much additional inflation at home by contributing to price (cost) inflation in the deficit country; a downward movement of the exchange rate by the deficit country could enable it to avoid much additional unemployment at home by contributing to resource unemployment in the surplus country. And the same point applies equally to other disequilibrium situations. There is no direct correlation between the distribution of adjustment responsibilities and the allocation of adjustment costs.

A number of economists have attempted to design optimal rules and conventions for the international adjustment process—in effect, to frame "codes of good conduct" for states that would minimize collective costs of adjustment.[27] Such efforts reflect the tendency of conventional economics to restrict consideration of governmental behavior mainly to normative policy judgments; they also reflect economic theory's exclusive preoccupation with the efficiency objective. Hence they embody the weaknesses as well as the strengths of the economist's traditional analytical approach. As guideposts to the maximization of global welfare they are particularly useful, especially insofar as their authors are careful to take explicit account of the various subjective elements inherent in codes of this kind (e.g., the technical problem of the uncertainty and unpredictability of adjustment costs, the practical difficulty of trying to distinguish between stochastic and nonstochastic disequilibria, and the imperative to make value judgments regarding the necessary trade-offs among values at the margin). But as organizing principles for real-world monetary relations, the usefulness of these codes is considerably diminished, since they ignore the equally fundamental problem of the distribution of economic welfare and decision-making authority. They fail to address the issue of how to minimize controversy over allocation of the collective costs of adjustment and the responsibility for taking action.

Generally, adjustment codes that have been framed by economists imply that each country ought to share in the responsibility for taking action and in the economic costs of adjustment more or less in proportion to its ability to contribute to the maximization of global welfare. Few governments, however, are apt to agree readily with such a cosmopolitan criterion. It is the fallacy of composition to assume that what is best for the world as a whole will also be seen as best by each state individually. In reality, states prefer to aim at a much different target: to minimize their own responsibilities and costs in the international adjustment process. "Nations do not willingly adjust."[28] From the perspective of the individual country, the best distribution is that which obliges the other fellow to take all the responsibility for adjusting and to pay all of the costs.

Why do nations not willingly adjust? Plainly, because governments choose their policies in the light of interests interpreted nationally, rather than in cosmopolitan terms. In selecting adjustment policies governments naturally interpret the national interest to mean the least possible sacrifice at home. As Robert Aliber has noted: "Countries in deficit do not wish to deflate incomes and employment. Countries in surplus do not wish their prices to rise. . . . For prestige and political reasons, countries wish others to take the initiative in restoring balance."[29] This is precisely why one cannot ignore the role of political sovereignty in monetary affairs—why it is so important to treat the state as an endogenous and purposive actor. Governmental policy is not in the hands of economists with a disinterested concern in the maximization of global welfare. It is in the hands of politicians with a very interested concern (at least in part because of their personal electoral ambitions) in the maximization of national welfare, as well as of national autonomy and prestige. The point bears repeating: distributional considerations matter.

An important factor contributing to these distributional considerations is the system of domestic power relationships within each state. It has been emphasized that the state is not a unitary actor. In practice, nongovernmental actors of all kinds are affected by the international adjustment process and are apt to lobby vigorously against any actions perceived as detrimental to their own special interests. Enterprises and workers threatened with unemployment will oppose deflationary monetary and fiscal policies in deficit countries. Fixed-income earners and creditors threatened with reduced purchasing power will oppose expansionary monetary and fiscal policies in surplus countries. Sectors of the economy heavily involved in foreign trade and investment will oppose the risks of exchange-rate flexibility and the inconveniences of restrictions or exchange control. And even elements of the public bureaucratic structure will tend to develop vested interests that lead them to resist certain adjustment options. (For example, central banks traditionally used to frown on revaluation because it would force them to write down on their books the domestic-currency value of their international monetary reserves.) Some observers have argued, with Cooper, that "international finance is an arcane subject and normally attracts little attention. The public ordinarily does not have strong feelings about it."[30] That may be true as concerns the broader issues of international monetary organization. But on the immediate issue of adjustment the public has strong feelings indeed in defense of its own diverse ambitions. This affects governmental behavior in at least three important ways. First, it encourages governments to use several instruments of adjustment simultaneously, in order to disperse and moderate negative impacts within the national community.[31] Second, it frequently causes policy to be indecisive or inconsistent, as indicated earlier, because of deadlocked judgments among domestic constituencies. And third, also as indicated, it creates an incentive on the part of governments to pass along as much as possible of the costs of adjustment to foreigners. The easiest way to reconcile conflict within any social collectivity is always at the expense of outsiders.

Many economists have suggested that all distributional considerations can be easily handled through agreed procedures for international consultation and cooperation, to ensure greater consistency among national policy targets and instruments. States have a mutual interest in cooperating for the sake of the efficiency objective. But cooperation among states can only suppress their conflicts of interest, not eliminate them. Consultation is not a substitute for a reallocation of resources. When nonstochastic disequilibria occur, some amount of real adjustment is required—and while consultation may be able to reduce the necessary economic costs, by moderating policy competition, it cannot eradicate them. These costs must be paid by someone: states must still agree on who will sacrifice what. And some states may not be willing to agree at all if the perceived costs of cooperation are too high. As Anthony Lanyi has pointed out:

> The costs of cooperation will, of course, differ among countries and circumstances. If the cost of cooperation is too great for a country at a particular time, it will prefer to take measures which, if often only in a minor and partial way, "break down" or diverge from the purposes and methods of the agreed-upon system.[32]

The process of adjustment, therefore, tends in practice to be much more a straigthforward matter of international monetary *power*, with each state seeking to avoid as much as possible any share of the costs and responsibilities of adjustment. Elsewhere I have written of the concept of "adjustment vulnerability," meaning the proportion of collective adjustment costs that a single state must pay in the event of international disequilibrium.[33] The greater a country's adjustment vulnerability, the weaker it is in international monetary relations. Conversely, low adjustment vulnerability implies considerable power (process or structure) to avoid the costs and responsibilities of adjustment by shifting them onto others. Less vulnerable states are continually tempted to transfer the "burden" of these costs and responsibilities onto the more vulnerable. The most vulnerable states are continually obliged to bear the greatest burden of all.

Consider, for instance, the continuing cost of adjustment, discussed in the previous chapter. The benefit of disequilibrium is the excess of real domestic absorption over real current income enjoyed by the deficit country at prevailing price levels and exchange rates. Normally this is thought to imply that the deficit country will be obliged to pay the continuing cost of adjustment by reducing real absorption relative to income. But that implication takes no account of possible changes in the international terms of trade (the ratio of export prices to import prices). To take an admittedly extreme but nonethcless instructive example, assume that adjustment is accomplished via a reduction of the money prices of imports, with no changes at all occurring in either the real quantity of imports or the money prices or real quantity of exports. In that case the nominal value of imports will be reduced relative to the nominal value of exports, yet the deficit country's real current absorption will be unchanged. The improvement of its terms of trade will shift all of the continuing cost of adjustment onto the surplus country (whose previously favorable terms of trade in effect represented the benefit of disequilibrium).

The point is that the continuing cost of adjustment, which as a first approximation is defined in terms of real current absorption forgone, must also be adjusted for any associated change in the terms of trade of the deficit country. Any tendency for its terms of trade to deteriorate during the adjustment process will add to the continuing cost for the deficit country. On the other hand, any tendency for its terms of trade to improve will constitute an offset to the necessity for the deficit country to reduce real absorption relative to income. The greater the tendency for its terms of trade to improve, the less will absorption have to be reduced at home, and the greater will be the continuing cost which the surplus country must bear instead. Admittedly, such circumstances are not always easy to imagine: the terms of trade of deficit countries usually deteriorate *a fortiori* during the adjustment process, rather than improve. But neither are such situations entirely inconceivable. In practice, countries in deficit frequently have enjoyed the power to transfer at least some of the continuing cost of adjustment to others through improvements in their terms of trade. What is required is some sort of monopolistic or monopsonistic power in international markets.[34]

During the nineteenth century, for example, when London stood at the center of the international monetary system (see Chapter 3), Great Britain in particular enjoyed such power. Ordinarily, when a deficit in the British balance of payments threatened to cause an outflow of gold from London, the Bank of England initiated the process of adjustment by tightening monetary policy. But this did not mean that Britain usually bore the continuing cost of adjustment. Quite the opposite. Very often the cost was successfully transferred from the United Kingdom to the nations at the periphery—the primary producers of the Western Hemisphere and other outlying areas. Restriction of credit in London tended to press especially heavily on the financing of trade in foodstuffs and raw materials, which were industrial Britain's chief imports. Since this tended to force dealers to compress their inventories, correction of the imbalance was frequently accomplished not by resource unemployment in the United Kingdom, but rather by a reduction in the prices of British imports. Most of the continuing cost of adjustment, in other words, was borne not at the center but at the periphery, where exporting nations were compelled to deflate.[35]

More recently, the industrial countries in general have enjoyed a similar power. Following the fourfold increase of world oil prices in late 1973, member-states of the Organization of Petroleum Exporting Countries (OPEC) ran a collective surplus on current account of approximately $65 billion in 1974. Some 80 percent of the counterpart trade deficit had been expected to fall on the industrial countries of Western Europe and North America, along with Japan. But as it happened, the combined trade deficit of these countries in 1974 actually amounted to only about $11 billion. The really serious deficits were experienced by the non-oil primary producers of the Third World, whose terms of trade fell precipitously—in part because of the high rate of inflation in the industrial world, which together with the oil price increases raised the prices of Third World countries' imports, but mainly because of the severity of the recession in the industrial world, which sharply reduced the prices of their exports. Again, it was the exporting nations at the periphery that had to bear most of the continuing cost of adjustment through an adverse shift in their terms of trade. These trends continued strongly in 1975.[36]

Consider now the transitional cost of adjustment. Of the several potential sources of transitional cost, only frictional changeover costs are necessarily borne by every country regardless of its international monetary power. Adjustment is by definition a mutual process, just as disequilibrium is a mutual experience. One country cannot be in payments deficit without a second being in surplus;

likewise, resources cannot be reallocated in one country without an equivalent and offsetting reallocation in the other. Since the process of adjustment necessarily involves a complementary reallocation of resources at the margin, the frictional costs of adjustment are necessarily borne by all adjusting countries. The magnitude of the frictional costs borne by each country will depend solely on the underlying structural attributes of each separate national economy.[37]

With regard to all the other potential sources of transitional cost, the distribution between countries may vary considerably depending on their international monetary power. This applies to potential increases of resource inefficiency at the microeconomic level as well as to potential increases of resource unemployment or price inflation at the macroeconomic level. Most of the burden of unemployment or inflation, or of distortions in the pattern of resource allocation, may well be borne by just a few countries, even though the adjustment process itself must be shared by all. Some countries may be able to pass through the adjustment process without being obliged to take any initiative at all or to pay any of these transitional costs. It all depends on the policies (or combinations of policies) chosen by the various governments in each particular circumstance. Most countries do have at least some power to transfer parts of the transitional cost of adjustment to others.

This power does not necessarily depend on a country's initial balance-of-payments position—that is, on whether a country happens to find itself initially in deficit or in surplus. Under the old Bretton Woods system, it was commonly thought that deficit countries bore most of the transitional cost of adjustment, because of the pressure of reserve losses. In principle, when exchange rates were pegged, there was virtually no limit to how much foreign exchange a government could accumulate in financing a surplus; there was a definite limit, however, to how much foreign exchange a government could sell in financing a deficit. The compulsions to act, therefore, were asymmetrical: deficit countries were usually obliged to be the first to take remedial action. From this it was inferred that deficit countries also had to pay the largest part of the transitional cost of adjustment.[38]

But this was a false inference, for as has already been emphasized, taking action to initiate adjustment is not the same as bearing the costs of adjustment, particularly if expenditure-switching policies can be relied upon to restore payments equilibrium. This has led some economists to suggest that perhaps it was the surplus countries that usually were obliged to pay most of the cost of adjustment under the Bretton Woods system, not deficit countries as generally supposed. One European economist, for example, has argued that "because it seems senseless to invest such an important part of their resources in reserves . . . [surplus countries] are led to initiate measures to correct disequilibrium . . . by yielding to inflation or revaluing their currency."[39] But this argument too confuses the distribution of adjustment responsibilities with the allocation of adjustment costs. In any event, under the Bretton Woods system surplus countries many times chose neither to initiate adjustment themselves nor to force deficit countries to adjust, but rather to extend the latter large and long-continued flows of credit—in effect, bribing debtors not to devalue or to impose restrictions or exchange control. Apparently creditors were willing to accept the continuing burden of disequilibrium because they found that bribes were less expensive than genuine adjustment. As one American economist wrote, "the potential lenders discovered that it was really in their interest to lend."[40]

On what, then, does the power to transfer transitional cost depend?[41] In fact, such power depends on the full range of resources that a country can call into action in the competitive payments struggle—the full range of asymmetric interdependencies in trade and finance that it can manipulate to advantage in the adjustment process. This is admittedly vague, but it has already been conceded that state power must remain an imprecise concept. What cannot be doubted is that such power exists, that states have an incentive to use it, and that it varies in different circumstances depending on the mechanism of adjustment in operation. The danger of conflict is real. So, therefore, is the challenge to the monetary order.

The Mechanism of Liquidity Creation

The previous chapter indicated that the essence of the liquidity problem is the need for an adequate supply (and rate of growth) of reserves. The essence of the confidence problem, on the other hand, is the need for some arrangement to cope with destabilizing shifts of confidence among different types of reserves. Insofar as the efficiency objective is concerned, the challenge to the monetary order is to ensure an optimal quantity and composition of international liquidity. Insofar as the consistency objective is concerned, the challenge is to minimize conflict over distribution of the benefits and costs of creating international liquidity—including the related gains and losses of political prestige and autonomy. Needless to say, this is a tough challenge too.

At the heart of this challenge is the concept of *seigniorage*.[42] Originally, seigniorage referred to the difference between the circulating value of a coin and the cost of bullion and minting, involving a once-for-all gain to the coin's issuer (the sovereign or "seigneur"). Later the term was extended to describe the gain of real resources, over and above costs of production and administration, associated with the creation and issue of any kind of money—including also international money. Alternative possible mechanisms for the creation of international liquidity each imply a different amount and distribution of seigniorage; these in turn imply varying consequences for national prestige and decision-making authority. Just as economists have attempted to design optimal rules and conventions for the international adjustment process, so many have tried to design optimal rules and conventions for the liquidity-creation process.[43] But just as the adjustment codes of economists fail to take account of distributional considerations, so usually do their proposals for the creation of liquidity. Most fail to address explicitly the issue of how to minimize controversy over allocation of the gains of welfare, prestige, and autonomy associated with the creation and issue of international reserves.

That the allocation of these gains matters to states should be clear. If governments naturally seek to minimize sacrifices at home from the payments adjustment process, so too they naturally seek to maximize benefits at home from the liquidity-creation process. Just as the problem of liquidity is really just the other side of the coin labeled "problem of adjustment," the conflict over the gains associated with seigniorage is really just the other side of the coin labeled "costs of adjustment." Governments have always been aware of the advantages accorded by control of the money supply. Within the national frontiers virtually every government, through its central bank, has long since asserted a monopoly over the power to issue currency, in order to be in a position to enjoy the associated seigniorage gains (in technical terms, monopoly "rents"). Likewise, across national frontiers, governments would like to be in a position to enjoy as large a share as possible of the seigniorage gains derived from control of the international money supply. And in this respect also, an important contributing factor is the system of domestic power relationships within each state. Key national constituencies have strong perceived interests in the choice of an international liquidity-creation mechanism—including, especially, the financial sector and the investors in international monetary assets. The consequence of all these factors is that the process of liquidity creation, like the payments adjustment process, tends in practice to be very much a straightforward matter of international monetary power.

All forms of international liquidity may be classified as either commodity reserves or fiduciary (fiat) reserves. *Commodity reserves* are those which have some intrinsic economic value quite apart from their value as money; the most prominent example of course is gold, although in the past other precious metals have also served as international reserves (see Chapter 3). Technically, commodity reserves also include paper assets that are generally accepted as international liquidity because they are based on and freely redeemable in a commodity or commodities of some kind. *Fiduciary reserves*, by contrast, have no intrinsic economic value apart from their value as money: their general acceptability as international liquidity rests upon the confidence of governments rather than upon any promise of redemption in commodities. Prominent examples of fiat reserves include national currencies that are formally or informally inconvertible into precious metals such as gold. Special Drawing Rights are also fiat reserves.

Alternative possible mechanisms for the creation of international liquidity—also known as "standards"—are distinguished by the type of reserve asset(s) that each would employ. Pure commodity standards include the gold standard and the so-called "commodity-reserve-currency" standard (which would employ a reserve asset based on an international stockpile of storable primary commodities, such as minerals and agricultural raw materials). Pure fiduciary standards include a reserve-currency standard (which would employ a single inconvertible national currency), a multiple-reserve-currency standard (which would employ two or more inconvertible national currencies), and an international-reserve-currency standard (which would employ an internationally created inconvertible currency). Mixed standards are also possible—and have existed. These include the gold-exchange standard, employing gold plus one or more national currencies convertible, directly or indirectly, into gold.

Pure commodity standards imply a relatively small amount of seigniorage, because of the comparatively high real-resource cost of producing and storing commodity reserves. Nevertheless, some net gain is implied, even if the commodity or commodities employed are produced under conditions of perfect competition, to the extent that producer income is increased over and above what would be the case in the absence of monetary demand for the commodity or commodities. This gain would be at the expense of users of each commodity, who would presumably be willing to bear the expense because of the commodity's usefulness as international money. It would accrue to all producers who are more efficient than marginal producers just able to earn a "normal" return. (In technical terms, the gain takes the form of "intramarginal rents.") Additional gain would accrue to producers to the extent that the commodity was produced under conditions of imperfect competition (monopoly). Thus, it is not surprising that pure commodity standards have been most enthusiastically advocated by the producers of the commodities that would be employed. As Cooper notes dryly, "the Union of South Africa and the Soviet Union have been the two most consistent supporters of returning to gold as the principal international reserve asset; these two countries are the first and second largest producers of gold in the world, and stand to gain the most in seigniorage from reliance on gold."[44] Likewise, the primary producing countries have been the most consistent supporters of proposals that have appeared from time to time for a commodity-reserve-currency standard; one express purpose of such proposals is to use the liquidity-creation mechanism to provide efficient price and income support to exporters of primary commodities.[45]

Pure fiduciary standards imply a relatively large amount of seigniorage, because of the much lower real-resource cost of producing and storing fiat reserves. This gain is a genuine saving of resources— a "social saving"—and must necessarily be distributed in some way. As Fritz Machlup has written:

> The discovery that international money can be produced with cheap ink and paper, and need not be produced with hard work applied to metal dug out of the ground, affords a large saving. . . . The saving in the production of the low-cost substitute must be distributed somehow. . . . the saving will benefit someone and its distribution must needs be arbitrary.[46]

In principle, there are two ways in which this social saving may be distributed. If the fiduciary reserve is produced under conditions of total monopoly, with no interest paid on reserve holdings, then the saving would accrue entirely to the issuer of the asset. If, on the other hand, the issuer is confronted by competition from other sources of reserves, then his net gain would be correspondingly reduced, since he would be obliged to pay a rate of interest on his liabilities in order to induce others to retain their holdings: part of the social saving would then accrue to holders in the form of such interest payments. Indeed, the greater the competition from other sources, the higher the interest rate would have to be. At the extreme, where the fiat reserve is produced under conditions approximating perfect competition and free entry, no significant gain at all would be expected to accrue, on a net basis, to the issuer. Asset holders, rather than the issuer, would receive the full benefit of the social saving.

With a reserve-currency standard, the fiduciary reserve would by definition be produced under conditions of total monopoly. Like the central bank within any national monetary system, the single state whose national currency performed the functions of international liquidity would therefore receive the full benefit of the social saving (the monopoly "rents"), as well as the associated gains of prestige and decision-making authority. The seigniorage benefit takes the form of a greater cumulative deficit in the country's balance of payments than would otherwise be possible—in effect, a kind of "free" command over foreign goods, services, and assets—owing to the willingness of other states to accumulate the reserve center's currency as reserves. The center would be able to finance deficits simply by issuing liabilities (i.e., by liability-financing) rather than by giving up reserves (asset-financing). The gain of decision-making authority consists of the greater flexibility and latitude (autonomy) in dealing with stochastic payments disequilibria afforded by this ability to liability-finance deficits. Additional income gains also would accrue specifically to the financial sector of the reserve center, insofar as domestic banks and other financial institutions had an effective monopoly over both the issue of monetary liabilities denominated in local currency and the exchange market for the currency. These gains have been called "private" or "denomination" seigniorage.[47] They take the form of extra earnings from foreign-exchange transactions, investment services, and other ancillary financial and commercial activities attributable to the international use of the national currency.

With a multiple-reserve-currency standard, many of these gains would be reduced by competition from alternative centers, and would be enjoyed instead by the holders of international reserves. Not only would reserve centers have to pay higher interest rates than otherwise, but competition among their financial sectors would also compress the private seigniorage gains attributable to the international use of their national currencies. Worse, the centers' advantage of flexibility in dealing with stochastic payments disequilibria would be partially or wholly offset by a policy constraint resulting from the threat of reduction or withdrawal of past accumulations of their liabilities (the confidence problem). This threat of the so-called "overhang" of liabilities could seriously impinge on an individual reserve center's ability to use expenditure-changing or expenditure-switching policies to maintain internal or external balance. The exact distribution of the social saving under these conditions would be uncertain. It would all depend on the degree and character of competition among reserve centers.

With an international-reserve-currency standard, the full social saving can be distributed consciously in accordance with any preconceived set of political or economic criteria. As before, there are two ways in which the distribution can be accomplished: either through the interest yield paid on holdings of the international reserve asset or, in the absence of a significant rate of interest, through the initial allocation of newly created reserves (which, as they are first spent, would produce an effect equivalent to a reserve center's seigniorage benefit). When Special Drawing Rights were first established in the late 1960s, for example, the interest yield on accumulated holdings was set at the insignificant rate of 1.5 percent per annum. Consequently, a great deal of attention was paid to the question of how newly created SDRs should be initially allocated. The method finally adopted called for allocation among governments in proportion to national quotas in the International Monetary Fund; the rationale for the method was that it would (hopefully) be distributionally neutral, in the technical sense of conforming to the demand for reserves to hold rather than to the demand for reserves to spend.[48] The decision of the IMF in 1974 to raise the interest yield on SDRs to a more commercially competitive level was also, in principle, distributionally neutral. However, many observers have argued that some alternative distributional criterion would be rather more appropriate for Special Drawing Rights: specifically, many have proposed that the social saving afforded by SDRs be deliberately directed toward the poorer nations of the world, to aid them in their economic development. This is the so-called "link" proposal to join the mechanisms of liquidity creation and development finance.[49] Not surprisingly, the proposal has been most consistently supported by governments of less-developed countries—though, until now at least, with conspicuously little success.

With a mixed standard such as the gold-exchange standard, the exact distribution of the social saving is (as with a multiple-currency-reserve standard) uncertain. The Bretton Woods system was a gold-exchange standard, and many economists have attempted to quantify the relative distribution of the social saving in that system as between holders (collectively) and issuers, usually as part of a broader survey of the costs and benefits of being a reserve center.[50] In general, the conclusion that can be drawn from these investigations seems to be that even in the case of the United States, which was the principal reserve center of the Bretton Woods system, some part of the net seigniorage benefit was effectively bid away by holders in the form of higher interest payments.[51] Furthermore, the United States also seemed to suffer a considerable loss of policy autonomy after the end of the 1950s, because of the growing overhang of foreign dollar liabilities: America felt severely constrained, particularly in its use of exchange-rate policy, by the threat of conversions of official dollar balances into gold (the confidence problem again). Yet even in these circumstances, the United States was not without power. Quite the opposite, in fact. This was a striking example of how different a country's command over the various forms of international monetary power may actually be. As long as the United States played by the prevailing rules of the game, its power to utilize the liquidity-creation mechanism to advantage (its process power) was progressively diminished throughout the course of the 1960s; its flexibility advantage was gradually offset by perceived policy constraint. Yet America's structure power remained as great as ever. In 1969, Henry Aubrey pointed out that "surely a creditor's influence over the United States rests on America's willingness to play the game according to the old concepts and rules. If the United States ever seriously decided to challenge them, the game would take a very different course."[52] That of course is precisely what did happen in 1971. The dollar was declared inconvertible, the game took a different course, and the United States regained its policy autonomy. America was able to use its structure power to radically alter the allocation of gains associated with the creation and issue of international liquidity.

Conclusions

The relationship between the monetary order and the element of competititon in monetary relations can be summarized in terms of the so-called "*n − 1* principle," also known as the "redundancy problem."[53] In a world of n sovereign states, only $n - 1$ external policies (be they adjustment policies or liquidity policies) can be independently determined. One country (the nth country) is redundant. If all n countries try to set their policies independently, these policies will almost certainly be inconsistent—and as a result, the stability of the monetary order itself will be threatened. To preserve monetary stability, some means must be found to ensure consistency among national policies. Hence the consistency objective.

As indicated in the Introduction, there are only four alternative organizing principles capable of ensuring at least a minimum degree of policy consistency among states. These are automaticity, supranationality, hegemony, and negotiation. One of these four principles, or some combination of them, must be applied both to the mechanism of balance-of-payments adjustment and to the mechanism for creating international liquidity; it must also accommodate and balance the consistency objective with the efficiency objective. By now it should be clear that these are no easy tasks. That, of course, is precisely why the problem of organizing international monetary relations is so difficult.

Chapter 3

A Brief History of International Monetary Relations

The difficulty of organizing the world monetary order is well illustrated by the history of international monetary relations. As it has evolved through time, the structural framework of monetary relations has been marked by a continuing tension between economic and political values. At times the element of cooperation in monetary relations has prevailed, at others the element of competition; at times the monetary game has succeeded in realizing its potential for joint gain, at others it has not. Governments for decades have sought the secret of how, in effect, to accommodate and balance the efficiency and consistency objectives. A brief review in this chapter of their prolonged efforts will suffice to demonstrate that that secret is by no means easy to uncover.

The Classical Gold Standard[1]

It is impossible to specify a precise date when the international monetary order began. The origins of international monetary relations, like those of money itself, are shrouded in the obscurity of prehistory. We know that there were well-defined monetary areas in many parts of the ancient world. But it is only with the rise of the Roman Empire that we begin to find documentary evidence of a very explicit international monetary order. The Roman monetary order, which was based initially on the gold coinage of Julius Caesar and later on the gold solidus (bezant, nomisma) for Byzantium, lasted some twelve centuries in all. Though confronted from the seventh century on with competition from a silver bloc centered on the newly emergent Muslim dinar, the Roman system did not break down completely until the sacking of Constantinople in 1203. The next five centuries were characterized by fluctuating exchange rates and a succession of dominant moneys—the "dollars of the Middle Ages," one source has called them[2]—including in later years the Florentine fiorino, the Venetian ducato, the Spanish reale, and the Dutch florin. After the beginning of the Industrial Revolution, it was the British pound sterling that rose to a position of preeminence in world monetary affairs.

As its name implies, the pound sterling was originally based on silver. In fact, however, England began practicing a loose sort of bimetallism—gold coins circulating alongside silver ones—even as early as the fourteenth century. (Gold coinage was first introduced into England in 1344, during the reign of Edward III.) Gresham's Law was coined during the reign of Queen Elizabeth I. Sir Isaac Newton, as Master of the Mint, tried to cope with the problem of bad money driving out good by calculating the value of the gold guinea (named after the region in West Africa where gold was mined) in terms of silver shillings. And in 1817 gold was formally declared legal tender in England alongside silver. From the time of the Napoleonic Wars, the United Kingdom moved rapidly from bimetallism to a single-money system. In 1798 the free coinage of silver was suspended and a £25 limit set on the legal-tender power of silver coins. In 1816 silver's legal-tender powers were further limited to £2. And after 1819 silver could no longer be used to redeem circulating bank notes: paper could be redeemed in gold coin only. From that date onward, the pound was effectively based on gold alone. The British were on a full gold standard.

Other countries, however, resisted the gold standard for several decades more. Most European nations, as well as the United States, remained legally bimetallic for at least another half century; most others, especially in Asia, formally retained silver standards. It was only in the 1870s that the movement toward a full-fledged international gold standard picked up momentum, and it is from this decade that the modern history of international monetary relations is customarily dated. In 1871 the new German empire adopted the gold mark as its monetary unit, discontinuing the free coinage and unlimited legal-tender powers of silver. In 1873 a parallel decision followed in the United States (the "Crime of '73"), and by 1878 silver had been demonetized in France and virtually every other European country as well. During this decade, the classical gold standard was born. During succeeding decades, it spread to encompass virtually all of the world's independent countries, as well as all of the various colonial empires of Europe.

The classical gold standard was a comparatively brief episode in world history, ending with the outbreak of World War I in 1914. It was defined by two key features. A country was considered to be "on" the gold standard if (1) its central bank pledged to buy and sell gold (and only gold) freely at a fixed price in terms of the home currency, and (2) its private residents could export or import gold freely. Together, these two features defined a pure fixed-exchange-rate mechanism of balance-of-payments adjustment. Fixed exchange rates were established by the ratios of the prices at which central banks pledged to buy and sell gold for local currency. Free export and import of gold in turn established the means for reconciling any differences between the demand and supply of a currency at its fixed exchange rate. Deficits, requiring net payments to foreigners, were expected to result in outflows of gold, as residents converted local currency at the central bank in order to meet transactions obligations abroad. Conversely, surpluses, were expected to result in gold inflows. Adjustment was supposed to work through the impact of such gold flows on domestic economic conditions in each country.

The mechanism of liquidity creation under the classical gold standard was very nearly a pure commodity standard—and that commodity, of course, was gold. Silver lost its role as an important reserve asset during the decade of demonetization in the 1870s. And national currencies did not even begin to enter into monetary reserves in significant quantities until after 1900. The most widely held national currency before World War I was the pound; its principal rivals were the French franc and the German mark. But even as late as 1914, the ratio of world foreign-exchange reserves to world gold reserves remained very low.[3] The monetary standard even then was still essentially a pure commodity standard.

After World War I, observers tended to look back on the classical gold standard with a sense of nostalgia and regret—a sort of Proustian *Recherche du temps perdu*. As compared with the course of events after 1918, the pre-1914 monetary order appeared, in retrospect, to have been enormously successful in reconciling the tension between economic and political values. During its four decades of existence, world trade and payments grew at record rates, promoting technical efficiency and economic welfare; yet, looking back, it seemed that problems of balance-of-payments adjustment and conflicts of policy between nations had been remarkably rare. The gold standard seemed to have succeeded to a unique degree in accommodating and balancing the efficiency and consistency objectives. For many, it had literally been a "Golden Age" of monetary relations.

The image of a Golden Age, however, was a myth, based on at least two serious misconceptions of how the gold standard had actually operated in practice. One misconception concerned the process of balance-of-payments adjustment, the other involved the role of national monetary policies. The process of balance-of-payments adjustment was said to have depended primarily on changes of domestic price levels. The model was that of the so-called "price-specie-flow" mechanism: outflows of gold (specie) shrinking the money supply at home and deflating the level of domestic prices, inflows expanding the money supply and inflating domestic prices. National monetary policies, although reinforcing the adjustment process, were said to have been actually concerned exclusively with defense of the convertibility of local currencies into gold. Central banks were said to have responded to gold flows more or less mechanically and passively, with a minimum of discretionary action or judgment. They simply played the "rules of the game," allowing gold flows to have their full impact on domestic money supplies and price levels. Combined, these misconceptions produced a myth of an impersonal, fully automatic, and politically symmetrical international monetary order dependent simply on a combination of domestic price flexibility and natural constraints on the production of gold to ensure optimality of both the adjustment process and reserve supply.

More recent historical research has revealed just how misleading this myth of the Golden Age really was. Regarding the role of monetary policy, for example, Arthur Bloomfield has convincingly demonstrated that central banks before 1914 were rarely quite as mechanical or passive as observers later believed.[4] In fact, central banks exercised a great deal of discretion in reacting to inward or outward flows of gold. The rules of the game could be interpreted in either a negative or a positive sense. In the negative sense, central banks could simply refrain from any actions designed to counteract the influence of gold flows on domestic money supplies; in the positive sense, central banks might have been expected to magnify the domestic monetary influence of gold flows according to their deposit-reserve ratios.[5] Bloomfield has shown that under the classical gold standard, central banks hardly ever adhered to the rules in the positive sense, and sometimes even departed from them in the negative sense. Of course, this was still an era of predominantly laissez-faire attitudes in government economic policy. Yet, even then, central banks were neither entirely unaware of, nor indifferent to, the effects of gold flows on domestic prices, incomes, or public confidence. To counteract such effects when it suited them, monetary authorities developed a variety of techniques for evading the rules of the game—including manipulation of the margins around exchange rates (technically, the "gold points"), direct intervention in the foreign-exchange market, and loans between central banks. Monetary policies in this period were never really either fully passive or simply automatic.

Similarly, regarding the process of balance-of-payments adjustment, Robert Triffin has convincingly demonstrated that domestic price levels rarely played as much of a role before 1914 as observers later believed.[6] In fact, the process of adjustment depended at least as much on changes of domestic income and employment as on price changes. But most of all, the process depended on capital movements. The role of international capital movements in adjusting to payments disequilibria was far more important than any role that the terms of trade may have played. As Triffin wrote:

> The importance of international capital movements, and of their fluctuations, is often obscured by the disproportionate emphasis often placed on comparative price and cost fluctuations as the major factor in balance-of-payments disequilibria and their correction. . . . In fact, however, international capital movements often did cushion—and even stimulate—vast and enduring deficits, or surpluses, on current account without calling for any correction whatsoever.[7]

However, capital movements were not something that all countries could avail themselves of with equal facility. Triffin drew a distinction between countries that were capital exporters and those that were capital importers. Capital-exporting countries usually could avoid the consequences of balance-of-payments deficits—domestic deflation or a possible threat to the gold convertibility of the local currency—simply by slowing down investment abroad. The customary instrument in this regard was the central-bank discount rate (in England, Bank rate); that is, the rate at which the central bank discounted collateral when lending to commercial banks. A rise of the discount rate, cutting back cash reserves of banks, could normally be relied upon to reduce the rate of capital outflow and improve the balance of payments. Borrowing countries, on the other hand, were far less able to control the rate of their capital imports, these being primarily determined by credit conditions in the capital-exporting countries. The Golden Age, therefore, was really limited only to the "core" of advanced nations of Europe and the so-called "regions of recent settlement" (including North America, Australasia, South Africa, and Argentina). Elsewhere, the gold standard was far less successful in preserving payments stability or avoiding policy conflict. Again in Triffin's words:

This success . . . was limited to the more advanced countries which formed the core of the system, and to those closely linked to them by political, as well as economic and financial ties. The exchange rates of other currencies—particularly in Latin America—fluctuated widely, and depreciated enormously, over the period. This contrast between the "core" countries and those of the "periphery" can be largely explained by the cyclical pattern of capital movements and terms of trade, which contributed to stability in the first group, and to instability in the second.[8]

Thus, not only was the gold standard neither impersonal nor fully automatic; it was also not politically symmetrical. In fact, the pre-1914 monetary order was arranged in a distinctly hierarchical fashion, with the countries of the periphery at the bottom, the core countries above, and at the peak—Britain. Great Britain dominated international monetary relations in the nineteenth century as no state has since, with the exception of the United States immediately after World War II. Britain was the supreme industrial power of the day, the biggest exporter of manufactured goods, the largest overseas investor. London was by far the most important world financial center, sterling by far the most widely used of the world's currencies for both current- and capital-account transactions.[9] It is sometimes claimed that the gold standard was in reality a sterling-exchange standard.[10] In one sense this appellation is misleading, insofar as most monetary reserves before 1914 (as mentioned above) were still held in gold, not sterling, and insofar as governments continued to be concerned with maintaining the gold value of their currencies, not the sterling value. Yet in another sense the fact cannot be denied: the classical gold standard *was* a sterling standard—a hegemonic regime—in the sense that Britain not only dominated the international monetary order, establishing and maintaining the prevailing rules of the game, but also gave monetary relations whatever degree of inherent stability they possessed.

This stability was ensured through a trio of roles which at that time only Britain had the economic and financial resources to play: (1) maintaining a relatively open market for the exports of countries in balance-of-payments difficulties; (2) providing contracyclical foreign long-term lending; and (3) acting as lender of last resort in times of exchange crisis.[11] These were not roles that the British deliberately sought or even particularly welcomed. As far as the Bank of England was concerned, its monetary policies were dictated solely by the need to protect its narrow reserves and the gold convertibility of the pound. It did not regard itself as responsible for global monetary stabilization or as money manager of the world. Yet this is precisely the responsibility that was thrust upon it in practice—acquired, like the British Empire itself, more or less absentmindedly. The widespread international use of sterling and the close links between the larger financial markets in London and smaller national financial markets elsewhere inevitably endowed Britain with the power to guide the world's monetary policy. Changes of policy by the Bank of England inevitably imposed a certain discipline and coordination on monetary conditions in other countries. As Leland Yeager has written:

> The fact that the Bank of England raised and lowered Bank rate almost solely out of concern for its own reserves hardly settles the issue of management.... The Bank *did* manage the nineteenth-century gold standard in the sense of dominating it— which is not to say that the Bank's actions were in accordance with modern ideas of contracyclical policy and not to deny that they appeared to be dictated by circumstances instead of being freely chosen.[12]

It is important to recall, however, that the stability ensured by British monetary management was confined largely to the core of advanced nations in Europe and the regions of recent settlement— countries that were themselves capital exporters or, when necessary, were capable of availing themselves of the lending facilities of London or other financial centers. The less-developed countries of the periphery were, as emphasized, far less able to control the rate of their foreign capital imports; moreover, they suffered from Britain's related power to avoid the continuing cost of adjustment by manipulating its international terms of trade (See Chapter 2). As Fred Hirsch has argued, Britain " 'managed' the system partly at the expense of its weakest members."[13] Over time, this was bound to become a source of serious policy conflict in the monetary order.

In fact, it may be argued that behind the deceptive facade of the Golden Age, the classical gold standard actually bore within itself the seeds of its own destruction. Not only did the order require the continued acquiescence of periphery countries in order to preserve a semblance of stability in the core; it also depended on the continued hegemony of Great Britain in the world's economic affairs. But as many economic historians have noted, this dominance was already beginning to fade, even as early as the turn of the century.[14] From the decade of the 1870s onward, British industrialists were faced with a mounting wave of competition in world export markets, first from Germany and the United States, and later from France, Russia, and Japan. From the 1890s onward, London was faced with growing competition from newly emergent financial centers like Paris, Berlin, and later New York; the pound found itself rivalled *inter alia* by the franc, the mark, and eventually the dollar. As a result of these developments, the British gradually lost a good part of their power to manage the international monetary order. Thus, when it was brought down by the outbreak of World War I, the classical gold standard had already become a rather fragile thing. It is perhaps too much to argue, as does one economic historian, that "the tree felled by the crisis was already rotten."[15] But signs of decay there most certainly were.

The Interwar Period[16]

When World War I broke out, all of the belligerent nations—and soon most others as well—took action to protect their gold reserves by suspending currency convertibility and embargoing gold exports. The classical gold standard was dead. Private individuals could no longer redeem paper currency in gold, nor could they sell it abroad. But they could still sell one paper currency for another (exchange control not being invented until the 1930s) at whatever price the exchange market would bear. The fixed exchange-rate mechanism of the gold standard, therefore, was succeeded by its absolute opposite: a pure floating exchange-rate regime. In the ensuing years, as currency values varied considerably under the impact of wartime uncertainties, the international monetary order could not even come near to realizing its potential for joint gain.

Accordingly, once the war was over and peace arrangements taken care of, governments quickly turned their attention to the problem of world monetary reform. Lulled by the myth of the Golden Age, they saw their task as a comparatively simple one: to restore the classical gold standard (or a close approximation thereof). The major conundrum seemed to be an evident shortage of gold, owing to the extreme price inflations that had occurred in almost all countries during and immediately after the war. These had sharply reduced the purchasing power of the world's monetary gold stock, which was still valued at its old prewar parities. One plausible solution might have been an equally sharp multilateral devaluation of currencies in terms of gold, in order to restore the commodity value of gold reserves. But that was ruled out by most countries on the grounds that a return to "normal" (and to the Golden Age) must include a return to prewar rates of exchange. Yet at the same time, governments understandably wanted to avoid a scramble for gold that would have pushed up the metal's commodity value through competitive deflations of domestic prices. Some other solution had to be found.

The "solution" finally agreed upon was to *economize* on the use of gold. An international economic conference in 1922 (the Genoa Conference) recommended worldwide adoption of a gold-exchange standard in order to "centralize and coordinate the demand for gold, and so avoid those wide fluctuations in the purchasing power of gold which might otherwise result from the simultaneous and competitive efforts of a number of countries to secure metallic reserves."[17] Central banks were urged to substitute foreign-exchange balances for gold in their reserves as a "means of economizing the use of gold."[18] Gold holdings were to be systematically concentrated in the major financial centers (e.g., London); outside the centers, countries were to maintain their exchange rates by buying and selling "gold exchange" (i.e., currencies convertible into gold, such as sterling) instead of gold itself. The monetary order was thus to combine a pure fixed exchange-rate mechanism of balance-of-payments adjustment modeled on the classical gold standard, with a new mixed commodity-currency standard to cope with the shortage of gold.

The gold-exchange standard came into formal existence early in 1925, when Britain reestablished the gold convertibility of the pound and eliminated restrictions on gold exports. Within a year nearly forty other nations had joined in the experiment,[19] either de jure or de facto, and most other independent governments joined not much later. But the experiment did not last long. In 1931, following a wave of bank failures on the European continent, the British were forced by a run on their reserves to suspend convertibility once again, and in the chaos that ensued the international monetary order broke up into congeries of competing and hostile currency blocs. The largest of these was the sterling bloc, comprising Britain, its overseas dependencies and dominions (except Canada, which had closer financial ties with the United States), and a variety of independent states with traditionally close trading and banking connections with Britain. This bloc was a shrunken remnant of the world that the British had dominated and in effect managed prior to 1914. Members were identified by two main characteristics: they pegged their currencies to sterling, even after convertibility was suspended; and they continued to hold most of their reserves in the form of sterling balances in London. A second bloc after 1931 was informally grouped around the United States (the dollar area), and a third around France (the "gold bloc"). In addition, there was a large group of miscellaneous countries (including, especially, Germany and the states of Eastern Europe) that abandoned convertibility altogether in favor of starkly autarkic trade and financial policies.

The decade of the 1930s, the decade of the Great Depression, was a period of open economic warfare—a prelude to the military hostilities that were to follow after 1939. Never had the conflictual element in international monetary relations been laid quite so bare. It was truly a free-for-all regime. With public confidence shattered, exchange rates tended to fluctuate widely, and governments consciously engaged in competitive depreciations of their currencies in attempting to cope with their critical payments and unemployment problems.[20] As in the years during and immediately after World War I, the monetary order failed to come even near to realizing its potential for joint gain. In 1936 a semblance of cooperation was restored by the Tripartite Agreement among Britain, France, and the United States for mutual currency stabilization. But this was only the barest minimum that might have been done to restore consistency to international monetary relations.[21] Genuine monetary reconstruction had to wait until after World War II.

Why did the interwar experiment fail? Why did the attempt to return to the Golden Age end so disastrously? Mainly because the Golden Age *was* a myth, a myth based on misconceptions and a fundamental misunderstanding of how much the world economy had really changed. Governments failed to read the signs of decay in the prewar era; more importantly, they failed to realize how anachronistic a restored gold standard would be in the new circumstances of the postwar era. Conditions in the 1920s simply did not lend themselves to the adoption of an impersonal and fully automatic monetary order. In reality, the experiment was doomed from the start.

In the first place, governments were in the process of abandoning their inherited attitudes of laissez-faire in general economic policy. Social and political conditions had changed. A Bolshevik revolution had succeeded in Russia; elsewhere, socialism was almost universally on the rise. Governments could no longer afford to tolerate a certain amount of price or income deflation or inflation simply for the sake of maintaining convertibility of their currencies at a fixed price. Domestic stability now had to take precedence if politicians were to hold onto their jobs. If before World War I central banks rarely adhered to the gold-standard rules of the game in the positive sense, after the war they rarely adhered to them even in the negative sense. Instead, a variety of new instruments were devised to counteract and neutralize the domestic monetary influence of external payments disequilibria, just the opposite of what was needed to make a restored gold standard work.

> The domestic effects of changes in gold and exchange reserves tended to be neutralized. . . .The basic reason for this tendency was undoubtedly a desire for greater stability. Each country sought to protect its domestic credit system from the influence of fluctuations originating outside. When the precepts of the gold standard ran counter to the requirements of domestic monetary stability, it was the latter that usually prevailed.[22]

In the second place, prices and wages were becoming increasingly rigid, at least in a downward direction, under the impact of rising trade unionism and expanding social welfare legislation. Domestic price flexibility was a key requirement for a restored gold standard. Without it (and with exchange rates fixed), a disproportionate share of the adjustment process had to consist of changes of domestic incomes, output, and employment. It was precisely in order to avoid such impacts, of course, that governments were becoming increasingly interventionist in economic affairs. But the consequences of such interventionism inevitably included a complete short-circuiting of the external adjustment mechanism that the same governments were laboring so hard to rebuild.

A third problem was the distortion structure of exchange rates established under the new gold-exchange standard. In insisting upon a return to convertibility at their prewar parities, governments were taking insufficient note of the fact that price relationships between national economies had been dramatically altered since 1914. Inconvertibility and floating exchange rates had broken the links between national price movements, and domestic inflation rates had varied enormously. When convertibility was finally reestablished after 1925, many governments found themselves with currencies that were overvalued and undervalued by quite significant amounts. Yet they were prevented from doing much about it by the straitjacket of fixed exchange rates. The pound, for example, restored to convertibility at its old prewar parity of $4.86, was overvalued by at least 10 percent; but since subsequent changes of the parity were ruled out by the gold-standard rules of the game, it was not surprising that the British balance of payments stayed under almost continuous strain until 1931, and British unemployment rates remained uncomfortably high. The French, on the other hand, who were an exception to the general rule in returning to gold (de facto in 1926, de jure in 1928) at just one-fifth of their prewar parity, undervalued the franc by perhaps as much as 25 percent. The result in this case was an almost immediate drainage of funds from London to Paris, adding to Britain's woes and, in the end, contributing importantly to the final collapse of the ill-fated experiment in 1931.

A fourth problem was the war's legacy of international indebtedness, which imposed a severe strain on monetary relations throughout the 1920s. The United States was the net creditor in a complicated network of obligations arising from wartime interallied loans and postwar German reparations; the biggest debtor, of course, was defeated Germany. As it turned out, most countries simply did not have the capacity to generate the net current-account surpluses necessary to effect their obligated transfers on capital account. In large measure, therefore, they had to rely instead on private capital outflows from the United States (much of which went to Germany) in a vast circular flow of funds. The Germans paid their reparations essentially with funds borrowed from America; Germany's creditors then used the same funds or other American loans to pay off their debts in the United States. How precarious all of this was became clear in 1929, when the stock-market crash and ensuing Great Depression abruptly cut off virtually all U.S. investment overseas. It is no accident that within two years reparations and interallied debt payments were abruptly cut off as well.

Finally, there was the problem of divided responsibility in the monetary order. If what ensured the apparent stability of the classical gold standard before 1914 was a single dominant center capable of acting as money manager of the world, what ultimately brought down its successor in 1931 was the emergence of competitive financial centers effectively rendering Britian's traditional hegemonic role impossible. Rivals to London had begun emerging even before World War I. During the 1920s this process continued, as Paris reasserted itself as a financial center and New York suddenly appeared on the scene. Still losing ground industrially and now saddled with an overvalued currency as well, Britain was no longer capable of playing the trio of roles that had provided the prewar monetary order with its semblance of stability. Unfortunately, neither were the French capable of shouldering such heavy responsibilities—they lacked the requisite economic and financial resources—and the Americans, who did have the resources, were as yet unwilling to do so. As a result, the system drifted without a leader. As Charles Kindleberger has written: "The United States was uncertain of its international role.... The one country capable of leadership was bemused by domestic concerns and stood aside.... The instability [came] from the growing weakness of one driver, and the lack of sufficient interest in the other."[23]

Could the two drivers, together with France, possibly have managed the monetary order cooperatively? Perhaps so. But this would have called for greater mutual trust and forebearance than any of the three seemed capable of at the time. Britain was still trying to lead, albeit from weakness, and the United States had not yet learned how to lead from strength. The French, meanwhile, resented both Anglo-Saxon powers, and all three were competing actively for short-term money flows—and even for gold itself. (After 1928, for example, the Bank of France added to the pressures on the British by suddenly opting to convert its sizable accumulation of sterling balances into gold.)[24] The result of this lack of coordination was a continual problem of large-scale transfers of private funds ("hot money" movements) from one financial center to another—the confidence problem. "This shifting of balances from one market to another [was] inevitable in a gold standard system without a single dominating center."[25] In the end, it was such a shifting of balances out of London in 1931 that finally brought the system down. In fact, it was not until 1936, with the Tripartite Agreement, that the three powers eventually got around to acknowledging formally their mutual responsibility for the monetary order. By that time, however, it was too late.

The Bretton Woods System

World War II brought exchange control everywhere and ended much of what remained of the element of cooperation in international monetary relations. But almost immediately, planning began for postwar monetary reconstruction. Discussions centered in the Treasuries of Britain and the United States, and culminated in the creation of the International Monetary Fund at a conference of 44 allied nations at Bretton Woods, New Hampshire, in 1944.[26] The charter of the IMF was intended to be the written constitution of the postwar monetary order—what later became knows as the Bretton Woods system. The Bretton Woods system lasted only twenty-seven years, however, and died in August 1971.

The Origins of the Bretton Woods System

The Bretton Woods system originated as a compromise between rival plans for monetary reconstruction developed on the one hand by Harry Dexter White of the U.S. Treasury, and on the other hand by Lord Keynes of Britain. In 1944 the differences between these two plans seemed enormous. Today their differences appear rather less impressive than their similarities. Indeed, what is really striking, a third of a century later, is how much common ground there really was among all the participating governments at Bretton Woods. All agreed that the interwar experience had taught them several valuable lessons; all were determined to avoid repeating what they perceived to be the errors of the past.[27] Their consensus of judgment was reflected directly in the contents of the IMF's Articles of Agreement.

Four points in particular stand out. First, it was generally agreed that the interwar period had demonstrated (to use the words of one authoritative source) "the proved disadvantages of freely fluctuating exchanges."[28] The floating rates of the 1930s were seen as having discouraged trade and investment and encouraged destabilizing speculation and competitive depreciations. Nations were loath to return to the free-for-all regime of the Depression years. But at the same time, they were also unwilling to return to the exchange-rate rigidity of the 1920s. The experience of those years was seen as having demonstrated the equal undesirability of the opposite extreme of permanently fixed rates. These, it was agreed, could "be equally harmful. The general interest may call for an occasional revision of currency values."[29] Accordingly, the negotiators at Bretton Woods were determined to find some compromise between the two extremes—one that would gain the advantages of both fixed and flexible rates without suffering from their disadvantages.

What they came up with has since been labeled the "pegged-rate" or "adjustable-peg" regime. Members were obligated to declare a par value (a "peg") for their currencies and to intervene in the exchange market to limit fluctuations within maximum margins (a "band") one percent above or below parity; but they also retained the right, whenever necessary and in accordance with agreed procedures, to alter their par values to correct a "fundamental disequilibrium" in their balance of payments. What constituted a fundamental disequilibrium? Although key to the whole operation of the Bretton Woods adjustment mechanism, this notion was never spelled out in any detail anywhere in the Articles of Agreement. The omission was to come back to haunt members of the Fund in later years.

Second, all governments generally agreed that if exchange rates were not to be freely fluctuating, countries would need to be assured of an adequate supply of official monetary reserves. An adjustable-peg regime "presupposes a large volume of such reserves for each single country as well as in the aggregate."[30] The experience of the interwar period—the gold shortage of the 1920s as well as the breakdown of fixed rates in the 1930s—was thought to have demonstrated the dangers of inadequate reserve volume. Accordingly, a second order of business at Bretton Woods was to ensure a supplementary source of reserve supply. Negotiators agreed that what they needed was some "procedure under which international liquidity would be supplied in the form of pre-arranged borrowing facilities."[31]

What they came up with, in this instance, was the IMF system of subscriptions and quotas. In essence, the Fund was to be nothing more than a pool of national currencies and gold subscribed by each country. Members were assigned quotas, according to a rather complicated formula intended roughly to reflect each country's relative importance in the world economy, and were obligated to pay into the Fund a subscription of equal amount. The subscription was to be paid 25 percent in gold or currency convertible into gold (effectively the U.S. dollar, which was the only currency still convertible directly into gold).[32] and 75 percent in the member's own currency. Each member was then entitled, when short of reserves, to "purchase" (i.e., borrow) amounts of foreign exchange from the Fund in return for equivalent amounts of its own currency. Maximum purchases were set equal to the member's 25-percent gold subscription (its "gold tranche"), plus four additional amounts each equal to 25 percent of its quota (its "credit tranches"), up to the point where the Fund's holdings of the member's currency equaled 200 percent of its quota. (If any of the Fund's holdings of the member's initial 75 percent subscription of its own currency was borrowed by other countries, the member's borrowing capacity was correspondingly increased: this was its "super-gold tranche.") The member's "net reserve position" in the Fund equaled its gold tranche (plus super-gold tranche, if any) less any borrowings by the country from the Fund. Net reserve positions were to provide the supplementary liquidity that was generally considered necessary to make the adjustable-peg regime work.

A third point on which all governments at Bretton Woods agreed was that it was necessary to avoid a recurrence of the kind of economic warfare that had characterized the decade of the 1930s. Some "code of action" was needed to "guide international exchange adjustments,"[33] some framework of rules to ensure that countries would remove their existing exchange controls and return to a system of multilateral payments based on currency convertibility. At Bretton Woods such a code was written into the obligations of Fund members. Governments were generally forbidden to engage in discriminatory currency practices or exchange-control regulation, although two exceptions were permitted. First, convertibility obligations were extended to current international transactions only. Governments were to refrain from regulating purchases and sales of foreign exchange for the purpose of current-account transactions. But they were not obligated to refrain from regulation of capital-account transactions; indeed, they were formally encouraged to make use of capital controls to maintain equilibrium in the face of "those disequilibrating short-term capital movements which caused so much trouble during the 'thirties.' "[34] And second, convertibility obligations could be deferred if a member so chose during a postwar "transitional period." Members deferring their convertibility obligations were known as Article XIV countries; members accepting them had so-called Article VIII status. One of the functions assigned to the IMF was to oversee this code of action on currency convertibility.

Finally, governments agreed that there was a need for an institutional forum for international consultation and cooperation on monetary matters. The world could not be allowed to return to the divided responsibility of the interwar years. "International monetary relations especially in the years before the Tripartite Agreement of 1936 suffered greatly from the absence of an established machinery or procedure of consultation."[35] In the postwar era, the Fund itself would provide such a forum. Of all the achievements of Bretton Woods, this was potentially the most significant. Never before had international monetary cooperation been attempted on a permanent institutional basis. Judged against the anarchy of the 1930s, this could be considered a breakthrough of historic proportions. For the first time ever, governments were formally committing themselves to the principle of collective responsibility for management of the international monetary order.

These four points together defined the Bretton Woods system—a monetary order combining an essentially unchanged gold-exchange standard, supplemented only by a centralized pool of gold and national currencies, with an entirely new pegged-rate mechanism of balance-of-payments adjustment. The Fund itself was expected to perform three important functions: regulatory (administering the rules affecting exchange rates and currency convertibility), financial (supplying supplementary liquidity), and consultative (providing a forum for the cooperative management of monetary relations). The negotiators at Bretton Woods did not think it necessary to alter in any fundamental way the mixed commodity-currency standard that had been inherited from the interwar years. Indeed, it does not even seem to have occurred to them that there might be any inherent defect in the structure of a gold-exchange standard. The problem in the 1920s, they felt, had not been the gold-exchange standard itself

but the division of responsibility—in short, a problem of management. "The nucleus of the gold exchange system consisted of more
than one country; and this was a special source of weakness. With
adequate cooperation between the centre countries, it need not have
been serious."[36] In the Bretton Woods system the IMF was to
provide the necessary machinery for multilateral cooperation. The
management problem would thus be solved and consistency in
monetary relations ensured.

Implicit in this attitude was a remarkable optimism regarding
prospects for monetary stability in the postwar era. Underlying the
choice of the pegged-rate adjustment mechanism, for instance,
seemed to be a clear expectation that beyond the postwar transitional period (itself expected to be brief) payments imbalances
would not be excessive. The adjustment mechanism was manifestly
biased in principle against frequent changes of exchange rates, presumably because of the experience of the 1930s; governments had to
demonstrate the existence of a fundamental disequilibrium before
they could alter their par values. At the same time, no government
was prepared to sacrifice domestic stability for the sake of external
equilibrium. Yet nations were left with few other instruments, other
than capital controls, to deal with disturbances to the balance of
payments. This suggests that the negotiators at Bretton Woods felt
that the major threat to stability was likely to come from private
speculation rather than from more fundamental price or income
developments. It also suggests that they were confident that most
disequilibria would be of a stochastic rather than nonstochastic
nature. Underlying the IMF's financial function seemed to be a clear
expectation that its centralized pool of liquidity would be sufficient
to cope with most financing problems as they emerged.

As matters turned out, this optimism proved entirely unjustified.
Monetary relations immediately after the war were anything but
stable, and the transitional period anything but brief.[37] Only the
United States, Canada, and a small handful of other countries (mainly
in Central America) were able to pledge themselves to the obligations of Article VIII right away. Most others were simply too
devastated by war—their export capacities damaged, their import

needs enormous, their monetary reserves exhausted—to commit their currencies to convertibility. Payments problems, especially in Europe and Japan, could hardly be described as stochastic; the Fund's initial pool of liquidity was anything but sufficient. After a short burst of activity during its first two years, mainly to the benefit of European nations, the Fund's lending operations shrank to an extremely small scale. (In 1950 the Fund made no new loans at all, and large-scale operations did not begin again until 1956.) The burden instead was shifted to one country, the only country after the war immediately capable of shouldering the responsibility for global monetary stabilization—namely, the United States.

Fortunately, this time, for reasons of its own (see below), the United States was willing. As dominant then as Britain had been in the nineteenth century, America rapidly assumed the same trio of managerial roles—in effect, taking over as money manager of the world. A relatively open market was maintained for the exports of foreign goods. A relatively generous flow of long-term loans and grants was initiated first through the Marshall Plan and other related aid programs, then through the reopened New York capital market. And a relatively liberal lending policy was eventually established for the provision of short-term funds in times of exchange crisis as well. Since monetary reserves were everywhere in such short supply—and since the IMF's pool of liquidity was manifestly inadequate—the United States itself became the residual source of global liquidity growth through its balance-of-payments deficits. At the war's end, America owned almost three-quarters of the world's existing monetary gold; and prospects for new gold production were obviously limited by the physical constraints of nature. The rest of the world, therefore, was more than willing to economize on this scarce gold supply by accumulating dollars instead. The dollar thus was enshrined not only as principal "vehicle currency" for international trade and investment but also as principal reserve asset for central banks. In the early postwar years, America's deficits became the universal solvent to keep the machinery of Bretton Woods running. It may be misleading, as I have indicated, to call the classical gold standard a sterling-exchange standard (though not, I have suggested, to call it a hegemony); it is not at all misleading to call the postwar monetary standard a dollar-exchange standard. Indeed, the Bretton Woods system became synonymous with a hegemonic monetary order centered on the dollar. Though multilateral in formal design, in actual practice (like the classical gold standard before it) the Bretton Woods system was highly centralized.

In effect, what the United States did was to abjure any payments target of its own in favor of taking responsibility for operation of the monetary order itself. Other countries set independent balance-of-payments targets; America's external financial policy was essentially one of "benign neglect."[38] Consistency in monetary relations was ensured not by multilateral cooperation but by America's willingness to play a passive role in the adjustment process, as the nth country, in effect: "other countries from time to time changed the par value of their currencies against the dollar and gold, but the value of the dollar itself remained fixed in relation to gold and therefore to other currencies collectively."[39] The growth of the world's liquidity supply was largely determined, consequently, by the magnitude of America's deficits—modified only to the extent that these deficits were settled in gold, rather than dollars, reflecting the asset preferences of surplus countries.

Like the British in the nineteenth century, the Americans did not deliberately seek the responsibility of global monetary management (In the interwar period they had evaded it.) On the other hand, unlike the British, once the Americans found themselves with it, they soon came to welcome it, for reasons that were a mixture of altruism and self-interest. Being money manager for the world fit in neatly with America's newfound leadership role in the Western Alliance. The cold war had begun, and isolationism was a thing of the past. The United States perceived a need to promote the economic recovery of potential allies in Europe and Japan, as well as to maintain a sizable and potent military establishment overseas. All of this cost money: the privilege of liability-financing deficits meant that America was effectively freed from balance-of-payments constraints to spend as freely as it thought necessary to promote objectives believed to be in the national interest. The United States could issue the world's principal vehicle and reserve currency in amounts presumed to be consistent with its own policy priorities—and not necessarily with those of foreign dollar holders. Foreign dollar holders conceded this policy autonomy to America because it also directly contributed to their own economic rehabilitation. America accepted the necessity, for example, of preferential trade and payments arrangements in Europe, despite their inherent and obvious discrimination against U.S. export sales; likewise, America accepted the necessity of granting Japanese exporters access to the U.S. internal market at a time when other markets still remained largely closed to goods labeled "Made in Japan." In effect, as I have argued elsewhere, an implicit bargain was struck.[40] America's allies acquiesced in a hegemonic system that accorded the United States special privileges to act abroad unilaterally to promote U.S. interests. The United States, in turn, condoned its allies' use of the system to promote their own economic prosperity, even if this happened to come largely at the expense of the United States. In the words of Marina Whitman:

> The United States was frequently willing to subordinate its short-term economic interests, narrowly conceived, to the long-term political and economic advantages of strengthened economies in other free-world nations. . . . Other countries, in turn, were willing to accord the United States certain special privileges (primarily that of printing international money) as a concomitant of the special responsibilities we took for the economic stability and military security of the non-Communist world.[41]

The History of the Bretton Woods System[42]

The subsequent history of the Bretton Woods system may be read as the history of this implicit bargain. The breakdown of the system in 1971 may be read as the bargain's final collapse. As Harold v. B. Cleveland has observed, the monetary order

> depended for its proper functioning on a political relationship between the United States and the other major industrial countries. . . . [It] was acceptable as long as Europe and Japan felt dependent, politically and strategically, on the good will of the United States. . . . But these conditions could not long endure. . . .

Economic and political changes made the hegemony of the dollar an anachronism.[43]

The chronology of Bretton Woods can be divided into two periods: the period of the "dollar shortage," lasting roughly until 1958; and the period of the "dollar glut," covering the remaining dozen years or so. The period of the dollar shortage was the heyday of America's dominance of international monetary relations. The term "dollar shortage," universally used at the time, was simply a shorthand expression of the fact that only the United States was capable of shouldering the responsibility for global monetary stabilization; only the United States could help other governments avoid a mutually destructive scramble for gold by promoting an outflow of dollar balances instead. As David Calleo has written: "Circumstances dictated dollar hegemony."[44] Dollar deficits began in 1950, following a round of devaluations of European currencies, at American insistence, in 1949. (Dollar surpluses prior to 1950 were financed largely by grants and long-term loans from the United States.) In ensuing years, deficits in the U.S. balance of payments (as conventionally measured) averaged approximately $1.5 billion a year. But for these deficits, other governments would have been compelled by their reserve shortages to resort to competitive exchange depreciations or domestic deflations; they would certainly not have been able to make as much progress as they did toward dismantling wartime exchange controls and trade restrictions. Persistent dollar deficits thus actually served to avoid monetary instability or policy conflict before 1958. Not since the Golden Age before World War I, in fact, had the monetary order been so successful in reconciling the tension between economic and political values. The period to 1958 has rightly been called one of "beneficial disequilibrium."[45]

After 1958, however, America's persistent deficits began to take on a different coloration. Following a brief surplus in 1957, owing to an increase of oil exports to Europe caused by the closing of the Suez Canal, the U.S. balance of payments plunged to a $3.5 billion deficit in 1958 and to even larger deficits in 1959 and 1960. This was the turning point. Instead of talking about a dollar shortage, observers began to talk about a dollar glut; consistency in monetary relations no longer appeared quite so assured. In 1958, Europe's currencies returned to convertibility. In subsequent years the former eagerness of European governments to obtain dollar reserves was transformed into what seemed an equally fervent desire to avoid excess dollar accumulations. Before 1958, less than 10 percent of America's deficits had been financed by calls on the gold stock in Fort Knox (the rest being liability-financed). During the next decade, almost two-thirds of America's cumulative deficit was transferred in the form of gold. Almost all of this went to governments on the continent of Europe.

It was clear that the structure of Bretton Woods was coming under increasing strain. Defects were becoming evident both in the mechanism of liquidity creation and in the mechanism of payments adjustment.

Credit for first drawing attention to the defects in the liquidity-creation mechanism of Bretton Woods is usually given to Robert Triffin for his influential book *Gold and the Dollar Crisis.*[46] The negotiators at Bretton Woods, Triffin argued, had been too complacent about the gold-exchange standard. The problem was not simply one of management. Rather, it was one of structure—an inherent defect in the very concept of a gold-exchange standard. A gold-exchange standard is built on the illusion of convertibility of its fiduciary element into gold at a fixed price. The Bretton Woods system, though, was relying on deficits in the U.S. balance of payments to avert a world liquidity shortage. Already, America's "overhang" of overseas liabilities to private and official foreigners was growing larger than its gold stock at home. The progressive deterioration of the U.S. net reserve position, therefore, was bound in time to undermine global confidence in the dollar's continued convertibility. In effect, governments were caught on the horns of a dilemma. To forestall speculation against the dollar, U.S. deficits would have to cease. But this would confront governments with the liquidity problem. To forestall the liquidity problem, U.S. deficits would have to continue. But this would confront governments with the confidence problem. Governments could not have their cake and eat it too.

Not that governments were unwilling to try. On the contrary, during the early 1960s a variety of ad hoc measures were initiated in an effort to contain speculative pressures that were mounting against the dollar. These included a network of reciprocal short-term credit facilities ("swaps") between the Federal Reserve and other central banks, as well as enlargement of the potential lending authority of the IMF (through the "General Arrangements to Borrow"). Both were intended to facilitate recycling of funds in the event of speculative currency shifts by private investors. They also included creation of a "gold pool" of the major financial powers to stabilize the price of gold in private markets. Later, in 1968, the gold pool was replaced by a two-tier gold-price system—one price for the private market, determined by supply and demand, and another price for central banks, to remain at the previous fixed level of $35 per ounce. These several measures were moderately successful in helping governments cope with the threat of private speculation against the dollar—the private confidence problem. The official confidence problem, however, remained as acute a danger as ever.

Meanwhile, in the mid-1960s, negotiations were begun whose aim was to establish a substitute source of liquidity growth, in order to reduce reliance on dollar deficits in the future. These negotiations were conducted among ten industrial countries—the so-called Group of Ten (G-10)—compromising Belgium, Canada, France, Germany, Italy, Japan, the Netherlands, Sweden, the United Kingdom, and the United States. What came out of the G-10 negotiations was the agreement to create Special Drawing Rights, an entirely new type of world fiduciary reserve asset.[47] The SDR agreement was confirmed by the full membership of the International Monetary Fund in 1968 and activated in 1969. Between 1970 and 1972 some 9.5 billion SDR units were allocated to members of the Fund. Governments were confident that with SDRs "in place," any future threat of world liquidity shortage could be successfully averted. On the other hand, they were totally unprepared for the opposite threat—a reserve surfeit—which in fact is what eventually emerged.

Any number of authors could be credited for drawing attention to the defects in the payments adjustment mechanism of Bretton

Woods. Virtually from the time the Charter was first negotiated, observers began pointing to the ambiguity surrounding the notion of fundamental disequilibrium. How could governments be expected to alter their par values if they could not tell when a fundamental disequilibrium existed? And if they were inhibited from altering their par values, then how would international payments equilibrium be maintained? I have already noted that the adjustment mechanism was biased in principle against frequent changes of exchange rates. In practice during the postwar period it became biased even against infrequent changes of exchange rates. At least among the advanced industrial nations, the world seemed to have returned to the rigidities of the 1920s. Governments went to enormous lengths to avoid the "defeat" of an altered par value. (A particularly sad example of this was the long struggle of the British government to avoid devaluation of the pound—a struggle that ended when sterling was devalued by 14.3 percent in 1967.) The resulting stickiness of the adjustment process not only aggravated fears of a potential world liquidity shortage. It also created irresistible incentives for speculative currency shifts by private individuals and institutions, greatly adding to the confidence problem as well.

Speculative currency shifts were facilitated at the time by the growing integration of money and capital markets in all of the advanced industrial nations. Large-scale capital movements had not originally been envisaged by the negotiators at Bretton Woods; as I have indicated, governments actually were encouraged to *control* capital movements for the purpose of maintaining payments equilibrium. In reality, however, capital movements turned out to be promoted rather than retarded by the design of the Bretton Woods system—in particular, by the integrative power of the par-value regime, and by the return to currency convertibility in Europe in 1958. (Japan did not pledge itself to Article VIII of the IMF Charter until 1964.) After 1958, capital mobility accelerated *pari passu* with the growth of the Eurocurrency market—that well-known market for currencies deposited in banks located outside of the country of issue.[48] From its origin in the mid-1950s, the Eurocurrency market rapidly expanded into a broad, full-fledged international financial market; subject to just a minimum of governmental guidance, supervision, and regulation, it became during the 1960s the principal vehicle for private speculation against official exchange parities. Increasingly, governments found it difficult to "defend" unadjusted par values in the face of the high degree of international capital mobility that had been generated.

The most serious adjustment problem during this period was, of course, the dollar glut—more accurately, the persistent payments imbalance between the United States and the surplus countries of Europe and Japan. On each side, complaints were heard about the policies of the other. America felt that its erstwhile European and Japanese allies could do more to eliminate the international payments disequilibrium by inflating or revaluing their currencies; the Europeans and Japanese argued that it was the responsibility of the United States to take the first steps to reduce its persistent deficit. Each felt discriminated against by the other. The surplus countries felt that America's privilege of liability-financing deficits, growing out of the dollar's reserve-currency role, created an asymmetry in the monetary order favorable to the United States. None of them, after all, had such a degree of policy autonomy. America, on the other hand, felt that the use of the dollar by other governments as their principal intervention medium to support par values—the intervention-currency role of the dollar—created an asymmetry in the monetary order more favorable to Europe and Japan. Many sources argued that the dollar was over valued. Yet how could its value in terms of foreign currencies be changed unilaterally unless all other countries agreed to intervene appropriately in the exchange market? The United States felt it had no effective control over its own exchange rate (no exchange-rate autonomy) and therefore did not feel it could easily devalue to rid itself of its deficit.

In fact, the debate over asymmetries masked a deeper political conflict. The postwar bargain was coming unstuck. In the United States, concern was growing about the competitive threat from the European Common Market and Japan to American commercial interests. The period of postwar recovery was over: Europe and Japan had become reinvigorated giants, not only willing but able to compete aggressively with America in markets at home and abroad. The cost of subordinating U.S. economic interests to the presumed political advantage of now strengthened allies was becoming ever more intolerable. Conversely, concern was growing in Europe and Japan about America's use of its privilege of liability-financing to pursue policies abroad which many considered abhorrent (one example was the U.S. involvement in Vietnam), the "exorbitant privilege," as Charles de Gaulle called it. The Europeans and Japanese had just one major weapon they could use to restrict America's policy autonomy—their right to demand conversion of accumulated dollar balances into gold. Robert Mundell has written that "the sole function of gold convertibility in the Bretton Woods arrangement was to discipline the U.S."[49] But by the mid-1960s this was a discipline that most major financial powers were growing somewhat reluctant to use. America's overhang of liabilities was by now far larger than its gold stock. A concerted conversion campaign could have threatened to topple the whole of the Bretton Woods edifice. Governments—with one major exception—did not consider it in their interest to exacerbate the official confidence problem and provoke a systemic crisis. The one major exception was France, which in 1965, in a move strikingly reminiscent of its behavior toward sterling after 1928, began a rapid conversion of its outstanding dollar balances into gold, explicitly for the purpose of exerting pressure on the United States.[50] France alone, however, was unable to change America's policies significantly.

At bottom, the Bretton Woods system rested on one simple assumption—that economic policy in the United States would be stabilizing. Like Britain in the nineteenth century, America had the power to guide the world's monetary policy. The absence of an effective external discipline on U.S. policy autonomy could not threaten the system so long as this assumption held. And indeed, before 1965, the assumption did seem quite justified. America clearly had the best long-term record of price stability of any industrial country; even for some time after 1958 the United States could not justly be accused of "exporting" inflation, however much some governments were complaining about a dollar glut.[51] After 1965, however, the situation reversed itself, as a direct consequence of the escalation of hostilities in Vietnam. America's economy began to overheat, and inflation began to gain momentum. The Bretton Woods system was tailor-made to promote the transmission of this inflation abroad. With exchange rates pegged, tradable-goods price increases in the largest of all trading nations were immediately radiated outward to the rest of the world economy. And with governments committed to defending their pegged rates by buying the surfeit of dollars in the exchange market, a huge reserve base was created for monetary expansion in these other countries as well. Now the United States could justifiably be accused of exporting inflation overseas.[52]

The gathering world inflation after 1965 exposed all of the latent defects of Bretton Woods. American policy was no longer stabilizing, yet other governments were reluctant to use the one power of discipline they had. (Indeed, after the creation of the two-tier gold-price system in 1968, the U.S. government made it quite plain that if a serious depletion of its gold stock were threatened, it would be prepared to close the window and refuse further sales.) The adjustment mechanism was incapable of coping with the widening deficit in the U.S. balance of payments (which soared to $9.8 billion in 1970 and an incredible $29.8 billion in 1971), and the confidence problem was worsening as private speculators were encouraged to bet on devaluation of the dollar or revaluations of the currencies of Europe and Japan. Ultimately, it was the United States that brought the drama to its denouement. Concerned about the rapidly deteriorating U.S. trade balance, as well as about rising protectionist sentiment in the Congress, President Richard Nixon was determined to force the Europeans and Japanese to accept an adjustment of international exchange-rate relationships that would correct the overvaluation of the dollar. Feeling that he lacked effective control over the dollar exchange rate under the prevailing rules of the game, the President decided that the rules themselves would have to be changed. Thus, on August 15, 1971, the convertibility of the dollar into gold was suspended, in effect freeing the dollar to find its own level in the exchange market. With that decision, the Bretton Woods system passed into history.

Conclusions

What conclusions may be drawn from this brief history of international monetary relations? In effect, the world monetary order has gone through two complete life cycles over the course of the last century. The first cycle began in the 1870s and, after interruption by World War I and attempts at restoration in the 1920s, finally terminated in the monetary chaos of the 1930s. The second, rising like a phoenix from the ashes of the interwar period and World War II, lasted a shorter period and self-destructed in 1971. In each of the two cycles the monetary order was effectively organized around a single hegemonic country; the early success of each in accommodating and balancing the efficiency and consistency objectives was directly attributable to the stabilizing influence of the dominant national power. Likewise, in each of the two cycles the managerial role of the dominant power was eventually undermined by the emergence of economic and political rivals; in each case, the fate of the monetary order was sealed when the hegemony underlying it became an anachronism.

Two, of course, is a small sample. Still, certain conclusions do seem justified by this brief survey. Robert Gilpin has argued that "the modern world economy has evolved through the emergence of great national economies that have successively become dominant. . . . Every economic system rests on a particular political order; its nature cannot be understood aside from politics."[53] The modern history of international monetary relations certainly appears to lend credence to this point of view. The evolution of the world monetary order can scarcely be understood aside from politics; manifestly, in each of its life cycles it has rested on a particular political order.

Indeed, one can argue that at the structure level of analysis, where rules and conventions are established, politics inherently dominates. The underlying shape of incentives and constraints inevitably reflects the prevailing pattern of interstate relations. The rules of the monetary game that evolved before World War I, for example, clearly reflected the superior structure power of Great Britain, just as the rules evolved after World War II reflected that of the United States. Equally, the occasional important amendments of the rules that have occurred—e.g., the Genoa Conference in 1922, the Tripartite Agreement in 1936, the SDR agreement in 1968—have clearly reflected substantial historical shifts in the distribution of structure power. Gilpin is undoubtedly right to argue that "in the short run, the distribution of power and the nature of the political system are major determinants of the framework within which wealth is produced and distributed." He is also undoubtedly right to argue that "in the long run, however, shifts in economic efficiency and in the location of economic activity tend to undermine and transform the existing political system. This political transformation in turn gives rise to changes in economic relations."[54]

At the process level of analysis, which focuses attention on the effects of marginal changes within a given set of rules and conventions, economics inherently dominates. In a dynamic world, allocative behavior in the economic process inevitably alters the prevailing pattern of interstate relations, by altering the distribution of state power (both process and structure). This is clearly what happened to the hegemonic pattern of interstate relations under the classical gold standard; equally, it is what happened to America's hegemony under the Bretton Woods system. In both instances, the operation of the monetary system gradually undermined the assumptions of the monetary order and, ultimately, precipitated changes in the structural framework of relations.

At both levels of analysis, the key questions are: (1) Precisely *how* does the economic process alter the pattern of interstate relations? (2) Precisely *how* does the altered pattern of relations translate itself into a new structural framework? In other words, how do we get "from here to there"? The dynamics and detail of regime change are not easy to predict.[55] Analysis cannot easily anticipate how, within a given set of rules and conventions, economic decisions will ultimately transform the distribution of state power; nor can it easily anticipate how, once the assumptions of the monetary order have been undermined, political decisions will ultimately transform the underlying shape of incentives and constraints. Much depends on such imponderables as the nature of private enterprises and public bureaucracies, the timing of their decisions, and the character of their bargaining processes. Within broad limits, there is much latitude for variation of specific outcomes.

These considerations emphasize again the importance of the distinction between order and system that was introduced at the outset of this book. No global monetary reform that fails to provide for compatibility of the order and system through time can possibly succeed in practice. Unfortunately, most reform discussions are too static, in the sense that they tend to think only in terms of a *given* monetary system—that is, they stress the need for compatibility of order and system only at a single point in time. The mechanism of interchange between national money systems is treated as a parameter, not a variable: attention is focused on designing the monetary order simply to "fit" the existing monetary system. In the words of one source, "a proposal is not feasible if it is not consistent with the market forces."[56] But if the history of international monetary relations teaches anything, it is that the monetary system is a living thing and that market forces can undergo quite dramatic changes through time. These changes may be exogenous (e.g., the increase of wage and price rigidity in the 1920s), or they may be endogenous, a function of the design of the monetary order itself (e.g., the increase of capital mobility in the 1960s). To be effective, monetary reform must either anticipate such systemic changes or, failing prescience, ensure a sufficient degree of flexibility in the monetary order to cope with them as they occur (by accommodating or suppressing them). An international monetary order that is too rigid to ensure continuing compatibility with the international monetary system will surely not endure.

Chapter 4

Issues and Actors in Monetary Relations Today

The death of the Bretton Woods system reopened the whole Pandora's box of monetary reform. A life cycle of the monetary order had ended. Here was an opportunity to redesign completely all the rules and conventions governing the financial conduct of nations—in effect, to write a brand-new constitution for the monetary system. The purpose of this chapter is to examine how governments responded to this opportunity after 1971 and, as a prelude to Part II, to outline the principal issues and actors in monetary relations today.

From Smithsonian to Jamaica

President Nixon's dramatic initiative of August 1971 touched off intensive bilateral and multilateral negotiations on the future of the monetary order. The first order of business, it was agreed, was to patch up the old Bretton Woods system as much as possible, until such time as a more fundamental global reform could be agreed upon and implemented. In an almost purely reflexive action, governments set out to restore some version of the par-value regime that had crumbled when the dollar was effectively freed to find its own level in the exchange market. Almost all major currencies were floating in the autumn of 1971. Casting about for some way to reestablish a regime of pegged rates, governments recognized that something had to be done to correct the overvaluation of the dollar and restore America's trade competitiveness in world markets. The question was how—and how much.

After four months of discussions, agreement on a new alignment of exchange rates was reached in December at a Group of Ten meeting at the Smithsonian Institution in Washington, D.C. The United States pledged to raise the official price of gold formally from $35 to $38 per ounce, effectively devaluing the dollar by 8.57 percent. Simultaneously, other governments realigned their exchange rates upward in coordination with the dollar devaluation, to achieve a total net weighted revaluation of other currencies relative to the dollar of approximately 12 percent. (The only concession to the brief experience of floating rates was a parallel agreement to widen the permissible band of fluctuations around par values from the previous 2 percent to 4.5 percent.) Called "the greatest monetary agreement in the history of the world" by President Nixon, the Smithsonian Agreement in fact did little to correct any of the underlying defects in either the payments-adjustment or liquidity-creation mechanisms of Bretton Woods. Not surprisingly, therefore, it began to come apart almost before the ink on it was dry. Private individuals and institutions were not convinced that the official par values set by the agreement came anywhere near to coinciding with "true market equilibrium values"—it was not even clear that there could be such a thing as "true equilibrium market values" in the then uncertain atmosphere of gathering world inflation—and waves of speculation soon broke over the new pattern of exchange rates. Within six months, the pound sterling was driven back to floating. In February 1973, the dollar itself was devalued for a second time, by 11.1 percent, to a new official gold price of $42.22 per ounce. And finally, in March 1973, all the major currencies were unpegged to float, either singly or in groups, in the foreign-exchange market. So ended "the greatest

monetary agreement in the history of the world." After fifteen
months of struggle to reestablish some sort of par-value regime,
governments decided, at least temporarily, to see what life would be
like with floating rates.[1]

Fortunately, the transition to floating rates in 1971-1973 was not
the occasion of a new free-for-all regime, as in the 1930s. Quite the
opposite, in fact. Despite latent policy conflicts, governments continued to cooperate in the understandable hope that they could
stave off a repetition of the disastrous experience of the interwar
period. Even while the Smithsonian Agreement was coming apart, a
more fundamental reform effort was initiated under the auspices of
the International Monetary Fund. In addition to attempting an
immediate realignment of exchange rates, the Smithsonian Agreement had called for a new look at the whole structure of global
monetary relations. Toward this end, the IMF created in July 1972 a
Committee of the Board of Governors (of the Fund) on Reform of
the International Monetary System and Related Issues—popularly
known as the Committee of Twenty (C-20). During the 1960s,
monetary negotiations had been conducted almost exclusively within
the Group of Ten. Many governments, however, especially those of
less-developed Third World countries, felt that the G-10 forum had
not been fully representative of their views or sensitive to their
interests. In the aftermath of the Smithsonian meeting, where they
had no formal representation at all, they were determined to broaden
national participation in any future negotiation process. Unlike the
Group of Ten, the Committee of Twenty, reflecting the composition
of the IMF's own twenty-member Executive Board, included not
only the G-10 industrial countries but also Argentina, Australia,
Brazil, Ethiopia, India, Indonesia, Iraq, Morocco, Venezuela, and
Zaire.[2]

The Committee of Twenty began business in September 1972
with high hopes that full agreement on a new structural framework
of relations could be reached before the end of 1973. Regrettably,
however, agreement proved elusive, and in June 1974 the Committee
wound up its affairs without final accord on a comprehensive plan
for reform. Instead, the Committee declared that henceforth the

task of putting a reformed international monetary order into prac-practice would have to be treated as an evolutionary process which could not be completed in only one or two years. In the words of the Chairman of the Deputies of the Committee of Twenty, "some aspects of reform should be pushed forward and implemented early, while other aspects could be developed over time."[3] No esti-mate was given of how long the Darwinian process of evolution might actually take.

There were two principal reasons for the Committee's failure to come up with a quick and easy blueprint for reform. In the first place, C-20's deliberations were stymied by serious conflicts of views between nations on outstanding questions. The basic issues of monetary reform had been under discussion for so long, in formal or informal settings, that by the early 1970s most governmental positions had tended to become frozen and inflexible. It was like the trench warfare of World War I: repeated assaults were made on the positions of others, but little ground was ever really given. The second cause for the Committee's failure was the emergence of unanticipated and unprecedented international economic problems, such as the rampant global inflation of 1973-1974 (the final explo-sion of the storm that had been gathering since 1965) and the energy crisis initiated by the oil-price increases of the Organization of Petroleum Exporting Countries (OPEC) in late 1973. The negotiators in the Committee of Twenty were taken unawares by these develop-ments. As is so often true of generals, they were caught preparing for the last war instead of for the next.

In place of a comprehensive plan for reform, therefore, the Committee ended up by producing nothing more than two quite limited policy initiatives. One was called *Outline of Reform*, detail-ing areas of disagreement as well as agreement among the negotiators; and the other was a "program of immediate action" that the Com-mittee decided could be pushed forward and implemented early.[4] Neither of these was designed to have anything more than a minimal impact on the structural framework of monetary relations. In fact, neither the existing payments-adjustment mechanism, now based on floating rates, nor the mechanism of liquidity creation inherited from the breakdown of Bretton Woods was altered significantly as a result of the Committee's arduous two-year effort.

The *Outline of Reform* summarized the limited areas of agreement among the negotiators by listing six general features that, at the time, all felt would be desirable in a reformed monetary order. These six features were:

(a) an effective and symmetrical adjustment process, including better functioning of the exchange rate mechanism, with the exchange rate regime based on stable but adjustable par values and with floating rates recognized as providing a useful technique in particular situations;

(b) cooperation in dealing with disequilibrating capital flows;

(c) the introduction of an appropriate form of convertibility for the settlement of imbalances, with symmetrical obligations on all countries;

(d) better international management of global liquidity, with the SDR becoming the principal reserve asset and the role of gold and of reserve currencies being reduced;

(e) consistency between arrangements for adjustment, convertibility and global liquidity; and

(f) the promotion of the net flow of real resources to developing countries.[5]

As should be clear, the first feature on the list encompassed the problem of adjustment; the second, the private confidence problem; the third and fourth jointly, the liquidity and official confidence problems; and the last, the problem of the "link" (see Chapter 2).* It should also be clear that, as listed, these features were not much more than vague generalities and platitudes. All the really hard questions were begged by these formulations. Having found it difficult to reconcile frozen governmental policy positions, the Committee apparently opted for glossing them over instead.

Probably for the same reason, the Committee's "program of immediate action" was remarkably modest, also begging all the hard questions. With respect to the adjustment problem, for example, the program's principal contribution was a set of guidelines for the

---

*The next-to-last item (e) merely called, logically enough, for harmony among the features.

management of floating exchange rates.[6] In principle, these guide-lines were supposed to avert the danger of competitive exchange-rate alterations in the absence of established par values. In practice, they had very little impact on the way the new floating-rate regime worked, since they were in no way legally binding on governments.

With respect to the liquidity and confidence problems, the pro-gram's principal contributions were a new method of valuing the SDR and a new higher interest rate on SDR holdings.[7] Both were intended to improve the SDR's attributes as a reserve asset. Under the original agreement creating Special Drawing Rights, the Fund valued the SDR in terms of the dollar at the par value of the dollar; exchange rates for the SDR against other currencies were derived from market rates for those currencies against the dollar. In practice, this meant that the value of the SDR in terms of any other currency was simply the market rate for that currency against the dollar. In an era of floating rates, this generated considerable uncertainty about the value of the SDR and a great deal of support for a different method of valuation. The method adopted by the Committee of Twenty, known as the "standard basket" technique,[8] established the value of the SDR in terms of a weighted "basket" of sixteen cur-rencies. (The currencies were those of the sixteen countries with a share of world exports averaging more than one percent over 1968-1972, with relative weights being set broadly proportionate to the share of these countries in international transactions.) The main advantage of the new valuation method was that it gave a more stable capital value to the SDR in terms of currencies in general, thus in principle making the SDR a relatively more attractive reserve asset to hold.

The new, higher interest rate on SDR holdings was also meant to enhance its relative attractiveness as a reserve asset. Originally set at the nominal level of 1.5 percent per annum, the yield on SDRs was now raised to 5 percent and linked to current rates of interest in private financial markets. This too made the SDR potentially more competitive with the dollar or other national currencies as a reserve asset to hold. However, neither this nor the improvement in the method of valuing SDRs had any practical impact on the asset prefences of reserve holders, since no new SDRs were issued after the initial 9.5 billion unit allocation in 1970-1972, and since few corresponding changes were made in the regulations preventing significant shifts between the SDR and other reserve assets. (See below.)

With respect to the problem of the "link," the Committee was unable to agree on whether, or how, the distributional criterion for SDRs might be altered to direct more of the social saving afforded by the SDR toward the poorest nations of the world. Instead, two new credit facilities were established in the IMF that were expected to be of principal benefit to less-developed countries, or LDCs. (These were in addition to the already existing "compensatory finance facility," designed to aid LDCs in the event of unanticipated fluctuations of their export proceeds.) Both were carefully circumscribed. One was a permanent "extended Fund facility" under which LDCs would receive longer-term balance-of-payments finance; and the other was a temporary "oil facility" to assist countries in balance-of-payments difficulties because of the 1973 oil-price increases. (The oil facility was phased out less than two years later, in March 1976.) In addition, a joint committee of the Fund and World Bank (the Development Committee) was created to pursue discussion of the issue of resource flows to developing countries.

Finally, to carry forward the "evolutionary" process of reform, a so-called Interim Committee of the Board of Governors on the International Monetary System was established—in effect, to pick up where the Committee of Twenty left off. (In fact, the Interim Committee was simply the Committee of Twenty by another name, with virtually the same countries participating in both.) The Interim Committee quickly set out to determine what additional aspects of reform could be developed in the near term. After a year and a half, agreement on yet another package of measures was reached at a special meeting of the Interim Committee in Kingston, Jamaica, in January 1976.[9] Some parts of the package required formal amendment of the IMF's Articles of Agreement: though quickly drafted by the Executive Board,[10] and approved by the Board of Governors,[11] the proposed Second Amendment (the first occurred when SDRs were established) was not expected to come into effect for at least eighteen months, until after completion of the necessary process of ratification by member countries.[12] Nevertheless, the Jamaica package was immediately hailed as a giant step forward in the reform process. Indeed, for many, reform now seemed just about complete. The chairman of the Interim Committee claimed that the measures "round off three years of effort to define a new international monetary system."[13] The U.S. Secretary of the Treasury was quoted as saying that the package "is a fundamental reform" that "ends successfully a three-year effort."[14] A typical newspaper headline proclaimed "A Monetary Order Is Born in Jamaica."[15]

The Jamaica package contained four essential ingredients. First, floating exchange rates were now legalized—an important change of principle, if not practice. Since under the original Bretton Woods agreement freely fluctuating exchange rates were outlawed, nations technically were living in sin after the struggle to reestablish some sort of par-value regime ended in March 1973. The *Outline* of the Committee of Twenty moved part of the way toward removing the stigma by recognizing floating rates as "a useful technique in particular situations." But in 1974 governments were still thinking in terms of ("stable but adjustable") par values. It was only with the Jamaica package that the stigma was removed completely. Governments henceforth could choose either to establish a par value or not, as they liked. Pegged and floating rates were given equal legal status. (Procedures were also laid down for a general return to a par-value regime, should that eventually be considered desirable by Fund members, but these were clearly not expected to be implemented in the near term.)

Second, a variety of agreed-upon measures were intended to reduce the reserve role of gold, as envisaged by the Committee of Twenty. There were four main provisions: (a) the official price of gold was abolished; (b) the obligation of IMF members to use gold in certain transactions with the Fund was eliminated; (c) one-sixth of the Fund's own holdings of gold (amounting to some 25 million ounces) was to be sold over a period of four years on the open market, with the major part of the profits to be lent on highly concessionary terms through a new IMF Trust Fund to poorer member countries;[16] and (d) another one-sixth of the Fund's gold was to be sold back ("restituted"), at the former official price, directly to member governments in proportion to their quotas.

Third, Fund quotas were to be increased by about one-third, with the share of OPEC countries in the total being increased from 5 to 10 percent, and the share of industrial countries being correspondingly reduced. (OPEC countries and LDCs together would now account for about one-third of Fund quotas.) This was of particular importance to OPEC governments, because voting in the IMF is decided on a weighted basis, with weights being proportional to each country's quota. Under the formula traditionally used for calculating Fund quotas, the OPEC countries were not entitled to an increased share. But the governments of OPEC felt that after the 1973 oil-price increases, their enhanced status as financial powers should be formally recognized in Fund voting procedures. A problem was that up to that time most Fund decisions had always required a weighted majority of 80 percent to be effective, and the United States, with just over 20 percent of the total, was the only member that could exercise a veto on its own. The Americans were obviously reluctant to lose their veto. The increase of quotas, therefore, was coupled with an agreement to increase the required majority for many Fund decisions from 80 to 85 percent. The United States thus retained its veto, and OPEC got its enhanced status.

Finally, two further measures were undertaken, in addition to the IMF Trust Fund, to promote a greater flow of resources to less-developed countries. One was permanent, a liberalization of the Fund's existing compensatory finance facility (offsetting the scheduled phasing out of the Fund's oil facility). The other was temporary, a 45 percent increase in the amount that countries could borrow under each of their four credit tranches in the IMF, pending approval and ratification of the overall one-third increase of Fund quotas. Although formally extended across-the-board to all Fund members, the temporary measure was in practice intended to be of principal benefit to poorer countries. In fact, it was the price demanded—and received—by the LDC members of the Interim Committee for their agreement to the other ingredients of the Jamaica package.

The Issues Today

Was a monetary order born in Jamaica? Was the U.S. Treasury Secretary right in saying that the reform effort had now ended "successfully"? Or was it more accurate to argue, as another source did at the time, that the package could best be characterized as "unfinished business"?[17] In fact, there seems little doubt that the Treasury Secretary's optimism was premature; indeed, little had changed. The Jamaica package left many questions unanswered. At best an uneasy compromise, it tended to suppress rather than resolve many of the outstanding issues of reform. Like the Committee of Twenty before it, the Interim Committee was stymied by serious conflicts of views and frozen governmental positions. The negotiators were caught in a "stalemate system."[18] Since no country was willing to take important risks to try to force a major change, once again formulations had to be found to gloss over their differences. In the words of one observer: "only empty phrases . . . were preserved in the final accord; the important principles were lost in the shuffle, or deliberately dropped."[19] To repeat from the Introduction, a monetary order is supposed to provide the control for the world monetary system by specifying which instruments of national policy may be used and which targets of policy may be regarded as legitimate. On these key points, however, the Jamaica package provided only conflicting signals. If a monetary order was born in Jamaica, it bore more resemblance to a free-for-all-regime than to any of the alternative organizing principles for international monetary relations.

The Mechanism of Payments Adjustment

Consider, for example, the adjustment mechanism. After Jamaica, this could be described as a regime of "managed floating." Par values, at least among the major countries, in practice had been abolished. Exchange rates, in principle, were no longer to be determined by government fiat but rather by movements of autonomous demand and supply in the foreign-exchange market. Central banks were expected to intervene in the market whenever necessary, to limit the frequency and amplitude of fluctuations of rates around their long-term trend ("clean floating"). But they were not to attempt to influence the long-term trends themselves in mutually inconsistent ways ("dirty floating"). In the words of the Second Amendment of the Articles of Agreement, central banks were to "avoid manipulating exchange rates or the international monetary system in order to prevent effective balance of payments adjustment or to gain an unfair competitive advantage over other members."[20] In the words of President Valéry Giscard d'Estaing of France, exchange rates were to be not "volatile" but "viscous."

This formula reflected a seminal diplomatic compromise between France and the United States at an economic summit meeting of the six largest industrial nations (America, Britain, France, Germany, Italy, and Japan) at Rambouillet, France, in November 1975. Up to that date, the United States had been arguing strongly for a totally unrestricted regime of floating exchange rates. France, on the other hand, had held out for a return to the "stable but adjustable" par-value objective accepted by the Committee of Twenty. Exchange-rate movements, the French felt, were much too extreme, indeed even "irrational," after March 1973; and on this point they were scarcely alone.[21] As Table 4-1 indicates, fluctuations between the dollar and other major currencies during 1973-1975 in fact ranged up to 20 percent or more over periods of just a few months. According to the French (and their supporters), fluctuations of this magnitude—as in the 1930s—were bound to discourage trade and investment and encourage destabilizing speculation. According to the Americans, conversely, a return to pegged rates would only recreate all of the undesirable defects of the Bretton Woods adjustment mechanism. Until November 1975, this dispute had held up all progress in the deliberations of the Interim Committee. Then, at Rambouillet, the two governments finally agreed to bury their differences, clearing the last obstacles to the Jamaica package two months later. Henceforth a distinction would be made between "disorderly" or "erratic" exchange-rate movements on the one hand, and movements caused by "underlying economic and financial conditions" on the other:

TABLE 4-1
Dollar Exchange Rates for Selected Currencies, 1973-1975
U.S. cents per foreign currency unit

	MAY 7, 1973	JULY 6, 1973	JAN. 7, 1974	MAY 10, 1974	SEPT. 6, 1974	FEB. 28, 1975	JULY 31, 1975
Belgium	2.482	2.905	2.309	2.675	2.529	2.943	2.601
Canada	99.770	100.230	100.760	103.955	101.300	100.190	96.587
France	21.918	26.130	20.120	20.665	20.720	24.010	22.878
Germany	35.058	44.300	34.700	41.380	37.440	43.925	38.838
Italy (100 lire)	16.935	17.360	15.815	16.030	15.095	15.925	15.019
Japan (100 yen)	37.675	38.250	33.330	36.030	33.050	34.920	33.579
Netherlands	33.805	40.225	33.845	39.130	36.754	42.700	37.638
Sweden	22.105	25.230	20.650	23.605	22.300	25.715	23.247
Switzerland	30.763	37.200	29.205	34.825	33.140	41.625	36.900
United Kingdom	249.150	256.000	222.800	243.050	231.090	243.050	214.391

PERCENTAGE CHANGE FROM PRECEDING DATE

		JULY 6, 1973	JAN. 7, 1974	MAY 10, 1974	SEPT. 6, 1974	FEB. 28, 1975	JULY 31, 1975
Belgium		17.04	−20.52	15.85	−5.46	16.37	−11.62
Canada		0.46	0.53	3.17	−2.55	−1.10	−3.60
France		19.22	−23.00	2.71	0.27	15.88	−4.71
Germany		26.36	−21.67	19.25	−9.52	17.32	−11.58
Italy		2.51	−8.90	1.36	−5.83	5.50	−5.69
Japan		1.53	−12.86	8.10	−8.27	5.66	−3.84
Netherlands		18.99	−15.86	15.62	−6.10	16.21	−11.85
Sweden		14.14	−18.15	14.31	−5.53	15.31	−9.60
Switzerland		20.92	−21.49	19.24	−4.84	25.60	−11.35
United Kingdom		2.75	−12.97	9.09	−4.92	5.18	−11.79

Source: Swiss Bank Corporation.

With regard to monetary problems, we affirm our intention to work for greater stability. This involves efforts to restore greater stability in underlying economic and financial conditions in the world economy. At the same time, our monetary authorities will act to counter disorderly market conditions, or erratic fluctuations, in exchange rates.[22]

The appropriate form of the exchange-rate regime had occupied much of the time of the Committee of Twenty.[23] The negotiators had wrestled long and hard over questions like these: What rules and conventions should guide central-bank intervention in the foreign-exchange market? What should be the respective adjustment obligations of surplus and deficit countries? What provision, if any, should be made for bringing pressures to bear on countries in persistent payments imbalance? And what should the IMF's role be in connection with the adjustment process? The Rambouillet compromise—brilliant diplomatic coup though it may have been—did little at all to answer any of these fundamental questions. In fact, as Edward Bernstein has commented, it "left open all the difficult problems of actually managing a system of flexible exchange rates."[24]

Central-bank intervention. The major problem here is *how to ensure* that governments will "avoid manipulating exchange rates . . . to gain unfair competitive advantage." The Second Amendment is silent on this: it does not even define what is meant by "manipulation" or "unfair" competitive advantage, let alone suggest rules by which these might be curbed or prevented. At Jamaica, much reference was made to the guidelines for management of floating rates laid down by the Committee of Twenty, but these, as indicated, were not legally binding on governments. At Rambouillet, much reference was made to a proposed new system of intergovernmental consultation and coordination on exchange-rate matters, but this too left many questions unanswered. The new system, according to one informed source, was supposed to provide for daily contacts among central banks to decide on short-term intervention strategies in the exchange market; plus weekly or monthly meetings of deputy finance ministers and quarterly meetings of finance ministers to review the longer-term trends of exchange rates.[25] No indication was given, however, of what countries would be represented in these meetings, nor of the institutional forum in which they would take place. Furthermore, no criteria were offered to guide officials in trying to distinguish between "erratic" and "underlying" exchange-rate movements. And most critically of all, there was not even a hint of how consistency of intervention policies was to be achieved if officials ever happened to disagree. As one observer noted, governments "sidestepped those issues by placing present hopes on refurbished procedures rather than reinforced principles."[26] But as I noted in Chapter 2, although intergovernmental consultations may be able to suppress conflicts of interest among states, they cannot eliminate them. It is still necessary to agree on who will sacrifice what, if governments are not to work at cross-purposes. On this point, the Rambouillet compromise was highly ambiguous.

It was also highly ambiguous on the related issue of how to ensure for the United States the same degree of exchange-rate flexibility as other countries in the new regime of managed floating. I noted in the last chapter the existence of an asymmetry in the Bretton Woods system, unfavorable to the United States, created by the intervention-currency role of the dollar. Because governments used the dollar as their principal intervention medium to support par values, the Americans could not change the exchange rate of the dollar unilaterally unless all other countries agreed to intervene appropriately in the exchange market; in addition, even when it could be changed, the dollar exchange rate could move by only half as much as the exchange rate between any other pair of currencies.[27] This sort of asymmetry persists even in a floating-rate regime if governments continue to intervene predominantly in dollars—as in fact they have done since 1973. "This persistent asymmetry is likely to be at least as damaging to the exchange rate autonomy of the United States under floating rates as it was under par values."[28] Richard Cooper has pointed out that in order to eliminate this sort of asymmetry, governments must either: (a) introduce a new nonnational private international currency for intervention purposes; (b) abandon exchange-market intervention in favor of an international clearing union of some kind; or (c) initiate intervention in a variety of national currencies ("multi-currency intervention").[29] In the Committee of Twenty, this issue was thoroughly examined, and both the first and third of Cooper's alternatives received serious attention, the second being rejected as less efficient than a regime of continuous market clearing.[30] Under the Rambouillet compromise, however, neither approach was formally endorsed: in fact, the dollar's continuing position as universal intervention currency does not even seem to have been brought into formal question. The United States, therefore, continued to suffer from the disability of more restricted exchange-rate flexibility than other countries.

Adjustment obligations. In the negotiations of the Committee of Twenty, both the United States and its principal negotiating adversaries in Europe agreed that a more symmetrical adjustment process was called for. However, because they were talking about different kinds of symmetry (see Chapter 3), they found it difficult to agree on a common approach to the problem. Each side was prisoner to its own perception of the past. As Peter Kenen wrote in 1973:

> As usual, the parties are arguing from history as each reads it. Americans believe that the U.S. deficits of the 1950s and 1960s were prolonged and led finally to the collapse of the par value system because surplus countries—the Europeans and Japan—could not be compelled to alter their policies, and the United States could not easily initiate a change in exchange rates. Europeans read this same post-war history to argue that the blame and obligation to change policies rested with the United States, yet it was not compelled to act because it was not losing reserves.[31]

In the Committee, the United States argued in favor of absolutely symmetrical adjustment obligations. Proceeding from its own perception of the 1950s and 1960s, the United States contended that surplus countries as well as deficit countries had to be compelled to alter their policies in the event of payments imbalances. Washington wanted to prevent a recurrence of the kind of sustained payments surpluses that Europe and Japan had enjoyed under the Bretton Woods system. The adjustment process had to be "tight" all around. To aid this, the United States proposed an objective (i.e., quantitative) reserve-indicator structure to trigger the adjustment process. Disproportionate movements of reserves in either direction would establish an automatic presumption that adjustment measures were required.[32]

The Europeans, by contrast, argued in favor of the "loosest" possible adjustment process, preferring procedures for multilateral review and consultation rather than automatic or presumptive indicators. These countries too were proceeding from their own perception of the 1950s and 1960s. They did not want to be compelled by preordained rules to give up surpluses if they did not consider it in their individual interest to do so.

The Committee's *Outline of Reform* did little to clarify this question of adjustment obligations—not least because of a signal failure to distinguish clearly between the responsibility to initiate the adjustment process and the obligation to bear adjustment costs. As I emphasized in Chapter 2, these are not identical: there is no direct correlation between the distribution of adjustment responsibilities and the allocation of adjustment costs. The negotiators in the Committee of Twenty never fully confronted this crucial distinction, and the point was also blurred in the compromise at Rambouillet. As a result, after Jamaica, it was still not evident what the respective obligations of surplus and deficit countries were supposed to be. Consequently, there was still a high potential for conflict over the burden or privilege of taking action to initiate the adjustment process and over the appropriate distribution of the economic costs of adjustment.

Pressures.   The Committee of Twenty agreed on the necessity for "graduated pressures to be applied to countries in large and persistent imbalance, whether surplus or deficit."[33] But it failed to agree on what specific forms such graduated pressures might take.[34] The European countries, consistent with their bias toward a "loose" adjustment process, preferred to limit pressures mainly to financial disciplines. In the case of surplus countries, these might take the form of interest-rate charges on excessive reserve accumulations, or a withholding of future SDR allocations; in the case of deficit countries, these might be charges on reserve deficiencies or higher interest rates on Fund borrowings. By contrast, the United States, consistent with its bias toward a "tight" adjustment process, argued for the availability (in extreme cases) of additional pressures on surplus countries, to take the form of temporary import surcharges or other trade or current-account restrictions. In view of the Committee's difficulties in reconciling European and American views on the adjustment process, it is not surprising that the negotiators were also unable to reconcile related differences on the question of pressures. This question too had to be left open when the Committee wound up its affairs. The Rambouillet compromise contributed nothing to its further clarification.

The role of the IMF.   In its *Outline of Reform*, the Committee of Twenty recommended establishment of a permanent IMF Council of Governors, with one member appointed from each of the Fund's twenty constituencies (the same twenty constituencies represented in the Committee of Twenty and the Interim Committee), to be charged with responsibility for central coordination and guidance of the international monetary order. The Council, the *Outline* declares, "will meet regularly, three or four times a year as required, and will have the necessary decision-making powers to supervise the management and adaptation of the monetary system."[35] As matters turned out, however, nothing nearly so ambitious was included in the Rambouillet compromise or the package at Jamaica. Machinery to establish a Council of Governors was included in the Second Amendment,[36] but like the procedures laid down for a general return to a par-value regime, this was not expected to be implemented quickly. Apart from that, the Second Amendment simply states that "(a) the Fund shall oversee the international monetary system in order to ensure its effective operation. . . . (b) In order to fulfill its functions under (a) above, the Fund shall exercise firm surveillance over the exchange rate policies of members."[37] Since no specific functions were spelled out to give substance to the term "firm surveillance," there really was a question as to just what (if anything) this might mean in practical terms. On this question, too, there was much ambiguity after Jamaica.

The Mechanism of Liquidity Creation

Consider, now, the mechanism of liquidity creation. After the breakdown of the Bretton Woods system, this could be described as a mixed standard embodying one commodity reserve asset (gold), several nationally issued fiduciary reserve assets (of which by far the most important was still the dollar), and one internationally created fiduciary reserve asset (the SDR). The postwar dollar-exchange standard, based on the formal convertibility of the dollar into gold, had already begun an informal metamorphosis as early as the mid-1960s under the impact of the dollar glut, as most foreign governments grew increasingly reluctant to employ the discipline of gold conversions against the United States (see Chapter 3). This metamorphosis was completed in 1971 when gold convertibility of the dollar was officially suspended. Thereafter, although an official dollar price of gold ($42.22 per ounce) continued to be used by governments for formal bookkeeping purposes, the dollar itself, like the SDR, existed only as a pure fiat reserve. This imposed a considerable ambiguity on the structure of the liquidity-creation mechanism. What precisely was now to be the relationship among the three main reserve assets? Where ultimately was control of the supply and rate of growth of reserves now to be located? And who now was to enjoy the benefits of creating international liquidity? The Jamaica package did little to answer any of these fundamental questions either.

Special Drawing Rights.   The Committee of Twenty agreed that the SDR should become the "principal reserve asset" of the monetary order, in order to achieve "better international management of global liquidity" (meaning formal international control of the supply and growth rate of reserves); that objective was endorsed by Interim Committee as well.[38] The Jamaica package, however, contributed little toward enhancing the status of the SDR, other than to confirm the SDR's growing importance as numeraire of the monetary order by abolishing the official price of gold. Under the original Bretton Woods agreement, the world numeraire was technically gold: par values were to be expressed "in terms of gold as a common denominator."[39] In practice, however, the world numeraire was the dollar, since the value of the dollar was itself presumed to be fixed in relation to gold. But after the dollar was devalued in 1971 for the first time in the postwar period, this presumption clearly no longer held; by the time exchange rates began to float in 1973, it had become positively anachronistic. The new method of valuing SDRs introduced by the Committee of Twenty facilitated replacement of the dollar by the SDR in all official exchange-rate quotations. The abolition of the official gold price at Jamaica left the SDR formally the only unit of account for official monetary transactions.

Beyond this, however, Jamaica did relatively little to promote the reserve role of the SDR. The reforms of the Committee of Twenty— the new method of valuation and the higher interest rate—made the SDR more attractive as a reserve asset to *hold*. But if governments were to accept corresponding demotion of gold and the dollar as reserve assets, the SDR had to be made more attractive as a reserve asset to *use*. This the Jamaica package largely failed to do.

Under the original 1968 agreement creating SDRs, tight restrictions controlled their use. Governments could not use their SDRs merely to alter the composition of their reserves. In most circumstances, it was necessary to demonstrate a genuine balance-of-payments *need* to the satisfaction of the IMF, which in turn had responsibility to *designate* countries with whom authorized SDR transactions could then be conducted. Designated countries were obligated to *accept* SDRs up to certain maximum limits, and countries using SDRs were obligated to *reconstitute* minimum holdings within a certain allotted time period.[40] Regulations of such complexity were bound to restrict the attractiveness of the SDR as an asset to use. The Jamaica package went some way toward reducing this high degree of complexity, by relaxing the requirement of need and by authorizing transactions without Fund designation.[41] But in other respects, the changes of provisions controlling SDR use that were included in the Second Amendment all tended to be quite marginal.[42] As a result, the scope for use of SDRs still remains, on the whole, much more narrowly defined than that of other reserve assets.

Other opportunities to improve the attributes of the SDR were also lost at Jamaica. In relation to the issue of the exchange-rate autonomy of the United States, for instance, the possibility of introducing the SDR for intervention purposes might have been considered.[43] As a nonnational currency, the SDR would by definition eliminate the sort of asymmetry that arises from the dollar's continuing position as universal intervention currency. What was required was relaxation of the rule, under the original SDR agreement, limiting SDR holdings to official monetary authorities only: if private financial institutions were also authorized to hold and trade SDRs, central banks could readily substitute SDRs for dollars in their intervention operations. But no such change was proposed at Jamaica. Likewise, in relation to the reserve-currency role of the dollar, as well as of gold, the possibility of establishing a "substitution account" to issue SDRs in exchange for outstanding dollar and gold reserve balance might also have been considered.[44] But, as indicated below, this change was not seriously contemplated either. In all respects, therefore, the future reserve role of the SDR remained in question. Jamaica came nowhere near accomplishing the ostensible objective of making the SDR the principal reserve asset of the monetary order. In Fritz Machlup's words, "The alleged objective . . . is shown to be a sham."[45]

Gold. What about the gold ingredient of the Jamaica package? As mentioned above, the various decisions concerning gold were *intended* to reduce the reserve role of gold, as envisaged by the Committee of Twenty and so promote the SDR's reserve role *indirectly*. And certainly it is true that some of those measures did serve that purpose—for example, abolition of the official gold price which, as I have said, confirmed the SDR's importance as world numeraire. On the other hand, it is less certain that some of the other gold measures had similar effects. Indeed, in certain respects these decisions may actually have served to enhance, rather than diminish, the reserve role of gold. It is not at all clear that gold was actually demoted at Jamaica.

From the time that dollar convertibility was suspended, and then exchange rates began to float, gold in central-bank vaults was effectively frozen. With the private-market price soaring well above $100 per ounce in 1973 to nearly $200 in late 1974, before dropping back to a $140-160 range in 1975, no central bank was willing to offer any of its gold in settlement of monetary debts. Why sell at $42.22 to other governments when the private market might be prepared to offer three or four times that amount? In a technical sense, therefore, gold was unofficially "demonetized": it was no longer a usable liquid asset. The ostensible purpose of the Interim Committee at Jamaica was to make gold demonetization official. In practice, however, the effect may have been just the reverse.

Like the Jamaica formula on exchange rates, the Interim Committee's decisions on gold reflected a diplomatic compromise—in this instance, an understanding reached under the auspices of the Group of Ten in Washington in August 1975.[46] Up to that date, the United States had been arguing forcefully for a total demonetization of gold; some other major countries, led by France, had been fighting to preserve at least some part of gold's traditional reserve role. In Washington, the American government won a unanimous commitment on abolition of the official gold price and on the other gold measures ultimately included in the Jamaica package; in addition, all governments agreed that "the total stock of gold now in the hands of the Fund and the monetary authorities of the Group of 10 will not be increased."[47] But for their part, the French and their allies won agreement to limit all commitments on gold to a period of two years only: "these arrangements will be reviewed by the participants at the end of two years and then continued, modified, or terminated. Any party to these arrangements may terminate adherence to them after the initial two-year period."[48] In effect, therefore, all final decisions were put off to another day. In the meantime, the future of gold remained unclear.

In fact, by restituting one-sixth of the Fund's gold holdings to member governments, the Jamaica package actually added to the total stock of gold in the hands of monetary authorities (considered apart from the IMF). Moreover, it was clear after Jamaica that at least a few central banks, in particular the Bank of France, intended to buy some of the Fund gold to be sold on the open market as well.[49] The more gold central banks own, the more incentive they have to make it a usable liquid asset again—in other words, to re-establish some sort of stable market-related price that would enable them either to find buyers for it or to use it as collateral for foreign loans when they need international liquidity to finance balance-of-payments deficits. A fall in the price of gold would not be in the interest of the rich countries with large monetary gold holdings; it would also not be in the interest of the poor countries that are supposed to be the beneficiaries of the IMF Trust Fund. Thus, a real possibility existed after Jamaica that these two groups would form a de facto coalition, together with gold-producing countries such as South Africa, to "fix" an informal official floor price or price range (by gentlemen's agreements) for all gold transactions in the future.

If this were to occur, gold would not be demoted at all. Quite the contrary, it would be effectively remonetized—and at three or four times its former official price, gold would account for a much larger share of world reserves than at any time since the start of the Bretton Woods system. In turn, this would make the agreed objective of better management of global liquidity a great deal more difficult to achieve. Gold would remain an independent source of liquidity growth in the long term, not under formal international control. And worse, in the short term the volume of liquidity could fluctuate capriciously to the extent that shifts of speculative sentiment in the private market influenced the market-related price for official gold transactions. The Interim Committee did not seriously consider the alternative possibility of funding national monetary gold holdings into a substitution account in exchange for SDRs; it did not even opt for the simple expedient of prohibiting net increases of collective central-bank gold reserves. As a result, as *The Economist* commented at the time, "confusion remains as to whether gold is being phased in or phased out of the world's monetary system."[50]

The dollar.   Perhaps the most deafening silence at Jamaica concerned the dollar. After all the time that had been devoted to discussion of the international status of the dollar in the Committee of Twenty, it was truly remarkable how little attention was paid to the issue in the Interim Committee. I have said that the intervention-currency role of the dollar was not brought into formal question at

Jamaica; neither, it appears, was its reserve-currency role, despite the agreed objective of better management of international liquidity. Indeed, the Jamaica package afforded no clues at all to the probable future role of the dollar.

The principal reason for this omission was the energy crisis which began in late 1973 and completely transformed the attitude of most governments toward the traditional liquidity and confidence problems. With oil consumers scrambling to pay for their higher-priced imports, much less importance, it seemed, now needed to be attached to the older issues of dollar convertibility and the overhang of dollar liabilities; much more attention, rather, needed to be paid to a newer problem labeled "petrodollars." Not that concern about the petrodollar problem was necessarily misplaced, as we shall shortly see. But it can be argued that de-emphasis of the convertibility and overhang issues was inappropriate, or at least shortsighted. Certainly it is difficult to see how the supply and rate of growth of global liquidity can ever be brought under formal international control unless something is done regarding the reserve role of the dollar. The SDR can never become the principal reserve asset in the monetary order so long as governments are still able to accumulate substantial amounts of dollars (or, for that matter, other national currencies) in their reserves at will. That, of course, is why the Committee of Twenty labored so hard over the problem of the dollar's status.

In fact, there are two distinct problems here. One is the question of what to do about the existing overhang of official dollar liabilities; the other is the question of how to prevent the emergence of new official liabilities. In the Committee of Twenty, the code word for the former problem was "consolidation"; for the latter, "settlements."

To eliminate the existing overhang, some form of consolidation in the IMF would obviously be required. Even at market-related prices, America's gold stock by the mid-1970s had grown far too small, relative to official dollar balances, to accomplish a direct conversion. Instead, central banks would have to accept SDRs in place of their present dollars, with the dollars themselves being funded in an IMF substitution account. The only substantive question, therefore, would concern the *terms* of the consolidation. Would the United

States be obligated to "retire" the dollars in the substitution account by their gradual amortization into U.S. reserve assets? Or might some or all of America's accumulated debt be forgiven? The Committee of Twenty carefully refrained from committing itself on this very touchy issue.[51]

On the other hand, the Committee negotiators were almost unanimously agreed on the necessity for restoring dollar convertibility, although they remained divided on the issue of whether to treat convertibility as a right or an obligation. The European governments, once again proceeding from their own perception of the 1950s and 1960s, were determined to prevent a recurrence of the extensive liability-financing of deficits that the United States had enjoyed under the Bretton Woods system. This was the asymmetry in the former system that had disturbed them most. America too, they argued, would henceforth have to experience the pressure of reserve losses. The system of settling imbalances would have to be as "tight" for the United States as it was for others. Thus, transfers of reserves would have to be mandatory, not merely voluntary as before. Surplus nations would not merely be guaranteed an *opportunity* to present dollars acquired in the exchange market for conversion; they would be *obligated* to settle their imbalances in this way. The United States, conversely, argued for a relatively "loose" settlement system, in which countries would have the right to accumulate dollar balances to whatever extent they wished. The American government justified this argument in terms of ensuring sufficient elasticity in the settlement system. But clearly what underlay the U.S. position was a determination to surrender as little as possible of its past "exorbitant privilege." In effect, it was the U.S. position that prevailed, since no formal decision on the issue was taken by the Interim Committee.

The distribution of benefits. The Jamaica package left completely open the question of the relationship among the three main reserve assets, and consequently the question of control of the supply and rate of growth of world reserves. The SDR did not become the principal reserve asset of the monetary order; gold was not necessarily demoted; and the status of the dollar was not fundamentally altered. The structure of the liquidity-creation mechanism remained ambiguous; the monetary standard remained mixed. And as in all mixed standards, the resulting distribution of the benefits of creating international liquidity continued to be highly uncertain.

Insofar as it was successful in preserving its past "exorbitant privilege," the United States continued to enjoy much of the seigniorage benefit of reserve creation, as well as the associated gains of prestige and decision-making authority. The dollar's inconvertibility meant that there was now even less control over the growth of dollar reserve balances than had previously existed (at least in principle) under the Bretton Woods system. In addition, the continuing dominance of the United States in world financial markets ensured that only a fraction of its seigniorage benefit would be bid away in the form of higher interest rates to foreign dollar holders.

Insofar as gold's reserve role was likely to be enhanced, rather than diminished, by the Jamaica package, some seigniorage benefit could also be expected to go to gold-producing countries. A once-for-all gain would also be enjoyed by gold-holding countries to the extent of the difference between the former official gold price and any new informal official floor price that might be set in the future. The largest gold-holding countries, of course, are to be found among the advanced industrial nations; these would enjoy the largest one-time increase of command over foreign resources. Since these countries also have the biggest quotas in the IMF, they would also profit most from the restitution of Fund gold that was agreed upon at Jamaica. "The Golden Rule, IMF Style," is the way one influential U.S. legislator put it: "IMF aid to the wealthy . . . the greedy rather than the needy."[52]

The needy less-developed countries had put their hopes in the link—the proposal to alter the distributional criterion for SDRs to gain for themselves more of the social savings afforded by the SDR. As indicated, the Committee of Twenty was unable to agree on this question. Instead, by raising the interest rate on SDRs, the Committee actually made the SDR, in effect, more distributionally neutral (see Chapter 2). Less benefit would now be gained from a larger share of any initial allocation. (In any event, no new allocations of SDRs were expected in the near term.) The LDCs were compensated by establishment of the Fund's extended facility and temporary oil facility. They were also given a new committee—the Development Committee—and the several measures adopted at Jamaica. The net impact of the Interim Committee's decisions, however, was not expected to be large. According to Johannes Witteveen, the Fund's managing director, the temporary, across-the-board increase of 45 percent in IMF lending authority adopted at Jamaica would make about $1.5 billion in additional funds available to LDCs in 1976; liberalization of the compensatory finance facility would provide another $1 billion; and profits from the Fund gold sales, to be funneled through the Trust Fund, might add perhaps $400-500 million more during each of the four years over which sales were planned.[53] This was not a great deal, and it left the LDCs fundamentally unaltered in their dissatisfaction with the prevailing distribution of the benefits of liquidity creation.

Unanticipated Economic Developments

I have said that the negotiators in the Committee of Twenty were taken unawares by the emergence of some unanticipated and unprecedented international economic developments. These included rampant global inflation, the energy crisis, and growing fragility in the private international financial structure—three clear illustrations of how dramatically the monetary system can change through time. Though all of these developments posed serious problems for the monetary order, none was directly confronted by the Interim Committee. In effect, the Committee ignored the point, made at the end of Chapter 3, that monetary reform must either anticipate such changes in the monetary system or else ensure a sufficient degree of flexibility in the monetary order to cope with them as they occur. The Jamaica package did neither.

Inflation. By the time of the Jamaica meeting, global inflation seemed to be receding somewhat from the record rates attained in 1973-1974. But there was still no sign that inflationary forces had abated entirely, despite severe world recession in 1974-1975. In fact, global inflation looked to have taken on a life of its own. This cast the problem of liquidity in a rather new light.

Early discussions of the defects in the Bretton Woods system always stressed the danger of a shortage of international liquidity, not a surfeit (see Chapter 3). The fear was always that governments would have too few reserves rather than too many. This attitude reflected the historical experience of the Great Depression: the key problem to worry about was unemployment, and inflation was generally considered a secondary matter. The crucial imperative was to create some new source of liquidity to enable governments to avoid deflationary expenditure reductions in the event of payments deficits. That is why SDRs were created. The phrase "international management of global liquidity" always meant growth, never contraction. Yet it is clear that if inflation persists as a global problem, a fundamental change of attitude on the liquidity problem will be required. Much more attention would have to be paid in the future than in the past to the mechanics of monetary restriction at the international level—not just to the provision of reserves for monetary expansion.

This emphasizes again the ambiguous relationship among the three main reserve assets of the monetary order, and consequently, the absence of control over the supply and rate of growth of liquidity. With particular reference to the work of the Interim Committee, it demonstrates again the limitations of the 1968 agreement creating SDRs. Although providing for SDR cancellations as well as allocations, that agreement insisted on such decisions being made for basic periods of five years (even though, exceptionally, the initial 1969 decision to allocate SDRs was made for only three years). This period could be much too long to permit adequate adjustment to changing economic circumstances. For the SDR to become the principal reserve asset of the monetary order, as the Interim Committee ostensibly intended, both the rules governing its use and the rules governing its allocations and cancellations would have to be improved. (Needless to say, there would also have to be a lot more SDRs in circulation—perhaps through the funding of national gold or dollar reserve balances in an IMF substitution account—for a cancellation of SDRs to have much economic significance.) Otherwise, the rules simply might not be flexible enough to ensure continuing stability of the monetary order through time.

Petrodollars. The story of the oil price increases of late 1973 is well known.[54] The subsequent rise in the cost of world oil imports resulted in enormous current-account surpluses for the OPEC countries as a group—$65 billion in 1974 alone (as compared with $6 billion in 1973), an estimated $40 billion in 1975, and further large surpluses expected thereafter, at least until 1978-1980. Estimates concerning the prospective magnitude of the cumulative buildup of OPEC petrodollars have ranged from an early World Bank estimate of some $650 billion (current dollars) in 1980 to some later, more sanguine projections running as low as $180-190 billion.[55] But even the figures at the lower end of this range clearly represent a significant sum of money; manifestly, the implications of such financial accumulations for the monetary order could well be profound. Two questions, in particular, seemed urgent once the energy crisis broke: (1) How could governments ensure that petrodollars would be effectively "recycled" to the oil-consuming countries that were most in need of them? (2) How could they ensure that OPEC surplus accumulations would not become a new source of instability in international monetary relations? Both questions, as I have indicated, seemed to overshadow the traditional liquidity and confidence problems.

The recycling issue reflected the fact that oil price increases affected different oil consuming countries differently. Some consumers were more dependent on oil imports than others; and some were less able than others to offset the higher cost of oil imports either by increasing exports of goods and services to OPEC members or by attracting loans and investments from them. Consequently, some oil consumers found themselves in serious payments difficulties after the energy crisis broke, while others enjoyed relatively healthier external accounts. In the long term, consuming countries knew they would have to evolve a new structure of mutual trade relations compatible with the emerging pattern of OPEC capital flows to consumers as a group. In the shorter term, however, the key need was to channel oil revenues from consumers initially receiving the benefit of OPEC capital flows to those most in need of them. It was not clear whether private international financial markets, on which the principal responsibility for this financial-intermediation function was initially thrust, could in fact be relied upon to do the job entirely on their own. There was no assurance that an allocation of loans based on traditional banking considerations (credit-worthiness, relative interest rates, etc.) would in any way coincide with the requirements of global balance-of-payments equilibrium. There was also no assurance that the private markets would be able to bear up under the strain of such a responsibility (see below). A need seemed evident, therefore, to supplement the private markets with bilateral and multilateral credit facilities among governments. One new facility did soon come into existence—the IMF oil facility, first established in 1974 on a scale of about $3.5 billion, and subsequently renewed in 1975 for a maximum of $6 billion—but this, as indicated above, was phased out early in 1976. A second facility, the so-called financial support fund, was supposed to be created in 1975 by the advanced industrial countries under the auspices of the Organization for Economic Cooperation and Development (OECD), on a potential scale of $25 billion, but was stillborn because of the refusal of the U.S. Congress to ratify American participation. Hence, three years after the energy crisis broke, there was still some question whether sufficient facilities existed to cope with the recycling issue.[56]

The second, related issue concerned the disposition of OPEC surplus accumulations. Although OPEC countries were already beginning in 1975 to diversify some of their investments, both geographically and in terms of asset structure, it was evident that for a long time to come a large proportion would undoubtedly continue, following tradition, to be concentrated in short-maturity assets (bank deposits, etc.). Already, by the end of 1975, the official monetary reserves of oil producers as a group had risen to roughly $55 billion—one quarter of the world total. By the end of the decade, given their prospective surplus earnings, it seemed that OPEC countries might accumulate reserves in excess of $100 billion; most would be concentrated in the hands of four Persian Gulf nations and Libya. It was not at all clear that the monetary order could remain stable with such a large proportion of international liquidity unilaterally controlled by such a small number of countries—particularly countries with such a record for economic and political volatility. How could the international community ensure that these funds would not be shifted about frequently in a chaotic and irresponsible fashion? The Interim Committee evidently hoped that a doubling of OPEC's voting power in the IMF would help induce them to behave responsibly in the disposition of their surpluses. But on this point also there was some question whether the action undertaken would in fact suffice to ensure stability of the monetary order.[57]

The private financial structure. Even before the Bretton Woods system broke down, specialists inside as well as outside of government were expressing concern over the fragility of the private international financial structure. After 1971, signs of stress in money and capital markets began to multiply rapidly, and observers recalled the general crisis and collapse of the international financial structure that followed the wave of bank failures on the European continent in 1931. Several factors now seemed involved, including the Eurocurrency market, multinational corporations, floating exchange rates, and the energy crisis.

In contrast to national financial markets, where governmental supervision ordinarily ensures that at least minimal standards of good financial practice are adhered to, the Eurocurrency market was never subject to systematic guidance or regulation by monetary authorities. Eurocurrency banks traditionally were free to take whatever risks they felt were warranted by their own pursuit of profit: low reserve ratios, exceptionally narrow margins between deposit and loan rates, and lending on poor credit ratings. Eurocurrency loans were generally unsecured, and banks frequently lent through intermediaries without knowing anything at all about the end-use of their money. As the market expanded over the years, such questionable practices tended to increase steadily. By the mid-1970s, the danger of major defaults was clearly evident. Much of the private international financial structure had become vulnerable to unsound financial judgments by any of a large number of individual banking institutions.

A second factor was the multinational corporation. These giant industrial and commercial enterprises, which have grown to become the dominant actors in the private international economy today, command immense financial resources that can be shifted at extremely short notice from one location or currency to another. Already, in the 1960s, the multinational corporation was responsible for a sharp increase in the degree of international capital mobility. Large movements of funds could now be generated by the smallest of incentives: changing credit conditions, a variation of exchange rates, even mere rumors or innuendos. The multinational corporation became the principal agent of private speculation against official exchange parities—albeit a quite defensive sort of speculator. Most corporate flows were not intended to profit directly from exchange-rate changes but rather, simply, to protect corporate treasuries (and treasurers) against the exchange losses threatened by potential currency adjustments. The result, however, was the same as if the speculation had been more aggressive, adding considerably to existing strains on the private international financial structure. These strains continued even after the end of the Bretton Woods par-value regime; indeed, if anything, they were increased by the uncertainties of global inflation and floating exchange rates. After 1971-1973, financial markets found it more difficult than ever to function efficiently in the face of volatile and unpredictable international capital movements.

A third factor was the phenomenon of floating exchange rates. The collapse of the Bretton Woods par-value regime also added to the hazards of private international financial operations. Several individual banks reported considerable losses in their foreign-exchange dealings after 1971. In 1974 a wave of international bankruptcies was narrowly averted following the failure of the largest private bank in Germany, Bankhaus I.D. Herstatt of Cologne, owing to foreign-exchange losses in excess of $200 million. After 1974 the threat of other Herstatts hung over the system like a specter.

Finally, there was the energy crisis. Much of the responsibility after 1973 for absorbing and recycling OPEC's huge surplus earnings was, as indicated, initially thrust on the private international financial structure. This too added to the hazards of private financial operations. In the past, the oil producers of the Persian Gulf and Libya had traditionally confined their placement of short-term funds to a comparatively small number of banks: there was a danger that the capital structures of these banks now simply would not support such a concentration of enormous deposits. And even assuming this difficulty could be overcome, there was the further problem of transforming this short-term oil money into the medium- and long-term loans that so many consumers needed to finance their oil imports. As such lending operations increased, banks became increasingly vulnerable to the danger of either a major default or a loss of deposits backing such relatively illiquid assets.

The fragility of the private international financial structure clearly posed a threat to the structure and stability of the monetary order—especially to the mechanism of liquidity creation. At the extreme, a general financial crisis would certainly engulf not just private banking institutions but central banks as well. The usability of alternative reserve assets, and the relationships among them, would be cast further into question; and control over the supply and rate of growth of reserves would certainly become even more ambiguous and uncertain. In 1974 and 1975, governments undertook to forestall such a crisis by introducing some moderate supervision and regulation of the financial practices of Eurocurrency institutions and multinational corporations. As indicated, they also sought to relieve private financial markets of part of the responsibility for recycling petrodollars. Informal moves were made to ensure the existence of a "lender of last resort" for financially pressed banks if a chain reaction of defaults were to put the international financial structure in jeopardy.[58] (A lender of last resort is, of course, simply classic recycling by another name—the private confidence problem in a new light.) Here too, however, as at the time of the Jamaica meeting, there was some question whether the actions undertaken would suffice to cope with the problem.

Short of a general financial crisis, the fragility of the private international financial structure posed a threat to effective international management of global liquidity. The Eurocurrency market has always constituted a backdoor route to payments financing and the growth of currency reserve balances—particularly dollar reserve balances. (The dollar is by far the most widely traded of all Eurocurrencies, accounting for about 70 percent of the full Eurocurrency market.) Even in the absence of a cumulative deficit in the U.S. balance of payments, central-bank holdings of dollars can be increased through the process of Eurodollar deposit circulation. Suppose a central bank holding dollars in New York decides to shift them to a Eurocurrency bank in, say, London. The London bank can lend those dollars to another bank; ultimately, to the extent that monetary authorities are either borrowing dollars or buying them in the foreign-exchange market, the dollars will reappear as new currency reserve balances. The total of dollar assets will have risen—yet no net change will have occurred in the dollar liabilities of the United States.[59] An increase of global liquidity takes place, but solely through the process of recycling central-bank deposits through the Eurocurrency market— what has been called the "carousel effect." The carousel, clearly, can go around and around: currency reserve balances can grow quite independently of the balance of payments of the reserve center. Equally clearly (to mix a metaphor), what goes up may come down: strains in the Eurocurrency market could lead also to a multiple shrinkage of currency reserve balances.

Interestingly enough, the significance of the carousel effect was not fully appreciated until as late as 1970.[60] In 1971 the carousel was brought partially under control when the central banks of the Group of Ten agreed to refrain from further deposits in the Euro-currency market.[61] But little was done subsequently to eliminate this "Euro-gap" in the management of global liquidity. Central banks outside the Group of Ten—especially the monetary authorities of the OPEC countries—were loath to give up the higher interest rates that could be earned on Eurocurrency deposits; after 1973, oil producers poured literally tens of billions of dollars into the market. The result is that the Eurocurrency market has now come to play a role once reserved exclusively for agencies such as the IMF. As one former central banker put it, "the private banking system took over the functions proper to an official institution possessed of the power to finance balance-of-payments disequilibria through credit-granting and to create international liquidity. . . . The function of creating international liquidity has been transferred from official institutions to private ones."[62] Limitations on Eurocurrency reserve placements are therefore essential if the availability of payments financing and the supply and growth rate of world reserves are to be brought under formal international control. In 1976, this had still not been accomplished.

The Actors Today

All countries have keen vested interests in the outstanding issues of international monetary relations—hence the element of cooperation in the monetary order. But not all interests are identical in all countries—hence the element of competition as well. Policy conflicts may arise from any of the five sources mentioned in Chapter 2. An evaluation of alternative organizing principles for the monetary order requires not only an understanding of the key issues of reform but also an appreciation of the key state actors in monetary relations. That is the purpose of the remaining pages of this chapter.

The United States

The United States is clearly the paramount state actor in international monetary relations. Though reduced, relatively speaking, from its postwar position of overwhelming dominance, America is still by far the world's leading national economy. America has the largest gross national product of any country (30 percent of the world total), the greatest volume of foreign trade (one-eighth of the world total), the broadest and deepest financial markets, the main international currency. Much of the debate in the Committee of Twenty, as we have seen, revolved around the notion of "symmetry." But asymmetries such as these—pervasive asymmetries that run deep in the structure of the international economy—are not the kind to be reduced or eliminated by formal monetary reforms. The United States may no longer be *primus motor* of the monetary order, but it is still *primus inter pares*.

Yet, at the same time, the United States is also one of the world's most closed national economies, with foreign trade accounting for less than one-twelfth of America's GNP. Despite the importance of overseas operations for many of America's largest corporations, the main orientation of the U.S. economy is still basically inward rather than outward.

These two facts combine to establish a fundamental American bias toward maintenance of policy autonomy in monetary matters. As a leading economy, the United States naturally prizes its ability to act abroad unilaterally to promote objectives believed to be in the national interest. As a closed economy, the United States naturally accords a lesser priority to external considerations relative to internal policy needs. The key objective is to minimize any balance-of-payments constraint on the government's decision-making authority, in order to maximize the country's freedom of action in domestic and foreign affairs. This was, of course, the great advantage of the Bretton Woods system from the U.S. point of view: there was relatively little effective discipline on U.S. policy autonomy (other than the limitation on exchange-rate autonomy stemming from the intervention-currency role of the dollar). From the Smithsonian Agreement to Jamaica, America's manifest goal was to preserve as much as possible of the special privileges it had learned to enjoy in the years after World War II. All of its proposals for reform after 1971 were framed with that basic vested interest in mind. As one observer wrote in 1974, "rather than offering anything new or daring, what the United States is really after is a better means of carrying on its previous and still ongoing political-economic role of world leader."[63]

This explains, for example, America's strong support in the Committee of Twenty and Interim Committee for floating exchange rates—the proposal that ultimately carried the day at Rambouillet and Jamaica. Floating rates are highly useful to a large, closed economy like the United States. When exchange rates are fixed, substantial variations of domestic expenditures (or of trade restrictions or exchange control) are required to correct even a small external deficit; "the tail wagging the dog" is the way it used to be put in the United States. Such burdens can be avoided when the exchange rate of the home currency is free to move. A good part of the costs and

responsibilities of adjustment can then be shifted onto others—
the comparatively small size of the foreign-trade sector, meanwhile,
ensuring that the domestic impact of any exchange-rate changes will
be relatively muted (see Chapter 5). A floating-rate regime was
perfectly consistent with America's basic interest in policy autonomy.

Likewise, America's evident determination in the reform negotiations to surrender as little as possible of its "exorbitant privilege,"
derived from the reserve-currency role of the dollar, could be explained in terms of this basic vested interest. Why submit to more
external discipline than necessary? Such an attitude obviously underlay Washington's expressed preference in the Committee both for a
"tight" adjustment process (presumably intended to relieve some of
the pressures to alter domestic policies that might arise in the event
of further U.S. payments deficits) and a "loose" settlement system
(presumably intended to allow more cumulative deficits in the
future, should such deficits seem convenient). Suspension of the
dollar's convertibility in 1971 eliminated the one major weapon that
foreign governments had for restricting America's freedom of action
in domestic and foreign policy. The United States was not eager to
submit to effective new constraints on its decision-making
authority.[64]

Europe

Europe's common interest in monetary affairs is practically the
mirror image of that of the United States: that is, to *reduce* American
policy autonomy and enhance its *own* freedom of action vis-à-vis the
Americans. The United States may still be the world's leading national
economy, but the relative position of the Western European countries
as a group—especially the nine-member European Community—has
vastly improved since the end of World War II. The combined output
of the Community is now not far below that of the United States; its
combined trade totals and monetary reserves now far exceed
America's. According to the Europeans, their enhanced relative position in the world economy ought to be reflected in the structure of
the monetary order as well. They are no longer satisfied to acquiesce
in the postwar bargain that accorded the United States special

privileges to promote American interests unilaterally; circumstances no longer dictate dollar hegemony. Why should they bear what seems to them to be a disproportionate share of the costs and responsibilities of adjustment? Europeans certainly have no wish to repeat the painful experience after 1965 of massive inflation imported from the United States. Rather, they want more policy autonomy for themselves to manage their own monetary affairs. That is their key perceived interest.

This too was evident in the Committee of Twenty and Interim Committee—in the emphasis on "loose" adjustment and "tight" settlements, for example, and also in the support given to the French government up to the Rambouillet compromise on the issue of exchange rates. European economies are not so closed as that of the United States; indeed, in some of the smaller countries of Europe, more than half of GNP is accounted for by foreign trade. In such an environment, the domestic impact of exchange-rate changes can be considerable: freely floating rates may be quite detrimental to the stability of prices and incomes at home (again, see Chapter 5). Accordingly, most European governments were more inclined toward "stable but adjustable" par values than was the United States. Limitations on exchange-rate fluctuations were more suited to their own national economic circumstances.

Of course, Europe is far from being a homogeneous entity. Beyond the common interest in greater policy autonomy, it is difficult to generalize about a "European" attitude on monetary issues. One can only speak of individual national attitudes (even then bearing in mind the caveat, from Chapter 2, that states are not unitary actors). The three major state actors in Europe are France, Germany, and Great Britain.

France. Probably the best articulated national attitude in Europe is that of France. Ever since the great finance ministers of the ancien régime, French governments have treated money as an instrument of high politics.[65] International monetary relations are not simply a matter of technical economics; rather, in the purest sense, they are a matter of political economy, of political relations. Even before scholars fully appreciated it, French governments sensed the preeminent role of power in the organization of the monetary order. France's decisions to convert its balances of sterling after 1928 and dollars after 1965 (see Chapter 3) were both dictated by defense of French policy autonomy and resentment of monetary dominance by Anglo-Saxons. (For France, prestige tends to be a more important policy objective than it is for most other countries.) In the negotiations after 1971, the French government led the fight to curb the policy autonomy of the United States. The French also led the fight to save the reserve role of gold, which may or may not have been lost at Jamaica. (As I mentioned, the Bank of France in particular clearly intended to buy some of the IMF gold to be sold on the open market.) One reason for this was France's interest in preserving the value of the large monetary gold stock held by the Bank of France (to say nothing of the reportedly even larger gold hoards of French private citizens). But an even more important reason seemed to be a desire to force a corresponding reduction in the reserve-currency status of the dollar—and thereby, presumably, to reduce the monetary dominance of the United States as well.

Germany.   Unlike France, Germany is relatively unconcerned about prestige in international monetary affairs. In fact, successive German governments have struggled—vainly, as it turns out—to prevent the Deutsche mark from becoming an international reserve asset. (The DM is now the second most widely held currency in official reserves, surpassing even sterling;[66] it is also the second most widely traded Eurocurrency, accounting for about 15 percent of the full Eurocurrency market.) The Germans have never been much impressed by the potential seigniorage benefit of reserve-currency status—something that does impress the French, for instance. What worries the Germans more is the danger of policy constraint from a growing overhang of foreign liabilities. For them, as for the Americans, the key objective is to maximize policy autonomy. As a low-inflation country in a high-inflation world, Germany was among the nations most seriously affected by America's exported inflation after 1965. As a relatively open economy (trade equal to nearly 30 percent of GNP) in a floating-rate world, it was also among the most seriously affected by the wide swings of exchange rates in 1973-1975.

Germany's attitude is that it should not have to bear such a large share of the costs and responsibilities of adjustment.

Great Britain. The British attitude is heavily influenced by the nation's history as a reserve center. Although the pound is now only a shadow of its former self, it is still widely used as both vehicle and reserve currency, and London is still a leading international financial center. (About half of all Eurocurrency business is done in the City of London.) For decades, the British have had serious difficulties with their balance of payments; yet even today they insist that the international status of sterling perforce gives them a special place in monetary affairs. Britain shares with other European countries an interest in greater policy autonomy vis-à-vis the United States. But because of its continuing role as a reserve center, Britain shares with the United States an interest in preserving the benefits of a reserve role for national currencies. This tends to impart a certain ambivalence to British contributions in monetary negotiations.

Role of the Community. Other European countries, overshadowed by their larger neighbors, tend to take their lead from one or another of these three major state actors. In the mid-1970s, Germany began to emerge as Europe's dominant monetary power, the leader of a financial grouping strikingly reminiscent of the currency blocs of the 1930s. This grouping—popularly known as the "snake"—grew out of efforts in the European Community to promote monetary unification among its nine members ("the Nine"). The effective result, however, was not to unify the Community's moneys at all, but rather to consolidate German leadership in European monetary affairs.

Efforts to promote monetary unification in the European Community began almost immediately after Charles de Gaulle's retirement in April 1969. In December 1969, de Gaulle's successor, Georges Pompidou, surprised his fellow heads of government at a Community summit meeting at The Hague by personally endorsing the goal of a monetary union. Agreement was reached within fifteen months on an experimental narrowing of the margins of fluctuations between member currencies, with Community currencies to continue moving as a group vis-à-vis outside currencies within the wider band set by the Bretton Woods par-value regime. This was the origin of the so-called "snake in the tunnel" (the snake being the group of Community currencies, the tunnel being the band vis-à-vis outside currencies). Owing to the monetary disturbances of 1971, the launching of the snake was delayed until April 1972—and almost immediately the system ran into trouble.[67] Sterling (together with its satellite Irish pound) floated out in June 1972, followed by the Italian lira in February 1973 and the French franc in January 1974. (The franc joined again in July 1975 and left again in March 1976.) The tunnel itself was lost in March 1973 when the par-value regime collapsed. Meanwhile, two nonmembers—Norway and Sweden—joined in the experiment, and Switzerland and Austria informally aligned their currencies with the snake as well.

By the middle of the 1970s it was clear that the experiment had failed. Monetary unification in the Community had not been promoted. All that remained, in effect, was a European "Deutsche mark zone," as a special study group appointed by the European Community (the Marjolin Committee) noted in 1975:

> The efforts undertaken since 1969 add up to a failure. The "snake" had exploded and the "narrowing of the margins of fluctuations" no longer exists except between those currencies which are more or less closely linked with the Deutsche mark.[68]

It is instructive to ask why the Community experiment failed. Originally, monetary unification had two motivations, one internal to the Community and one external. The internal motivation was to take another step on the road toward full economic and political union in Europe. The external motivation, consistent with Europe's common interest in greater policy autonomy, was to lessen dependence on the dollar and enhance the Community's own monetary independence. It had long been evident that lacking a common currency of their own, the European countries were obliged to rely on the dollar instead to achieve a kind of informal monetary integration.[69] Since this also meant integration with the United States, it implied a partial loss of monetary sovereignty. Formal currency unification was viewed as the necessary condition for elimination of

dollar hegemony. In addition, a common currency, which would undoubtedly become attractive to others for vehicle and reserve purposes, might also enhance Europe's bargaining strength in international monetary negotiations.

The experiment failed, in the words of the Marjolin Committee,
for three principal reasons: "unfavourable events, a lack of political
will, and insufficient understanding."[70] The "unfavourable events"
included inflation and the energy crisis; the "insufficient understanding" referred to a total lack of prior analysis, at either the
national or the Community level, of the conditions necessary for
making a common currency operational. But the most critical of the
three reasons was clearly the "lack of political will." At a lower level,
national administrative hierarchies resisted all encroachments on
their bureaucratic power and privileges; central bankers, in particular,
were unwilling to become submerged in a European "Federal Reserve
System." And at a higher level, national political leaderships resisted
all encroachments on their traditional decision-making authority;
governments were unwilling to transfer any significant portion of
their formal sovereignty to Community institutions. Neither the
internal nor the external motivation was sufficient to overcome
these crucial political obstacles. As a result, monetary unification
itself lost all of its power of momentum. As Fred Hirsch wrote:

> In this sense one can conclude that European monetary inte-
> gration is not a serious issue. It belongs to that category of com-
> mitments that are endorsed by national authorities at the highest
> level, but are in fact ranked low in their priorities when it comes
> to the test.[71]

Other Advanced Nations

Other industrial or semi-industrial countries outside of Europe
share, to a greater or lesser extent, the same interest as the Europeans
in greater policy autonomy. But as one goes down the scale of industrial power, one finds an increasing acceptance of the constraints of
the monetary order.

Japan.   Japan is manifestly the most powerful industrial country
outside the United States and Europe. Like the Europeans, the

Japanese are no longer satisfied to acquiesce in the postwar bargain with America. Japan too wants to strengthen its freedom of action vis-à-vis the United States. On most issues in the Committee of Twenty and Interim Committee, Japanese views ran closely parallel to those of European governments—in particular, to those of Germany. Like Germany, Japan is relatively unconcerned about prestige in international monetary affairs; also like the Germans, the Japanese have long struggled (with somewhat greater success) to prevent their currency from becoming an international reserve asset. Japan, however, is never doctrinaire about its views (unlike, for instance, France) and more recently has shown some signs of revising its traditional attitude toward a possible reserve role for the yen. As in other spheres, Japanese policy tends to be flexible and pragmatic. Above all, the Japanese prize cooperation. Being as dependent as they are on foreign-trade relations, they are more sensitive than most to the risks of international policy conflict.

Canada. Though not so powerful industrially as Japan or the larger countries of Europe, Canada figures prominently in international monetary negotiations by virtue of its sizable foreign-trade volume and well-developed financial markets. Canadian views on monetary relations are heavily conditioned by the country's close ties with the much larger American economy; "being in bed with an elephant" is the way Canadian Prime Minister Pierre Trudeau once put it. To distance themselves somewhat from the elephant, the Canadians experimented at length with a floating exchange rate— despite being in technical violation of the IMF Charter—from 1950 to 1962, and again after 1970. In the Committee of Twenty and Interim Committee, Canada was, not surprisingly, quietly sympathetic to the efforts of Europe and Japan to increase their own policy autonomy in relation to the United States.

Australia, New Zealand, South Africa. Being even less powerful industrially than Canada, Australia and New Zealand are correspondingly more resigned to the inevitability of some external constraints on their domestic decision-making authority. South Africa also accepts the existence of some constraints on its monetary autonomy, but that nation has one crucial vested interest which clearly distinguishes it from most other countries in monetary affairs: its position as the most important gold producer in the world. Approximately three-quarters of all gold mined outside of the Soviet Union comes from South Africa; approximately one-third of all South African export revenues are derived from gold sales. These facts give the South Africans an obvious incentive to promote gold's continued use as a reserve asset, and to support all efforts to set an informal official floor price or price range for gold transactions in the future. South Africa has always opposed official demonetization of gold.

Less-developed Countries

Although even less homogeneous than the world of industrialized powers, the Third World has two vested interests that plainly set it apart in monetary affairs. First and foremost is an interest in an increased flow of resources from the rich to aid the development process. In the discussions of the Committee of Twenty and Interim Committee, this was the sine qua non for LDC agreement on any package of reforms. As indicated earlier, actual accomplishments fell rather short of Third World ambitions: LDCs did not get the "link" they had been seeking, and the financial benefits of the decisions taken at Jamaica were not expected to be large. The poor still had reasons to be dissatisfied with the prevailing distribution of the benefits of liquidity creation. Yet when measured against past experience, their accomplishments were not without significance. LDCs still had reasons to feel that progress had been made, particularly in the establishment of the Development Committee. "LDCs scored a major success in getting established a Joint Ministerial Committee of Bank and Fund which will in the future concern itself with the transfer of real resources from rich to poor countries. To this extent they succeeded in linking international monetary reform with the economic development of poor countries."[72]

The second common interest of less-developed countries is to increase their involvement in international monetary negotiations and their voice in the management of monetary institutions. I have pointed out that in the G-10 discussions during the 1960s, and even at the Smithsonian Institution, LDCs had no formal representation at all. LDC views and interests were not so much ignored as rejected as irrelevant. Until quite late in the negotiations leading to the creation of Special Drawing Rights, for instance, the less-developed countries were not expected to be allocated any SDRs at all. "Confidence in deliberately created reserve units would be likely to be the better maintained the more the units were limited to a coherent group of countries and the more they were backed only by major trading and financial countries."[73] It was only through the intervention of the IMF Managing Director in the negotiation process that provision was made for allocation of the new reserve asset to all Fund members. When the G-10 forum was broadened to the Committee of Twenty (and subsequent Interim Committee), LDCs thought that the relevance of their views and interests had now, at last, been conceded. But after Rambouillet, where poor countries neither took part in the discussions nor were promised any role in the proposed new system of intergovernmental consultation on exchange rates, the degree of LDC involvement in monetary negotiations and institutions was again thrown into question. Here, too, actual accomplishments appeared to fall somewhat short of ambitions.

OPEC

Until the energy crisis, the OPEC countries were regarded—and regarded themselves—simply as part of the Third World, with the same views and interests in monetary affairs. After 1973 this was no longer possible. OPEC countries still shared the same ambition to increase their influence in the negotiation process and in the management of monetary institutions—an ambition at least partially satisfied by the doubling of their voting power in the IMF—but they no longer had such a keen interest in increased financial transfers from the rich. On the contrary, now that they had joined the rich, their problem was to protect what they had—that is, to protect their prospective surplus accumulations against such risks as inflation, exchange-rate depreciation, expropriation, and default. Financial security now was their basic vested interest. In this respect at least, OPEC was more in accord with the advanced nations than with the poor. Henceforth, OPEC would have to be considered quite a distinct actor in international monetary relations.

Conclusions

It is evident that governments do sometimes learn from their mistakes. After the United States decided to suspend the convertibility of the dollar in 1971—four decades almost to the day after Britain's similar decision in 1931—nations did *not* replicate the experience of the interwar period. The monetary order did not degenerate into competing currency blocs; states did not engage openly and massively in economic warfare. Instead, the conflictual element in monetary affairs was suppressed, as governments undertook a controlled process of reform of the legal and conventional framework of relations. The element of cooperation held firm.

On the other hand, it is also evident that the learning process has limits. The reforms that were accomplished in the period from the Smithsonian Agreement to Jamaica hardly comprised a complete new constitution for the monetary system. In fact, they left monetary relations still quite close to a free-for-all regime. The reform process still had a long way to go with respect to both the mechanism of payments adjustment and the mechanism of liquidity creation. This chapter has reviewed the major issues and actors in monetary relations today. We now turn to a detailed evaluation of each of the four alternative organizing principles for the world monetary order.

PART II

Alternative Organizing Principles

Chapter 5

Automaticity

Automaticity as an organizing principle for the monetary order means a self-disciplining regime of rules and conventions binding for all nations. The rationale for automaticity is that it reduces the risk of policy conflict between states by narrowing the element of discretion in governmental behavior. The more fully automatic a monetary order is, the more likely it is to satisfy the consistency objective. At the extremes, two fully automatic monetary orders may be imagined—one based on the model of the classical gold standard, the other a regime of absolutely flexible exchange rates. Each corresponds to one of the two "pure" mechanisms of payments adjustment described in Chapter 1. This chapter discusses each of these two polar alternatives in turn, and then considers some possible compromises between the two, incorporating varying degrees of discretion in governmental behavior.

The Gold Standard

The myth of the Golden Age dies hard. There are still many who, lulled by the image of an impersonal, fully automatic, and politically symmetrical nineteenth-century monetary order, would turn back the clock to a reconstructed gold standard. One source, for instance, argues that "if gold had not existed as the basis of the monetary system, it ought to have been invented. . . . The choice of gold as the basis of the monetary system . . . is the right solution."[1] Another flatly asserts that "gold stands in precedence like a god above all national currencies."[2] In recent years, restoration of the gold standard has been advocated by a number of public figures both inside and outside government. Perhaps the most prominent of this number—certainly one of the most influential—was the first president of the Fifth French Republic, Charles de Gaulle:

> We consider that international exchanges must be established, as was the case before the great world-wide disasters, on an unquestionable monetary basis which does not bear the mark of any individual country.
>
> What basis? Actually, it is difficult to envision in this regard any other criterion, any other standard than gold. Yes, gold, which does not change in nature, which can be made either into bars, ingots or coins, which has no nationality, which is considered, in all places and at all times, the immutable and fiduciary value par excellence. Furthermore, despite all that it was possible to imagine, say, write or do in the midst of major events, it is a fact that even today no currency has any value except by direct or indirect relation to gold, real or supposed. Doubtless, no one would think of dictating to any country how to manage its domestic affairs. But the supreme law, the golden rule—and indeed it is pertinent to say it—that must be enforced and honored again in international economic relations, is the duty to balance, from one monetary area to another, by effective inflows and outflows of gold, the balance of payments resulting from their exchanges.[3]

The Case for the Gold Standard

A reconstructed gold standard, like its classical model, would combine a pure fixed exchange-rate mechanism of balance-of-payments adjustment with a pure commodity standard for liquidity creation. Monetary reserves would consist of gold alone, and governments would be expected to play the gold-standard rules of the game—"the supreme law, the golden rule"—by allowing gold flows to have their full impact on domestic money supplies and economic conditions. Currency values would not be permitted to vary; nor could the authorities make any use at all of selective expenditure-switching devices such as trade restrictions or exchange control. Discretionary actions or judgment would be minimized. The monetary order would operate mechanically and passively.

In principle, a gold standard would accommodate the consensual and conflictual elements in monetary relations by enforcing a close harmony of all national economies and economic policies. Basically an "integrationist" solution to the problem of monetary organization, it is designed to minimize the risk of policy conflict between states by maximizing external constraints on governmental decision-making authority. Both the efficiency and consistency objectives would presumably be promoted.

Key to the efficiency objective is the rigidly fixed exchange-rate mechanism, which by definition eliminates exchange risk, thus removing one of the chief obstacles to transfers of purchasing power between countries. International trade and investment can be pursued to the point where technical efficiency and global economic welfare are maximized. Key to the consistency objective is the pure commodity standard, which by definition eliminates national control over the supply and rate of growth of international liquidity. Gold is the only reserve asset currently or prospectively in use that is issued neither by national governments nor by an international agency. It is thus the only reserve asset whose quantity is not directly influenced by discretionary governmental behavior. Other reserve assets, being fiduciary in nature, are susceptible to management influences of a nonautomatic sort. (It is for this reason that discussion of other liquidity mechanisms is postponed until subsequent chapters.) The gold standard is the only truly automatic monetary standard. According to its enthusiasts, therefore, it is also the only monetary standard truly capable of minimizing the risk of policy conflict among states.

Advocates of the gold standard are generally skeptical about the potential for policy self-restraint on the part of central banks. Most take it for granted that left to their own devices, national monetary authorities will tend to create too much money and generate inflation. The advantage of the pure commodity standard is that it operates as a "Golden Brake" on the rate of monetary expansion. Excessive growth of the money stock at home, relative to money growth abroad, will be automatically curbed along "price-specie-flow" lines by outflows of gold reserves. Such outflows will act as a corrective for inflation, by shrinking the domestic money supply; more importantly, they will also act as a *deterrent* to potentially inflationary policies. Central banks will presumably hesitate to indulge in excessive monetary expansion if they fear the prospect of significant reserve losses. "The relative scarcity of gold and the resulting inadequacy of its monetary supply in face of an insatiable demand acted as nature's balance that tended to mitigate the debasement of the environment."[4] Gold acts as a natural discipline on inflationary monetary policy.

This is not necessarily a criticism of central banks. The fact that inflation is associated with an expansion of the money supply does not mean that money growth itself must be the independent variable, the causal factor that "initiates" all price increases; nor does it mean that all imbalances in the money market must necessarily arise from the supply side. In fact, money growth may merely reflect the passive response of the monetary authorities to *other* proximate influences on the level of prices, such as government deficit finance, union wage pressures, oligopolistic pricing policies, or commodity shortages. Some or all of these may be the genuine independent variables, the causal factors that trigger off the inflation process. Changes in the money stock may be as much endogenous as exogenous, reflecting political or social pressures on the central bank to avoid the hardships of offsetting monetary deflation once price increases have been initiated. As Charles Kindleberger has reminded us, "The easiest way to clear the market for money is to expand the money supply."[5] The authorities may simply take the path of least resistance by validating ("financing") price increases after they occur.

The point of the gold standard, however, is that by tying the level of the domestic money supply to the country's stock of international reserves, it stiffens resistance to all such inflationary pressures. Fixed exchange rates alone cannot do that. To the extent that the liquidity mechanism continues to permit creation of fiduciary reserve assets, a potential for excessive monetary expansion still exists. It is still necessary to limit growth of stock of international reserves. Fixed exchange rates make it difficult for countries to deviate from the average rate of inflation in the world—but that average inflation rate itself may be quite a bit higher than zero. Governments may simply coordinate their inflationary monetary policies. The one solution, according to gold-standard advocates, is to eliminate the fiduciary component of reserves. That is the only *sure* way to guarantee that central banks will exercise proper self-restraint.

Criticisms of the Gold Standard

Though advocated by many, the gold standard is criticized by even more. And with sound reason—five sound reasons, in fact.

In the first place, the model is politically naïve. It denies the real-world asymmetry of politically sovereign states, an asymmetry certainly no less striking today than it was in the years before 1914, when the myth of the Golden Age was born. More fundamentally, it denies the importance of political sovereignty itself in international monetary relations. In practice, it is difficult to imagine governments ever subscribing in full to "the supreme law, the golden rule." Can they really be expected to surrender all of their tools of domestic and foreign monetary management? The question is not just rhetorical. Even in the nineteenth century, when laissez-faire attitudes dominated economic policy, governments were not entirely indifferent to the effects of gold flows on domestic money supplies and economic conditions. They are hardly likely to be more indifferent in the last quarter of the twentieth century, when laissez-faire attitudes predominate far less. Over the last fifty years, governments have assumed responsibility for an ever wider range of macroeconomic and microeconomic policy targets. It is difficult to imagine them now suddenly putting the stability of their home economies at the mercy of blind and often disruptive forces imported from abroad: deflating incomes and prices passively whenever gold happens to flow out (whether deflation is justified by domestic economic conditions or not), inflating incomes and prices whenever gold happens to flow in. I have said that the gold standard is an "integrationist" solution to the problem of monetary organization. It is also a non-viable solution, foundering on the hard rock of conflicting national interests. No monetary order can remain stable that naïvely denies the endogenous and purposive role of state actors in world monetary affairs. Governments cannot realistically be expected to tolerate such a total infringement of their national policy autonomy.

They certainly are unlikely to tolerate loss of control over the external value of their currencies. The privilege of setting the price of the home currency in terms of some common international numeraire is another way of expressing a government's sovereign political right to create money. One implies the other. The exchange rate establishes the goal of monetary policy by linking prices expressed in national money to international prices. If the privilege to vary the exchange rate were denied absolutely, so too would be the right to manage the local money system. Despite the formal existence of separate national moneys, effectively there would be but a single global currency. The existence of separate national moneys, however, is the very starting point of the analysis of international monetary relations: it is the "hidden assumption" from which all else proceeds. If the assumption is denied, so too is the problem. This may be an attractive approach to analysis, but it is a naïve and unrealistic one.

The second reason for criticizing the gold standard is closely related to the first. If governments cannot be expected to surrender all of their policy autonomy, then the discipline supposedly imposed on inflationary monetary policies by fear of reserve losses will necessarily be incomplete. At one level, governments may sterilize the domestic monetary influence of external payments imbalances (assuming, once again, adequate external reserves or credit facilities to finance their payments deficits, plus an adequately large pool of government securities for open-market operations domestically or sufficient latitude for adjusting private bank reserve requirements). At another level, they may resort to devaluation or to more selective expenditure-switching devices. To the extent that any of these options is even temporarily successful in enabling the national authorities to cope with reserve losses, the deterrent to potentially inflationary policies is critically weakened; consequently, inflationary pressures may easily be transmitted outward from one country to another. In turn, this severely undermines the rationale for the gold standard itself, as Fritz Machlup has noted:

> This judgment is so seriously in contradiction to common opinion that one cannot expect to convince easily those who have from their school days always believed in the gold standard as the best preventive of inflation. All I can do here is to repeat and emphasize the proposition that, when political resistance to contraction is greater than to expansion (and this is true everywhere nowadays) and when therefore the contractionary effects of the adjustment mechanisms are largely or completely offset in deficit countries, the net effect of the adjustment mechanism on all countries taken together is necessarily inflationary.[6]

The third reason for criticizing the gold standard is that it is costly, as compared with any fiduciary monetary standard. Obviously, it is inefficient to dig gold out of a hole in the ground just to transport it to another location and bury it in a hole again. The real-resource cost of producing and storing fiat reserves is far lower, as even most gold-standard enthusiasts are prepared to concede. But that is beside the point, they argue: the real point is not cost but security—the greater certainty of acceptability as compared with any fiduciary reserve asset. Gold is the ultimate "war chest." In the words of one observer, "people will always unconditionally accept gold as the final haven of monetary refuge."[7] Argues another: "A reserve money that is entirely dependent on international agreements for its issue and acceptability (e.g., the SDR) is a fair-weather system. . . . One cannot imagine that a fiduciary asset which is necessarily political would be considered as safe and as dependable as gold."[8] But such arguments deny completely the element of cooperation in international monetary affairs—the efficiency objective in the mixed-motive money game. Keynes once called gold a "barbarous relic." Is it really necessary to base a monetary order on an anachronism, a remnant of earlier, less enlightened times?

The fourth reason is the uncertainty of gold supply. Net additions to monetary gold stocks are equal to new physical production less sales for nonmonetary uses. "Supply and demand are subject to the vicissitudes of speculative whims, cold war politics, racial disturbances, power politics, the vicissitudes of discovery, technological advances or exhaustion of the mines, and the monopolistic policies of the gold cartel operating in a rigged market."[9] One might also add fluctuations of demand for industry and the arts. It would be a lucky accident indeed if the residual of all these factors just happened to correspond to the reserve needs of the monetary order. (If domestic prices were sufficiently flexible, that would not matter. Variations in the physical stock of monetary gold would be offset by corresponding movements of national price levels to ensure optimality of the reserve supply in nominal terms. But prices are not sufficiently flexible—and have not been since at least the end of the last century.) In fact, knowledge of the determinants of monetary gold supply is extremely limited.[10] Gold is an inadequate foundation on which to build effective international management of global liquidity.

Finally, there is the problem of the gold price. Restoration of the gold standard would mean replacing all existing fiduciary reserve assets with gold. As in the 1920s, however, at prevailing prices gold is in evident short supply. An official gold price would therefore have to be reestablished at a sufficiently high level to permit direct conversion of all outstanding currency and SDR reserve balances.[11] Such a price increase would be objectionable for the once-for-all gain enjoyed by gold-holding countries, as well as for the enhanced seigniorage benefit afforded gold producers. It would also further weaken the already incomplete discipline that is supposed to be imposed on domestic monetary policies. As John Williamson has argued, once governments have learned that they can change the price of gold whenever discipline becomes irksome, gold becomes a kind of "funny money" with the capacity to provoke massive speculative shifts of funds in anticipation of price changes (once again, the confidence problem).[12] Far from stabilizing monetary relations, the gold standard would in fact threaten to become a source of even greater instability in the international economy.

Flexible Exchange Rates

At the opposite extreme from the gold standard is the regime of absolutely flexible exchange rates. This approach too is advocated by many sources. "Flexibility of exchange rates is the perfect solution for keeping a country's balance of payments in equilibrium," argues one.[13] Says another: "Flexible exchange rates are essential to the preservation of national autonomy and independence consistent with efficient organization and development of the world economy."[14] (That is, flexible exchange rates are essential to promote both the consistency and efficiency objectives.) The case for flexible exchange rates has enjoyed widespread intellectual respectability ever since publication of a famous article by Milton Friedman in 1953.[15] The case won political respectability when the United States became its advocate in the Committee of Twenty and Interim Committee (see Chapter 4). Today it is no longer possible to dismiss free floating casually because of its "proved disadvantages," as the negotiators at Bretton Woods did in 1944. The case for flexibility must now be considered seriously on its merits.

The Case for Absolutely Flexible Exchange Rates

The case for flexibility is essentially the converse of the case for the gold standard. A gold standard would accommodate the consensual and conflictual elements in monetary relations by maximizing external constraints on governmental decision-making authority—an "integrationist" solution to the problem of monetary organization. Flexible exchange rates, conversely, would accomplish the same objective ostensibly by *minimizing* all external constraints on governments—a much more "disintegrationist" solution. Just one explicit constraint would be placed on national economic policy autonomy. Authorities would be obliged to refrain from any direct intervention in the exchange market to influence the price of the home currency in terms of foreign currencies. Otherwise, they would be free to assume responsibility for as wide a range of macroeconomic and microeconomic policy targets as they like. They would not have to put their domestic economies at the mercy of forces imported from abroad, nor would they be forced to resort to such devices as trade restrictions or exchange control in order to promote and maintain internal balance. Flexibility of the exchange rate would automatically provide "insulation" of the home environment by substituting for direct changes of incomes and prices in the adjustment process. As Harry Johnson stated the case:

> The problem with [fixed exchange rates] is that they demand a surrender of national sovereignty in domestic economic policy, which countries have shown themselves extremely reluctant to accept. . . . The main argument for flexible exchange rates at the present time is that they would make this surrender of sovereignty unnecessary, while at the same time making unnecessary the progressive extension of interventions in international trade and payments that failure to resolve this issue necessarily entails.[16]

The insulation argument is not an unlimited one, as even the most ardent advocates of flexibility are prepared to admit. Johnson went on to add: "A flexible exchange rate is not, of course, a panacea."[17] A floating rate cannot insulate an economy from "real" external disturbances—fluctuations of the balance of payments owing to changes of foreign tastes, technology, factor endowments, and so forth. In such circumstances, a marginal reallocation of domestic resources will, of course, be required (e.g., from nontraded to tradable-goods production in the event of, say, a shift of foreign tastes that reduces demand for one of a country's leading export products). All the floating rate can do is ease the real adjustment and help switch expenditures between foreign and domestic output by facilitating an alteration of relative prices. The insulation that flexibility is said to provide is from "monetary" external developments—fluctuations in the balance of payments owing to inflation or deflation abroad. In such circumstances, floating rates are supposed to permit the rate of economic activity at home to be determined in total independence of the constraint on the balance of payments, in effect giving national authorities an extra degree of freedom in the formulation of domestic macroeconomic policy. It is in this sense that flexibility is claimed to make the surrender of sovereignty unnecessary.

Flexible exchange rates eliminate the need for any mechanism of liquidity creation. If governments are inhibited from all interventions in the exchange market, by definition they require no stockpile of international monetary reserves (though they may, if they wish, continue to hold reserve assets to back their domestic money supplies).

The monetary order comprises simply the pure floating-rate mechanism of balance-of-payments adjustment. The efficiency objective is supposed to be promoted by automatic operation of the price mechanism in the foreign-exchange market, with autonomous demand and supply adjusting continuously to maintain equilibrium in each country's external accounts. The consistency objective is supposedly promoted by the self-denying ordinance on exchange-market intervention, which is presumed to cut off all risk of policy conflict at its source. No longer need all nations be concerned about the possible lack of self-restraint on the part of some central banks. Excessive monetary expansion in a given country will simply be off-set by an appropriate movement of its exchange rate. Inflationary (or, for that matter, deflationary) pressures will simply be "bottled up" in the country of origin. This "bottling-up" argument, obviously, is simply the converse of the insulation argument.

Like the case for the gold standard, the case for flexibility is advocated by many—and criticized by even more. Here too the reasons for criticism are many and sound.

Political Naïveté of the Case

In the first place, like the case for the gold standard, the case for absolute flexibility is politically naïve. True, at least ostensibly, it makes more of a concession to the importance of political sovereignty in monetary relations than the gold standard does. But absolute flexibility still requires a much greater infringement on national policy autonomy than governments can realistically be expected to tolerate. The privilege of setting the price of the home currency in terms of some common international numeraire is, I have said, just another way of expressing a government's sovereign political right to create money. National authorities are no more likely to accept total loss of control over their exchange rates in the context of a floating-rate regime than they are in the context of the gold standard. The price of the currency is simply too essential for domestic monetary management.

Exchange rates are not like other prices: a currency is not just another commodity or financial asset. In the words of Robert Mundell: "The exchange rate is a price, but it is not a price like the price of cabbage."[18] In fact, the exchange, rate is an extremely crucial economic variable that helps to determine the whole pattern of resource allocation as well as the level and distribution of income in each economy. So long as governments continue to assume responsibility for macroeconomic and microeconomic policy targets, they will inevitably take a view about the external value of their currency. They simply will not accept absolute denial of the privilege to vary exchange rates.

Besides, governments are not limited in the means at their disposal for varying exchange rates. Whether they intend it or not, their policies influence currency values. If they do intend it, they can deliberately manage their exchange rates even when inhibited by a self-denying ordinance on direct foreign-exchange intervention. There is more than one way to skin a cat. Governments themselves undertake a considerable volume of international transactions, particularly on capital account. By varying the timing of their payments and receipts, they can effectively manipulate the movements of a floating rate. Likewise, selective expenditure-switching devices may be used to achieve the same end; even expenditure-changing policies may be utilized. The modern theory of balance-of-payments policy teaches that "there is no effect from direct intervention policy that could not also have been obtained through the appropriate manipulation of monetary policy under a pure float."[19] To prevent all such indirect manipulation, much more is required than a mere inhibition on direct intervention policies. Governments would also have to be barred from discretionary use of any of their macroeconomic or microeconomic policy instruments—in effect, they would have to submit to a set of external constraints as strong as any implied by a gold standard. Ostensibly more "disintegrationist" than the gold-standard proposal, the case for flexibility is in reality as integrationist as its converse. It is also, therefore, just as politically naïve.

Shaky Theoretical Foundations

Advocates of flexibility concede that governments may be *capable* of indirect manipulation of exchange rates. But, they argue, that is

not the point: the point is that governments would have no motivation to *use* that capability in a floating-rate world, since they would
be automatically insulated from monetary disturbances originating
abroad; inflationary or deflationary pressures would simply be
bottled up in the country of origin. Exchange rates may be unlike
other prices. Still, governments would not need to worry about
them. Insulation would guarantee them an extra degree of freedom
in their domestic economic policies.

The proposition is appealing—but deceptive. Neither the insulation argument nor its twin, the bottling-up argument, rests upon
firm theoretical foundations. In fact, both collapse on close examination. As Kindleberger has suggested, "the extra degree of freedom . . .
is illusory. . . . There is no free lunch."[20]

The insulation argument was originally derived from a model of
balance-of-payments behavior which excluded all capital flows (i.e.,
from a model of the trade balance alone); and even though the model
was later extended to incorporate capital mobility,[21] its conclusions
remained essentially unchanged. Because capital flows could not
affect domestic money supplies in the absence of central-bank intervention in the exchange market, theorists assumed that the home
economy would always be effectively insulated from external monetary developments. The assumption, however, was erroneous.

We know that in the context of fixed exchange rates, capital
flows influence domestic economic conditions via official exchange
intervention: unless offset by domestic sterilization operations, purchases or sales of foreign exchange by the central bank directly alter
the monetary reserve base of the domestic banking system and thereby generate changes of internal income and expenditures. Conversely,
we also know that in the context of floating, where there is no
official exchange intervention, there are no changes of the domestic
monetary reserve base. But that does not mean that the home
economy is therefore fully insulated from any influence of capital
flows. Quite the contrary, in fact. Suppose foreign interest rates
rise, inducing an outflow of capital from home. This directly
depreciates the exchange rate, in turn inducing an improvement of
the country's trade balance and stimulating an increase of internal

incomes and expenditures. Domestic economic conditions are affected despite the absence of official exchange intervention.

This suggests that the argument for insulation must be qualified. As Peter Kenen says, "Flexible exchange rates cannot insulate economies from changes in their neighbors' interest rates."[22] Flexibility may still provide greater insulation than a fixed-rate regime, but it is a difference in degree only, not in kind, and it is not an insulation that is gained automatically. Deliberate manipulation of domestic policy variables is required to offset any autonomous influences on domestic economic conditions stemming from international capital flows. As one source has concluded:

> The insulation problem is thus seen as dependent on domestic economic policy rather than a purely automatic mechanism. Flexible exchange rates may provide some degree of automatic insulation even with a high degree of capital mobility. However, it is more likely that any greater independence or freedom for domestic policy makers under flexible exchanges would derive less from *automatic* insulation and more from the broader range of policy alternatives brought about by the elimination of an official commitment to peg the price of gold or foreign exchange.[23]

Once this qualification is acknowledged, not much remains of the extra degree of freedom supposedly afforded the national authorities. "The gain in autonomy for monetary and fiscal policy is an illusion. Along with one more variable, there is one more target—the exchange rate."[24] The balance-of-payments constraint still remains, albeit in a modified form. Governments must still pay attention to their exchange rate, because of the key importance of this variable to the relationship between capital flows and domestic economic conditions.

The same point can be approached from a different direction by considering the bottling-up argument. Is it true that all nations need no longer be concerned about possible lack of self-restraint on the part of some central banks? We know that when exchange rates are fixed, powerful mechanisms exist to transmit inflationary pressures from one country to another.[25]

First, there is the direct *price mechanism* of transmission. Price levels in different countries are closely linked by global trade in goods and services, owing to the influence of international competition and the law of one price for one product in all markets (making due allowance for transport costs). Inflationary pressures anywhere in the world tend to be spread rapidly and directly between countries through import and export prices at fixed exchange rates; in turn, increases of tradable-goods prices are spread through the rest of the domestic price structure both vertically (i.e., to prices of raw materials and intermediate goods and to prices of products using tradable goods as inputs) and horizontally (i.e., to prices of nontraded substitutes and to complementary goods).

A second factor is the direct *income mechanism* of transmission. This operates through the impact of current-account surpluses on the level of aggregate domestic demand. Even apart from any internal monetary expansion associated with central-bank purchases of foreign exchange, as described above, current-account surpluses generated by inflation in foreign markets add directly to private incomes at home and thus tend to exert additional upward pressures on the level of domestic prices.

Finally, there is the *monetary mechanism* of transmission. This operates through the internal monetary influence of official exchange intervention, as described above. Inflation from abroad is transmitted to the economy at home through liquidity effects, as individuals and enterprises increase their aggregate expenditures to adjust the real value of their money balances to desired levels.

When exchange rates are free to float, all three of these mechanisms of transmission are short-circuited. But this does not mean that floating rates cannot transmit inflation. Quite the contrary. Flexibility enthusiasts overlook an important asymmetry in this regard. Foreign monetary developments can follow either an upward or a downward path; that is, they can take the form of either inflation or (in a world of downward wage and price rigidity) unemployment. In the event of foreign inflation, stability of the domestic price level can be safely assumed because it is virtually inconceivable that the equilibrating effects of the ensuing exchange-rate appreciation will be offset by compensatory reductions of wages and prices at home. The foreign inflation will be bottled up in the country of origin.

But what happens in the event of foreign unemployment (monetary deflation)? In that case, stability of the domestic price level cannot be safely assumed, because of the likely impact of the ensuing depreciation of the exchange rate on income claims by particular groups in the local economy. The equilibrating effects of the depreciation will very likely be offset by compensatory wage and price increases at home, since a decline of the exchange rate is understood to increase local-currency prices in the tradable-goods sector (and since these increases are unlikely to be balanced by decreases in other sectors, at least in the short term). The authorities will then be placed under precisely the same pressures as in a fixed-rate regime to permit the growth of domestic money supply required to validate the imported price rises. There is nothing in the nature of a floating-rate regime to suggest that central banks would be any less passively accommodating than when exchange rates are fixed. Indeed, with the discipline of potential reserve losses removed, there is good reason to suppose that they would, if anything, be even more tolerant of inflation.[26] Accordingly, the assumption that a floating-rate regime can provide an effective barrier to international transmission of inflation must be appropriately qualified. Unemployment in one country can inflict involuntary inflation on its neighbors, and so raise the average rate of world inflation.

Indeed, *any* foreign development—real as well as monetary—that causes a depreciation of the local currency is apt to lead to the same outcome. Suppose, for example, that shifting tastes abroad reduce demand for one of a country's leading export products. If resources in the country were sufficiently mobile and prices sufficiently flexible— in other words, if there were no substantial lags in the adjustment process—the outcome would, as indicated earlier, be a quick decline in the relative prices of nontraded goods and a reallocation of domestic resources at the margin from nontraded to tradable-goods production. In reality, however, since resource mobility and (downward) price flexibility tend to be rather limited, at least in the short term, the immediate result is more likely to be unemployment in the affected export industry, depreciation of the exchange rate, and a rising level of local-currency prices. And this, in turn, is likely to be quickly translated into cost-push inflation which the central bank will find difficult to resist. In this way, involuntary inflation can be inflicted on a country *whatever* the cause of the initial depreciation of its exchange rate. Owing to short-term domestic rigidities and delays in the adjustment process, floating rates are indeed capable of transmitting inflation internationally.

Moreover, given the well-known tendency of the balance of payments to follow a so-called "J-curve" in response to changes of exchange rates, the inflationary process can actually become cumulative. In the short run, currency depreciation generally tends to worsen a country's trade balance rather than improve it; only after a lapse of some time does the favorable impact of the depreciation begin to take hold. One source estimates that among industrial countries as much as half the full improvement of the trade balance tends to be delayed three years or more, principally because of various lags in the adjustment process—recognition lags, decision lags, production lags, delivery lags.[27] Hence, it is clear that even before the trade balance can begin to improve, the inflationary impact of the depreciation will already be firmly "locked into" the domestic wage and cost structure. And this in turn can generate yet further depreciation of the currency, inflicting yet more involuntary inflation on the country. The process may be repeated time and again, and price rises could continue ad infinitum in a cumulative upward "ratchet" effect. Floating rates are, potentially, a veritable perpetual-motion inflation machine:

> In today's world of inflation, depreciation is likely to raise prices in the depreciating country, leaving them unchanged in the appreciating country. . . . Depreciation and appreciation . . . will thus raise world prices on balance in ratchet style, and generate dynamic inflationary forces inside separate countries.[28]

Does this mean that floating rates are potentially more inflationary than fixed rates? Not necessarily. "There is no simple answer to the question whether a regime of fixed or more flexible exchange rates is more or less 'inflationary' *per se*."[29] In fact, among economists the question continues to generate a great deal of warm debate.[30] The point being stressed here is simply that there is no sound basis for arguing that floating rates must necessarily be *less* inflationary than fixed rates. Floating rates provide an effective barrier to the international transmission of inflation only in a theoretical model of perfect resource mobility and price flexibility. In the real world, where adjustments are not instantaneous, the collectivity of nations must be concerned about possible lack of self-restraint on the part of some central banks. Governments cannot ignore the domestic impacts of exchange-rate fluctuations.

Microeconomic Inefficiency

In addition to being politically naïve and resting on shaky theoretictal foundations, the case for flexibility is weak on straightforward economic grounds. Freely floating rates do not necessarily promote the efficiency objective, despite the claims of flexibility enthusiasts. In fact, global economic welfare may be more seriously damaged than under a fixed exchange-rate regime. Floating rates may be inefficient at both the microeconomic and macroeconomic levels.

At the microeconomic level, a floating-rate regime is less efficient than a genuinely fixed-rate regime to the extent that it adds to exchange risk and thus hampers the transfer of purchasing power between countries. "The special exchange-risks associated with foreign commerce come not from the existence of separate national monies but from the variations over time in their relative values."[31] The greater these potential variations, the greater the risks attached to international transactions and to investment in the production of tradable goods. Such uncertainty is a unique and additional cost of foreign commerce, since it is entirely absent when business activity is confined to a single national money system. Floating exchange rates have a fundamental "anti-trade" bias to the extent that they increase such uncertainty and thereby foster an avoidance of investment in tradable-goods industries. Enterprises may be led to more and more inward-looking, domestic-oriented business decisions. As a result, international trade and investment may be discouraged below the point where technical efficiency and global economic welfare are maximized.

For some observers, this is reason enough to reconsider the case for a single global money or its equivalent, discussed briefly in Chapter 1. A single global money would give international traders and investors the advantages of a unified medium of exchange, unit of account, and store of value, thereby minimizing total transactions costs. "The benefits of international money are not negligible and should not be ignored."[32] For advocates of flexibility, however, the anti-trade bias of floating rates is a mirage for two reasons.

First, to the extent that floating rates do add to exchange risk, enterprises can protect themselves against it at relatively low cost. A principal means for doing this is the forward-exchange market, the market for foreign exchange bought and sold for future delivery.[33] The forward market is an integral part of the foreign-exchange market, which also includes the market for "spot exchange" bought and sold for immediate delivery. (The price in the forward market, which is set at the time that the contract is made, is known as the "forward rate" and is quoted in exactly the same manner as the "spot rate" of a currency.) Forward markets are vital to traders and investors anxious to protect their international operations against exchange risk. Anticipated foreign-exchange receipts can be sold forward to protect against the risk of possible depreciation; anticipated payment obligations can be matched by forward purchases to protect against possible appreciation. This is known as the process of "covering."[34] Exchange risk is converted into a sort of insurance premium equal to the cost of cover.

Advocates of flexibility do not expect that the cost of forward cover would be excessive in a regime of floating rates. "If there were a demand for more extensive forward market and hedging facilities than now exist, the competitive profit motive would bring them into existence."[35] Accordingly, the cost of cover would be bid down to tolerable levels. True, the cost would not become zero: at the margin, some trade and investment would still be discouraged. But this is trade and investment that, in the opinion of flexibility enthusiasts, should not take place anyway—and would not take place but for the price-fixing policy of governments, a policy which in effect subsidizes foreign business activity at the expense of the entire national com-

munity. Any loss of productive efficiency would be outweighed by a
gain of economic equity:

> A system of officially pegged exchange rates involves a certain
> type of distribution of the burden of exchange-risk insurance over
> the entire community. Those individuals and firms in the economy
> that receive relatively little benefit from international trade and
> investment must nevertheless share more-or-less equally the
> macroeconomic costs of pegging the rate. This constitutes an
> inequity. . . . A system of floating rates, on the other hand, would
> place the cost of insuring against exchange risk squarely on the
> shoulders of those directly profiting from international com-
> merce. . . . Floating rates, then, appear to provide a far more
> equitable distribution of the cost of exchange-risk insurance.[36]

The trouble with this line of defense is not that it is logically
invalid—in fact, it is perfectly sound—but rather that it claims too
much. Efficient forward markets might be expected to develop under
floating rates, and the distribution of the cost of exchange-risk insurance would surely be made more equitable as a result. But this still
would not dissolve the anti-trade bias of floating rates. Forward markets can only eliminate the uncertainty of the foreign-exchange
element of *individual* international transactions; they cannot insure
businessmen against the risk that shifting rates in the future will
potentially favor uncovered competitors. Nor can they provide the
kind of "fixed" frame of reference that businessmen feel they need
in order to plan future transactions and investments.[37] Commercial
decisions are not made with each separate deal calculated afresh.
Enterprises engage in activities, not single transactions. For planning
and investment purposes they require some sense of competitive
conditions over a period longer than that of a single purchase or sale.
Forward markets cannot give them this sense, as businessmen learned
with regret after the transition to generalized floating in 1971-1973.
Enterprises showed a great deal of ingenuity after 1973 in devising
ways to cope with forms of exchange risk that could not be covered
in the forward market.[38] But one lesson that their recent experience
teaches is that even with all their ingenuity, they are unable to dispell entirely the uncertainty created by floating exchange rates.

This causes flexibility enthusiasts to fall back to their second line of defense. Their second reason for denying the anti-trade bias of floating rates has to do with the role of private speculators in the foreign-exchange market. Speculation in foreign exchange is defined as any transaction intended to take advantage of the possibility of changes in the price of a currency over time. The speculator deliberately takes a risk by assuming an "open" position in a currency (i.e., a position of unequal assets and liabilities). Advocates of flexibility concede there may be uncertainty in a regime of floating exchange rates, but they claim the uncertainty will be minimized by the stabilizing effect of speculation. A freely floating rate, they contend, is not necessarily an unstable one. Speculative purchases and sales can be counted on to keep it from straying very far from its true market equilibrium value. "The movement of the rate would be facilitated and smoothed by the actions of private speculators, on the basis of their reading of current and prospective economic and policy developments."[39] As a result, potential variations will be small and exchange risk will be minimal.

Will speculation be stabilizing or destabilizing under floating exchange rates? This is a question that has long agitated scholars specializing in international finance. In his 1953 article, Friedman argued that speculation *must* be stabilizing: unless speculators buy when a currency is low relative to its equilibrium value and sell when it is relatively high, they will lose money on average and go out of business; consequently, only stabilizing speculators will remain.[40] Subsequent writers, however, have identified a number of examples of destabilizing profit-making speculation that are both plausible in principle and relevant in practice.[41] After more than two decades of intense debate in the technical literature, what now seems quite clear is that only profit-*maximizing* speculators *must* be stabilizing, as Friedman insisted; destabilizing speculators do not necessarily lose money. But to be profit-*maximizers*, speculators must have perfect foresight about prospective economic and policy developments— and that is precisely what they cannot realistically be expected to have in the world in which we actually live, where the only constant is change. Thus, speculators cannot realistically be expected always to be stabilizers, as even many flexibility enthusiasts have now conceded. In the end, the question can be answered only on empirical grounds:

> In view of this analysis, it would seem wisest ... to abandon the emphasis of the Friedman analysis on the proposition that "destabilizing speculators must lose money." Instead, attention should be concentrated ... in the particular case of the debate over flexible versus fixed rates of exchange [on] the empirically important question [of] whether the speculation inherent in the maintenance of a fixed rate will generate more or less destabilizing speculation than would occur with a floating rate.[42]

What has been the empirical evidence to date? As we know, exchange-rate movements in 1973-1975 were quite large (see Chapter 4). Does this suggest the presence of destabilizing speculation in the exchange market? Not necessarily. In fact, what the evidence suggests is a *paucity* of private speculation. Individuals and enterprises, concerned over the signs of stress in the private international financial structure, became very reluctant after 1973 to risk assuming open positions in foreign exchange. And even banks became very cautious after the Herstatt affair in 1974. Banks traditionally function in the exchange market as "professional risk bearer"; they "make" the market by assuming (at a price, of course) risks that the non-bank public prefers to avoid. With even banks refusing to assume such risks (or being prevented from doing so by government regulation), the exchange market became extremely thin, and price movements as a result became notably volatile.[43]

This suggests that the debate since 1953 may have been misplaced. Instead of asking whether speculation would be stabilizing or destabilizing, perhaps the question ought to have been: would there be *any* kind of speculation? It is possible, of course, that the widespread reluctance in the private sector after 1973 to assume currency positions was a temporary phenomenon, reflecting the extraordinary unknowns of systemic breakdown and reconstruction. Beyond a period of transition, the volume of speculative activity could pick up considerably and might even turn out to be stabilizing. But that remains to be proved. Flexibility enthusiasts have yet to demonstrate their case.

Macroeconomic Inefficiency

At the macroeconomic level, a floating exchange-rate regime is less efficient than a fixed-rate regime to the extent that it adds to the economic costs of balance-of-payments adjustment and thus hampers the adjustment process. I have already suggested in Chapter 1 that an efficient monetary order could not rely on exchange-rate flexibility exclusively. The total transitional cost of adjustment could turn out to be much higher than necessary, because of the danger that movements of exchange rates would be either exaggerated or perverse. The salience of this danger was confirmed by the experience after 1973. Because of the combination of lags in the adjustment process (the J-curve) and a paucity of stabilizing speculation, exchange-rate changes even if in the "right" direction tended to overshoot equilibrium. As one observer remarked, these developments "reinforce concern that large overshoots may be characteristic of more or less free floating and bring in its wake large and unnecessary dislocations in both domestic and international markets."[44] Such an adjustment process is hardly optimal.

The argument can be carried further. From one point of view, the adjustment process under floating rates is not just suboptimal but absolutely impotent. This view, which derives from the recently developed "monetary" approach to macroeconomic theory, places central emphasis on the relationship of aggregate expenditures to changes in the real value of money balances (the "real-balance effect"), treating the process of payments adjustment as a purely monetary phenomenon.[45] Exchange rates can have only a transitory impact on the balance of payments because of their effect on real money balances (e.g., depreciation reducing the value of real money balances by raising prices, appreciation doing the opposite). Over the long term, as individuals and enterprises alter their aggregate expenditures to adjust real balances back to desired levels, the initial modification of relative prices stemming from an exchange-rate change will be offset by a corresponding modification of domestic price levels, and the balance of payments will revert to its previous position. No lasting adjustment occurs.

In the context of discussions of alternative exchange-rate regimes, this new view has been most prominently championed by Robert Mundell and Arthur Laffer.[46] One self-proclaimed disciple has summarized the key elements of their argument as follows:

> It is thus the contention of Mundell and Laffer ... that devaluation has no "real" effects, but results only in the price inflation in the devaluing country relative to the country or countries against which the devaluation occurs. By reducing the amount of goods its money can buy, the devaluing country creates an excess demand for its money. If it simply prints more money, there is no balance of payments improvement—which was what devaluation was supposed to achieve. If it doesn't, its citizens will simply import money (by exporting bonds) to satisfy the excess demand, and this will show up as a brief "improvement" in the balance of payments.[47]

According to Mundell-Laffer, therefore, floating rates are superfluous, and the world would be better off with a regime of fixed exchange rates—that is, with a single global money or its equivalent. "A world currency system would be vastly preferable to flexible exchange rates. . . . Far from being inferior to freely floating rates, truly fixed rates have a distinct edge."[48] Of course, that opens again the question of the liquidity-creation mechanism. Someone has to control the rate of world monetary expansion. For Mundell-Laffer, however, that is no problem. The answer is simply to restore the gold standard—which brings us full circle, back to where this chapter began. Mundell-Laffer's disciple is undoubtedly right when he predicts that their proposal will "raise the hackles of a generation of economists who were raised to think that the 'gold standard' was one of yesteryear's most awful superstitions."[49] Their advocacy has yet to swing many converts to the cause.

The principal criticisms of the gold-standard proposal have already been outlined. The one new element introduced by Mundell-Laffer is the asserted impotence of the adjustment process under floating rates. The weakness of their analysis lies in the hypothesized close relationship between exchange-rate changes and movements of relative price levels. Few economists doubt that over the very long term (i.e., decades) changes in exchange rates do tend to offset—or be offset by—corresponding changes of domestic price levels.[50] The question is: how rapidly does the offset occur? Mundell-Laffer argue that it occurs very quickly, owing to the high degree of integration of the world economy and the law of one price for one product in all markets. But in fact the offset tends to occur rather slowly, because world markets are not nearly so well integrated as Mundell-Laffer assume. Multinational corporations and other enterprises in oligopolistic industries do not quickly "pass through" the changes of prices implied by exchange-rate changes. Empirical evidence suggests that most, if not all, of the initial changes of relative prices stemming from exchange-rate changes "stick" in the short and even medium term.[51] In turn, this implies that the adjustment process under floating rates is not nearly so impotent as Mundell-Laffer assert. It may, indeed, be quite potent.

But potency is not the same as optimality. Freely floating exchange rates cannot *optimize* the adjustment process, any more than absolutely fixed rates can (see Chapter 1). Neither extreme can minimize the real costs of balance-of-payments adjustment. Rather, what is needed is some compromise between the two—one that would maximize the advantages of both while minimizing their disadvantages. The problem is to find the *optimal* degree of exchange-rate flexibility.

The Optimal Degree of Flexibility

The search for the optimal degree of exchange-rate flexibility is not new. Optimal flexibility was the goal of the negotiators who designed the postwar par-value regime at Bretton Woods. It was likewise the goal of the many scholars and officials who in the decades after 1944 proposed to reform or replace the par-value regime.[52] There is an almost infinite array of possible compromises between the two polar alternatives of rigidly fixed or absolutely flexible exchange rates.[53]

Such compromises may be distinguished by the degree of discretion afforded official intervention in the foreign-exchange market: whether governments are required or permitted to fix precise limits for their exchange rates, whether they set such limits close or far apart, whether they announce them publicly, whether they revise them periodically, how they revise them, and so on. The search for optimal exchange-rate flexibility is really the search for the optimal degree of official intervention in the exchange market.

Obviously, the variety of possible combinations of automaticity and discretion in exchange-rate regimes is enormous. Space limitations prevent us from considering here more than a representative sample of choices from such a rich menu. The following discussion, after some brief comments on the meaning of optimal exchange-rate flexibility, will concentrate on four key classes of compromise arrangements: (1) the par-value regime; (2) the "band proposal"; (3) the "crawling peg"; and (4) managed floating.

Optimal Exchange-Rate Flexibility

The optimal degree of exchange-rate flexibility may be defined in terms of either of two dimensions—time and space. With respect to the former, the question is: over what period of time should rates be held fixed before they are allowed to vary? With respect to the latter, the question is: over how large an area should rates be held fixed and not allowed to vary?

The former question is the more familiar of the two. It is, in fact, what much of the discussion of the relative merits of fixed and flexible exchange rates in this chapter (as well as in Chapter 1) has been all about.[54] There are costs in allowing rates to change too quickly or continuously, including the loss of the benefits of international money (including, in particular, the benefit of a fixed point of reference for international transactions) and the potentially higher real costs of balance-of-payments adjustment. There are also costs in preventing rates from changing quickly or continuously enough, including the possible accumulation of undesirable distortions in the pattern of global resource allocation (investments in real capital and human skills that will have to be written off) and the economic cost of inapposite adjustment policies. If the exchange-rate mechanism is to be designed to promote the efficiency objective, some means must be found for balancing these two sets of costs at the margin, in order to minimize them. Rate changes must be neither too continuous nor too discontinuous. (In other words, some meaning must be found for the phrases "too quickly" and "not quickly enough.") At the same time, if the consistency objective is to be promoted, governments must not be given too much latitude for discretionary behavior that would avoid or transfer the costs and responsibilities of adjustment to others. The exchange-rate mechanism must not become a new source of policy conflict among states. These are not easy balances to strike.

The latter question goes under the name of the theory of "optimum currency areas"—a relatively recent development in the economics literature.[55] In the years immediately following Friedman's 1953 article, the controversy over fixed versus flexible exchange rates was debated in the abstract, and currency areas were assumed to be more or less alike. It was only in the 1960s that writers began to ask whether fixed or flexible rates might be more appropriate for some currency areas and less appropriate for others. National money systems are obviously not all alike. An exchange-rate regime that suits one local system may be quite unsuitable for another. The dimension of space is clearly relevant, as soon became clear in the literature. The question gradually emerged: what is the appropriate domain of a currency area?

There are two possible approaches to answering this question. One stresses the global or cosmopolitan point of view, while the other proceeds from a more national perspective. Earlier contributions to the theory took the first approach, as if the world were about to be designed anew, and focused on the hypothetical question of where lines ought to be drawn between separate currency areas to maximize global economic welfare. Different writers singled out the particular economic characteristics they considered crucial to the analysis (e.g., factor mobility, degree of openness, product diversification). Unfortunately, no one of these criteria turned out to be entirely free of ambiguity; collectively, as one source observed, "they tend to cancel each other out."[56] As a result, the approach proved to be of only limited usefulness in practical policy discussions. As one source has concluded: "It seems that theories based on [this approach] have to be rejected as a guide for practical policy."[57]

The alternative approach begins with the world as we know it, focusing on existing money systems as indivisible units, and asks which of these are candidates for participation in broader currency unions. According to this approach, which is characteristic of more recent contributions to the theory, an optimum currency area is defined by the balance at the margin of the costs and benefits of having a common currency (or its functional equivalent: genuinely fixed exchange rates within the group, together with some degree of joint flexibility vis-à-vis the outside world). The conclusion that may be drawn from these contributions is that this is not an easy balance to strike, either.

In large part, the balance appears to depend on the degree of harmony or discord of national macroeconomic policies, particularly with respect to the trade-off between unemployment and inflation. It also appears to depend to a large extent on the size and degree of openness of each national economy and the source of likely disturbances to the balance of payments. A large closed economy has little interest in fixing its exchange rate to those of its neighbors, since rather substantial variations of domestic expenditures, or of trade restrictions or exchange control, are then required to correct even small external deficits; with a floating rate, much of the costs and responsibilities of adjustment can be shifted onto others, while the comparatively small size of the foreign-trade sector ensures that the domestic impact of any exchange-rate changes will be relatively muted. Small open economies, conversely, have little interest in a floating rate, which may be quite detrimental to the stability of prices and incomes at home, unless the majority of shocks to the balance of payments can be expected to arise in the outside world; in that event, countries can avail themselves of the relatively greater degree of insulation from external disturbances afforded by exchange-rate flexibility to reduce their adjustment vulnerability.

"It is rather widely accepted that a country has the strongest case for freely floating exchange rates when the disturbances to its balance of payments typically come from outside its borders and the weakest case when they come from inside."[58] If most shocks come from inside, then a fixed exchange rate is preferable because of its greater ability to spread some part of the burden of adjustment to others. A common currency can serve as "shock absorber for the nation."[59]

These considerations have quite a bit of practical policy relevance. They explain, for example, America's strong support in the Committee of Twenty and Interim Committee for floating exchange rates, as indicated in the last chapter. They also explain Canada's prolonged experiments with a floating rate in the 1950s and 1960s, when a principal objective of Canadian policy was to shield the domestic economy and reduce its vulnerability to shocks originating in its larger American neighbor to the south. These considerations also help explain the efforts of many smaller, more open economies after 1973 to avoid the adverse domestic impact of potentially excessive exchange-rate fluctuations by pegging their currencies to those of countries to which they had close trade and financial ties. The 1931 experience was repeated: when generalized floating began, currency blocs tended to form. In Euope, nonmembers as well as members of the European Community took advantage of the "snake" experiment to align themselves with Germany's dominant Deutsche mark. In the Third World, the great majority of LDCs chose to peg to one or another of the major world currencies.[60] These decisions clearly reflected the greater interest of small countries in exchange-rate stability.

Not that small countries were entirely content with these arrangements. Indeed, especially among LDCs, there was a distinct feeling of dissatisfaction with the necessity to peg to a single major currency at a time when, as part of their drive for economic development, they were trying to diversify rather than concentrate the geographic pattern of their foreign trade and financial ties. For many, diversification had already proceeded to the point where there was no clear-cut candidate for pegging. This has been called the "outer exchange-rate problem."[61] When fluctuations occur in the cross-rates among major currencies (outer exchange rates or "outrates"), LDCs find life much more complicated than in the "good old days" of the Bretton Woods system:

> Under conditions of diversification, pegging to a single currency will result in variations in the *effective* exchange rate of the small country. Those variations will result from fluctuations among key currencies and will have nothing to do with the balance-of-payments position of the small country . . . . Allowing fluctuations among key currencies will introduce one more source of uncertainty about the terms of trade, servicing the foreign debt, and the balance of payments for small countries that previously benefited from convertibility at fixed exchange rates.[62]

To cope with the outer exchange-rate problem, a number of LDCs have chosen to peg their currencies to one or another basket of major currencies or to the SDR (itself a basket of currencies).[63] But such arrangements are still considered inferior to a stable and open regime of fixed exchange rates among all of the major currencies. LDCs still believe that they are obliged to bear a disproportionate share of the burden of adjustment in a world of floating rates.[64]

This demonstrates just how difficult it is, in practice, to identify the appropriate domain of a currency area. For one observer, this suggests that "the theory of optimum currency areas is primarily a scholastic discussion which contributes little to practical problems of exchange rate policy and monetary reform.[65] But that is really much too harsh a judgment. More apropos is the suggestion that the theory "provides useful information for the formation of 'good,' even though non-optimum currency areas, and it tends to raise the general level of discussion of fixed versus flexible exchange rates."[66] In particular, it emphasizes the close interrelationship of space and time in the discussion of fixed versus flexible exchange rates. Both dimensions—the geographic as well as the temporal—are clearly important in the search for optimal flexibility. Both must be kept in mind in attempting to design a viable exchange-rate regime.

The Par-Value Regime

At Bretton Woods, the negotiators attempted to design a viable exchange-rate regime by introducing the concept of fundamental disequilibrium (see Chapter 3). The par-value regime was an explicit compromise between the two polar alternatives of rigidly fixed or absolutely flexible exchange rates. Governments were to maximize the advantages of the former by declaring and maintaining a par value for their currencies within narrow margins; they were to maximize the advantages of the latter by altering their par values whenever necessary to correct a fundamental disequilibrium. In principle, this was supposed to suffice both to optimize the adjustment process and avoid the risk of policy conflict. In practice, however, as we know, the mechanism was not at all free of serious defects.

The main defect, of course, was the ambiguity surrounding the notion of fundamental disequilibrium. It was no accident that the postwar adjustable-peg regime tended to become biased toward rigidity, at least among the advanced industrial nations. This was an inevitable result of the requirement that governments *demonstrate* the existence of a fundamental disequilibrium before altering their par values. Conrad Oort has called attention to

> the political asymmetry between positive action and nonaction on parities. Governments are rarely criticized for not changing the par value. . . . A change of the par value, on the other hand, is a conscious overt policy action that is unavoidably accompanied by all the trappings of a major public decision: . . . the very fact that it is a discontinuous change, resulting from an overt act of policy, cannot fail to elicit public reaction. . . . No government will on its own initiative . . . change the parity unless it is convinced that at least the direction of change is right. No government wants voluntarily to put itself in a position of having to reverse a decision of that kind within a period of, say, two years.[67]

Delays are inherent in any policy context where a positive decision to change something is required. Political pressures from domestic (or even foreign) actors whose special interests are threatened naturally favor procrastination on the part of decision makers; and this tendency toward inertia is reinforced as well by bureaucratic delays as the necessary evidence for a change is accumulated. As Oort comments, "Solid evidence . . . by definition comes too late for prompt action."[68] Under the Bretton Woods system, the emphasis was always on the "peg" rather than on the "adjustable."

This in turn created irresistible incentives for speculative currency shifts by private individuals and institutions. The high degree of capital mobility that developed under Bretton Woods provided the means for large-scale speculation against official parities. The rules of the par-value system provided the stimulus. On the one hand, the narrow bands around par values (1 percent above or below parity) meant that speculators incurred little risk in selling a weak currency or buying a strong one. The most they could lose, by guessing wrong, was 2 percent (e.g., if they sold a weak currency at its lower limit and later repurchased it at its upper limit). On the other hand, the inevitable delays in decision making by policymakers meant that speculative profits might potentially be quite large, since once a change was decided, it could be counted upon to be fairly substantial. (In any event, exchange rates could not be adjusted rapidly enough to neutralize all opportunities for windfall capital gains.) In effect, therefore, speculators were offered a "one-way option" to bet against the ability of central banks to maintain declared exchange values. As Harry Johnson wrote:

> The adjustable peg system gives the speculator a "one-way option": in circumstances giving rise to speculation on a change in the rate, the rate can move only one way if it moves at all, and if it moves, it is certain to be changed by a significant amount— and possibly by more, the stronger is the speculation on a change. The fixed-exchange-rate system courts "destabilizing speculation," in the economically-incorrect sense of speculation against the permanence of the official parity, by providing this one-way option; in so doing it places the monetary authorities in the position of speculating on their own ability to maintain the parity.[69]

In this basic sense, the par-value regime was the worst of all possible compromises. Instead of deterring speculative currency shifts, it provoked them. In the words of one central banker, it was a "speculocratic standard."[70] As a result, the environment for trade and investment was anything but stable, and the process of balance-of-payments adjustment was anything but optimal. The world economy benefited neither from a fixed frame of reference for international transactions nor from a continuous adjustment of payments disequilibria. The advantages of neither fixed nor flexible exchange rates were maximized. Rather, it was their disadvantages that were most evident.

The Band Proposal

Today, most observers recognize the defects of a par-value regime of the Bretton Woods type.[71] "The so-called adjustable-peg system has shown itself to be a poor compromise between fixed and flexible exchange rates."[72] Even the Committee of Twenty, when it urged a return to par values, put as much emphasis on the "adjustable" (i.e., the need for less inertia in decision making) as on the "peg." The key problem, it is now understood, is how to achieve a greater degree of flexibility in the exchange-rate mechanism without losing the presumed advantages of fixed currency values.

One possible solution that has been suggested is the so-called "band proposal," which would modify the par-value regime by widening the permissible margin of fluctuations around par values to something greater than the 2 percent originally stipulated at Bretton Woods.[73] Three advantages are claimed for the band proposal. First, by increasing the potential risks of speculation against official parities, wider bands would decrease the one-way option for speculators and thereby reduce the volume of speculative currency shifts. Second, the proposal would provide more scope for movements of market exchange values to smooth and hasten the process of payments adjustment. And third, it would add to the independence of domestic macroeconomic policy (to the extent that the theoretical insulation argument for floating rates is actually valid in practice). Retention of declared par values, meanwhile, would presumably preserve the advantages of a fixed point of reference for international transactions.

With the wisdom of hindsight we can see that the band proposal is really a rather modest type of reform. At the time it was first broached in the 1960s, however, it was considered quite radical indeed. As Fritz Machlup has explained, "There was a time when economists thought that this type of flexibility would be the most they could ever expect the responsible officials to accept."[74] As late as 1970, the executive directors of the IMF declared themselves unwilling to accept anything more than a "slight" widening of margins around par values.[75] When the G-10 countries meeting at the Smithsonian in 1971 agreed to broaden the band from 2 to 4.5 percent, their decision was hailed as a breakthrough of historic proportions.

Today, the limitations of the band proposal are more fully appreciated. Two problems in particular stand out. First, there is a problem of size. How wide should the band be? If the limits are set too close together, the advantages claimed for the proposal are lost; if they are set too far apart, the world economy loses its fixed frame of reference. Proponents of variations of the band proposal have called for margins as narrow as 2 percent or as wide as 10 percent in either direction; some have even called for asymmetrically wider bands.[76] But none has been able to say with any precision what specific quantitative criteria might be used to optimize the width of the band.

The second problem is what happens when market rates reach the limits of the bands. Implicit in the band proposal is the same attitude of optimism regarding prospects for monetary stability that characterized the original Bretton Woods agreement. No significant change in the postwar bias toward rigidity is mooted. The one modification of the par-value regime is intended merely to enhance governmental capacity to cope with large reversible disturbances to currency values around essentially horizontal trends. The major threat to stability is still private speculation; most disequilibria are evidently still expected to be stochastic rather than nonstochastic. Yet if the postwar experience has taught us anything, it is that disequilibria are at least as likely to be persistent as otherwise, owing to numerous monetary or structural disturbances. Currency trends are only rarely horizontal over long periods of time. The band proposal offers nothing to help governments cope with irreversible, cumulative disturbances. Once market rates get stuck at the limits of the bands, the regime once again creates irresistible incentives for speculative currency shifts. "An exchange rate at the edge of a rigidly fixed band is not much different from a rigidly fixed rate."[77] The same one-way option is offered to speculators. In the end, therefore, the band proposal solves very little. The standard is still speculocratic.

The Crawling Peg

This reasoning has led some observers to advocate an alternative approach to reform of the par-value regime—the "crawling peg."[78] Rather than widen the bands around par values, this approach would increase the rate of change of par values themselves, substituting very small and frequent parity changes for large and infrequent alterations. (In other words, the pegs would "crawl.") The small size of prospective parity changes, it is claimed, would have the advantage of decreasing potential profits of speculators and would thereby reduce the volume of speculative currency shifts. The frequency of the parity changes, on the other hand, would have the advantage of reducing inertia in decision making, thus enabling governments to cope more effectively with cumulative payments disequilibria on a gradual and continuing basis. The benefits of greater exchange-rate flexibility would be gained without, presumably, losing the advantages of a fixed frame of reference for trade and investment.

This type of proposal was also considered quite radical when it was first broached in the 1960s. And likewise today its limitations have come to be more fully appreciated. Here also two particular problems stand out, each virtually a mirror image of the two problems with the band proposal just mentioned.

First, here also there is a problem of size. How large should individual parity changes be, and how frequently should they be authorized? If changes are too small and infrequent, the advantages claimed for the crawling peg are lost; if they are too large and frequent, the world economy again loses its fixed frame of reference. Variations of the proposal have called for differing combinations of automaticity and discretion in initiating parity changes. But here, too, none has been able to say with any precision what specific quantitative criteria might be used to optimize the rate of crawl.[79]

The second problem is: what happens in the event of large sudden disturbances of a nonstochastic nature? Implicit in the crawling-peg proposal is also a kind of optimism—the belief that monetary or structural disequilibria will cumulate, at worst, only slowly and gradually. But another lesson of the postwar experience is that large and sudden disturbances (e.g., large-scale price changes, sudden shifts of macroeconomic policy, civil or military disturbances) can and do often occur. Crawling pegs are not well designed to handle such crisis situations. If speculators suspect that greater adjustments of parities may be required than are authorized under prevailing rules, speculative currency shifts will once more be encouraged, and the environment for trade and investment will again be destabilized.

Managed Floating

In view of this problem, numerous observers have proposed combining the crawling-peg and band proposals into a "crawling band," in order to gain the advantages of flexible adjustment to large and sudden disturbances as well as to longer-term cumulative disequilibria.[80] Each half of the combination would solve the adjustment problem of the other. (This is one way to interpret the "stable but adjustable" par value formula of the Committee of Twenty.) But then one might reasonably ask: why maintain the fiction of par values at all? If the exchange-rate mechanism is to incorporate such a high degree of flexibility, might it not be more realistic, as well as less complicated, just to drop declared limits to official intervention altogether—that is, to adopt a regime of managed floating instead? That was evidently the reasoning behind the decisions at Rambouillet and Jamaica. Properly managed, a regime of floating rates can be the exact equivalent of a crawling band, with the added advantage of simplicity. Instead of altering official parities according to a de jure formula within publicly announced margins, central banks can intervene in the exchange market and accomplish precisely the same results de facto merely by observing the same limits on changes of exchange rates. Is there any reason to preserve an artificial construct of par values and bands?

In practice, there might be two reasons, one relating to the efficiency objective, the other to the consistency objective. With respect to the former, it could be argued that the construct remains necessary to preserve the presumed advantages of fixed currency values: par values and bands conserve a fixed frame of reference for trade and investment, and so promote technical efficiency and economic welfare. I have already mentioned the difficulties experienced by businessmen after 1973 in trying to dispell the uncertainty created by floating exchange rates. Many observers believe that such uncertainty can only be dispelled by restoring and maintaining precise limits to official exchange-market intervention. But surely the "certainty" that results is of a particularly spurious sort. Since governments can never be expected to fix currency values absolutely, the stability offered by par values is purely an illusion. Changes in exchange-market relationships are bound to occur, and such changes could prove to be smoother in the absence of declared intervention limits than in their presence. Pegged rates are not necessarily stable rates, as the postwar experience amply testifies; and floating rates, as I have said, are not necessarily unstable. It all depends on how each type of regime is managed. A regime of floating rates is not necessarily inferior to a crawling band in providing a stable environment for international transactions—*if* it is properly managed.

Likewise, with respect to the second reason, relating to the consistency objective, it could be argued that the construction of par values and bands remains necessary in order to avoid policy conflict. Floating may give governments too much leeway for discretionary behavior; indeed, in the eyes of some observers, official intervention in the exchange market would inevitably be "dirty" rather than "clean." But surely this argument also contains an element of the spurious. Since the sources of disagreement among states are so numerous, inconsistency of national policies is possible under any type of regime. Again, it all depends on how each type of regime is managed.

With respect to both objectives, therefore, the case for managed floating reduces to the question of whether floating can be managed "properly." Can rules and conventions for governmental behavior—

a "code of good conduct"—be designed that will both ensure a stable environment for business operations and avoid policy conflict? That is the heart of the matter.

To be effective, a code of good conduct for a world of floating rates must fulfill four conditions. First, it must be comprehensive. It must encompass not only direct interventions in the foreign-exchange market but also, for reasons indicated earlier, all deliberate indirect manipulations of exchange rates. Governments must not be permitted to accomplish covertly what they are restrained from seeking overtly. "Success in eliminating overt policy conflicts in the exchange markets might indeed simply shift the scene of such conflicts."[81] In addition, the code must go beyond the narrow question of exchange rates per se to the broader issues of the respective obligations of surplus and deficit countries and the pressures, if any, to be brought to bear on countries in persistent payments imbalance. As I indicated in Chapter 4, these questions were left unanswered by the Rambouillet and Jamaica agreements. Yet they too are fundamental to the form of the exchange-rate regime.

Second, the code must negotiate successfully between the Scylla of excessive detail and Charybdis of vague generality. Excessive detail can make a monetary order too rigid, rendering it incapable of coping with changes in the monetary system. "Problems and institutions do change over time, and specific rules often prove outdated and inadequate, or even harmful."[82] Excessive detail can also provoke opposition or noncompliance from governments, if they feel that their policy autonomy is unduly threatened. Policymakers prefer to have as many "safety valves" as possible; to deny them any margin at all for discretionary behavior is, once again, to indulge in the naïve denial of the endogenous and purposive role of state actors. The more detailed a code of action becomes, the more likely it is that when vital national objectives are at stake, the rules will be bent, broken, or ignored.

On the other hand, there are also dangers in trying to rely entirely on vague generalities and broad principles (as, for example, the Rambouillet and Jamaica agreements tried to do). For a code of action among governments to be practicable, it must be broadly accepted as *legitimate*, and to be accepted as legitimate, it must be quite clear in defining the rights and obligations of all nations. Lack of clarity leaves scope for the self-interested exercise of state power: the outcome will reflect as much the distribution of power in international relations as the influence of the prevailing rules. And since the distribution on power in international relations is obviously unequal, many nations will as a result feel discriminated against—as, for instance, many LDCs have felt discriminated against under floating rates because of the outer exchange-rate problem. As an old French saying has it, "In relations between the strong and the weak, it is freedom that oppresses and law that liberates." To avoid feelings of discrimination, the code must avoid ambiguity about who is required to sacrifice what, and when. Only by doing so can it win effective legitimacy.

A corollary of this point is that rights and obligations must not be too asymmetrical. Since in any interstate arrangement, governments naturally focus most on the disadvantages for themselves and the advantages for others, many are still apt to feel discriminated against unless the costs of their cooperation do not seem excessive. As Anthony Lanyi has written:

> The less often excessive costs are placed on particular countries, the less often will they take actions diverging from the purposes and methods of the system. The more equally costs of cooperation are distributed among countries—for instance, the more equally the cost of balance-of-payments adjustment is divided between deficit and surplus countries—the less is the *chance* that excessive costs will be placed on a particular country. Therefore, the more equally the costs of cooperation are distributed, the better is the chance that the system will be maintained unimpaired.[83]

The third condition is that the code must reduce inertia in decision making. Rules for governmental behavior may take two basic forms: (1) rules that specify circumstances in which certain policy actions are required (what may be called "thou-shalt" rules); and (2) rules that specify circumstances in which certain policy actions are prohibited ("thou-shalt-not" rules). The Bretton Woods system was of the "thou-shalt" type, requiring a positive decision to do something;

and the same is true of the band proposal and the crawling peg. All three have an inherent bias toward rigidity because of the inevitable delays associated with such a requirement. Managed floating, by contrast, can be based on either type of rule—and that is perhaps its most attractive feature. Governments have a choice, and if they choose to base their behavior on rules of the "thou-shalt-not" type, they can effectively eliminate most of the inertia in decision making. Decisions not to act do not require the same accumulation of evidence in the bureaucracy; they also capitalize on the natural procrastination of decision makers in the face of pressures from powerful vested interests. Hence, the bias toward rigidity can be fully eliminated, and the advantages of flexible exchange rates maximized.

For example, consider the rules for central-bank intervention in the exchange market. One particularly attractive idea for a code of good conduct in this area is the so-called "reference-rate proposal" of Wilfred Ethier and Arthur Bloomfield.[84] The proposal consists of two rules:

(1)   No central bank shall sell its own currency at a price below its reference rate by more than a certain fixed percentage (possibly zero) or buy its own currency at a price exceeding its reference rate by more than a fixed percentage. (This is the sole restriction placed upon central-bank intervention.)

(2)   The structure of reference rates shall be revised at periodic pre-specified intervals through some defined international procedure.

The key rule is the first. As Ethier and Bloomfield suggest, this rule "turns the basic idea of a par value inside out: it gives a point of reference away from which the market exchange rate must not be deliberately forced by official intervention, as opposed to a pegged rate that the authorities must defend."[85] Consequently, it eliminates the bias toward rigidity of a "thou-shalt" type of rule, maximizing the advantages of flexible exchange rates. It also eliminates the one-way option for speculators, since governments are no longer obliged to defend any particular currency rate (thereby making it a matter of indifference whether governments announce their reference rates publicly or not).[86] Yet, at the same time, it restricts the scope for "dirty" interventions by central banks. Governments are not given too much latitude for discriminatory behavior that would avoid or transfer the costs and responsibilities of adjustment to others; the risk of policy conflict is thus minimized. Yet nothing restricts the scope of "clean" floating. Governments are free to limit the frequency and amplitude of fluctuations around long-term trend as much as they can. In fact, they are free to choose from among a wide variety of specific arrangements to guide their individual currencies (e.g., free floating, pegged rates, wider bands, group floating, etc.). Such a rule therefore allows for the geographic as well as the temporal dimensions of exchange-rate optimality. This is clearly the type of rule on which to build a viable code of good conduct for a world of floating rates. What is needed, to fulfill the condition of comprehensiveness, is to extend the principle to encompass not just direct interventions in the exchange market but all forms of deliberate indirect exchange-rate manipulation.

The final condition is that the code of good conduct must contain some mechanism for resolving policy conflicts and inconsistencies when and if they arise. Assuming the reference-rate proposal is adopted, the mechanism would also be needed to conduct periodic revisions of reference rates, to ensure that their structure is at all times reasonably close to true market equilibrium values. Such a mechanism is not easy to design.[87] In effect, it would encapsulate all dimensions of the oligopolistic struggle between nations inherent in the international money game; for that reason, it would necessarily become the focus of an explicit bargaining process. The problems of managing such a bargaining process can hardly be overestimated. I shall have more to say about these problems in subsequent chapters.

Assuming all four conditions are fulfilled (a crucial assumption), there seems no reason why a regime of floating rates cannot be managed "properly." Thus, there is also no reason why a regime of managed floating should not be adopted in lieu of a wider band, a crawling peg, or some combination of the two. Managed floating can maximize the advantages of both fixed and flexible exchange rates and minimize their disadvantages. In fact, it appears to come closer to the objective of optimal exchange-rate flexibility than do any of the other regimes examined.

Conclusions

The defect of automaticity as an organizing principle is that it expects too much and delivers too little. Fully automatic monetary orders demand more from politically sovereign states than governments can realistically be expected to surrender. At the same time, they deliver less in terms of economic welfare than their advocates would have us believe. They promote neither the consistency nor the efficiency objective. They are politically naïve and economically suboptimal. Neither a resurrected gold standard nor a regime of absolutely flexible exchange rates is a viable option.

The real problem is to find some compromise between the two polar alternatives that will approach an optimal degree of exchange-rate flexibility. Put differently, the problem is to find the optimal degree of discretion for official intervention in the foreign-exchange market. Of the four classes of compromise arrangements suveyed in this chapter, the preferred alternative is clearly a regime of managed floating, based on a "code of good conduct" fulfilling four key conditions. Managed flexibility can come closer than any other regime to both maximizing economic welfare and avoiding policy conflict. In a well-organized international monetary order, this would certainly be one essential ingredient.

Chapter 6

Supranationality

Supranationality as an organizing principle for the monetary order means a regime founded on collective adherence to the decisions of an autonomous international organization. The rationale for supranationality is essentially the same as that for automaticity: it reduces the risk of policy conflict between states by narrowing the element of discretion in governmental behavior. The more that formal decision-making powers can be transferred to a supranational institution, the more likely it is that the monetary order will be able to satisfy the consistency objective. At the extreme, one can imagine a monetary order based on a full-fledged world central bank. This chapter discusses the case for a world central bank and then considers some possible compromise arrangements embodying more limited functions for an international monetary institution.

A World Central Bank

The case for a world central bank has been argued by a variety of prominent figures both inside and outside of government. As a former Chairman of the Federal Reserve Board of Governors has summarized it: "In the world of today, a strong world central bank is becoming more and more essential to support orderly economic growth in a constructive international context."[1] (That is, a world

central bank is becoming more and more essential to promote both
the consistency and efficiency objectives.) Over the years, the name
that has come to be most closely associated with the case is that of
Robert Triffin, who has long urged an approach to monetary reform
that would ultimately lead to transforming the International Monetary Fund into a world central bank. For Triffin, this is the most logical
solution to the problem of international monetary organization.

> The internationalization of foreign exchange reserves under
> the aegis of the International Monetary Fund [is] the most logical
> solution of this problem. It would facilitate the adjustment of
> the Fund's lending operations to the legitimate liquidity require-
> ments of an expanding world economy, and help stabilize the
> world monetary system against the vicissitudes of national mone-
> tary management.[2]

The case for a world central bank has gained special weight in many
circles owing to the eloquence and persistence of Triffin's determined
advocacy of this sort of approach.[3]

The key requirement of the case is subordination of all national
central banks to a supranational monetary authority—a central bank
for central banks. Even more than the gold-standard approach, this is
obviously an "integrationist" solution to the problem of monetary
organization. The consensual and conflictual elements in monetary
relations would be accommodated in the pure case by transferring all
formal monetary powers to the world central bank. Gold and foreign-
exchange reserves would be consolidated and replaced by a single
fiduciary asset issued by that bank, and national money supplies
would be strictly controlled by the bank through loans to national
monetary authorities and open-market operations. Like a national
central bank, the world central bank would perform two essential
functions. In the short term it would be a lender of last resort, providing an elastic supply of reserves ("crisis" liquidity) to governments
to finance payments imbalances when and if circumstances warrant.
In the long term it would be a money creator, providing a steady
growth of ultimate reserves ("trend" liquidity) to accommodate the
needs of the world economy as a whole. At all times the total stock
of international reserves would be determined exclusively by the

world central bank. All responsibility for global monetary management and all power to discipline national monetary policies would be centralized in the single autonomous institution.

In principle, the world central bank approach is consistent with a variety of alternative mechanisms of balance-of-payments adjustment (other than freely floating exchange rates or a reconstructed gold standard). The critical element of the structural framework of relations is the pure fiduciary standard, which gives the world central bank effective leverage over the process of payments adjustment through its control of the supply (and rate of growth) of international liquidity. The efficiency objective is promoted by the bank's ability to optimize the adjustment process and resolve the confidence problem through rational control of a homogeneous reserve supply. The consistency objective is ostensibly promoted by the bank's ability to constrain governmental decision-making authority and thereby suppress potential policy conflicts among states.

The logic of the case for a world central bank is drawn essentially from economic history. As mentioned in Chapter 1, the clear historical tendency in all national societies has been to limit the number of currencies—and eventually to standardize the domestic money system on just a single currency issued and managed by the national authorities. Commodity moneys (e.g., gold coins) have been replaced by fiduciary moneys, and decentralization and laissez-faire have been replaced by centralization and control, in recognition of the key role played by the money supply in the economic growth and stability of nations. At the international level, the beginnings of a similar historical evolution can be seen in the transformation of the gold standard in this century into a gold-exchange standard, placing ever-increasing amounts of fiduciary reserve assets (e.g., dollars) alongside the commodity reserve asset (gold). The argument for a world central bank is essentially the argument for carrying this historical evolution to its ultimate and logical conclusion. As Triffin has stated the case:

> The displacement of commodity money by fiduciary money and of commodity reserves by fiduciary reserves reflects the effort of man to control, instead of being controlled by, his environment in the monetary field as well as in others.

The displacement of *national* fiduciary reserves by *international* fiduciary reserves should similarly be viewed as one aspect of the adjustment of the former tribal, feudal, and national institutions through which this control could previously be asserted, to the ever-changing realities of a more and more interdependent world.

Both phenomena should be viewed in a vaster historical perspective: the long march of mankind toward its unity and a better control of its own fate.[4]

Stated in these sweeping terms, the argument can hardly be criticized. Who can oppose anything that gives man more control over his destiny? If global economic efficiency were our only concern, a world central bank would certainly be unobjectionable. But the trouble is that global efficiency is not our only concern: the monetary order must also take account of the distribution of economic welfare among nations and other political values, and this the case for a world central bank simply does not do. Supranationality, like automaticity, tries to deny the importance of political sovereignty in international monetary relations. Like automaticity, therefore, it suffers critically from the defect of political naïveté. In practice, national governments are no more likely to surrender their formal policy autonomy to some supranational institution than to a set of automatic rules. A world central bank is no more viable as an organizing principle than a gold standard or absolute flexibility. It too founders on the hard rock of conflicting national interests.

To criticisms of this kind, Triffin responds by quoting Erich Fromm: "In individual as in social life, it is the logic of facts that determines reality, not the logic of wishful thinking."[5] Triffin continues:

This is why I have little doubt about the inevitability of a continued evolution of our international monetary institutions in a direction so clearly charted by the historical development of *national* monetary systems in every country of the world, and by similar trends already perceptible in the changing structure of the *international* reserve system itself over the last half century.[6]

But is this not also wishful thinking? National monetary systems developed as they did because national societies constituted distinct political entities and because sovereign governments recognized that it was in their individual interest to assert a local monopoly over the power to issue money (see Chapter 1). At the international level, both of these conditions are lacking. The international community is not a distinct political entity, and there is no sovereign global government to enforce the will of a world central bank. These are the real facts. Their logic is that there is nothing at all inevitable about the trends that Triffin describes.

At bottom, the case for a world central bank rests on a fallacy. A world central bank is supposed to promote the consistency objective by constraining governmental decision-making authority. But so long as governments remain politically sovereign, the risk of policy conflict persists: only the form of the conflict is altered. Supranationality transforms inconsistencies that would otherwise be revealed in the foreign-exchange market into inconsistent demands on the supranational monetary authority. The nub of the problem, which creation of a world central bank fails to resolve, is the endogenous and purposive role of state actors in international affairs. This is the reality that must be confronted if any reform of the framework of monetary relations is to be viable.

Does this mean that there can be no role at all for an autonomous international organization in the world monetary order? Not at all. As Robert Keohane has reminded us: "Between the poles of unilateral national behavior and an unrealizable supranationalism, quite a few moderately effective organizational possibilities may exist."[7] The choice is not limited just to the extremes. Even though states naturally desire to preserve as much decision-making autonomy as they can (reflecting the conflictual element in monetary relations), they also have an incentive (reflecting the consensual element) to curb their competition as much as possible, in order to avoid conflict and promote the efficiency objective. One way to do this is to transfer certain limited functions to an autonomous organization and to agree collectively on adherence to its decisions. In the last chapter, I indicated that between the extremes of rigidly fixed or absolutely flexible exchange rates, the problem is to find the optimal degree of exchange-rate flexibility. A similar point holds here. Between the extremes of a free-for-all regime and a world central bank, the problem is to find the optimal degree of *supranationality* in monetary affairs—that is, the optimal range of functions for an international monetary institution (or institutions).

The Position of the IMF

Like the search for the optimal degree of exchange-rate flexibility, the search for the optimal degree of supranationality in monetary affairs is not new. This too was a goal of the negotiators at Bretton Woods, as well as of many of the reform plans that have been proposed in the decades since 1944.[8] At Bretton Woods (as indicated in Chapter 3), the IMF was established as the central institution of the monetary order and was endowed with three important functions: regulatory (administering the rules affecting exchange rates and currency convertibility), financial (supplying supplementary liquidity), and consultative (providing a forum for the cooperative management of monetary relations). In the third of a century since Bretton Woods, two basic types of questions have been raised about the Fund: (1) Should the IMF be supplemented or replaced by another international organization (or organizations)? (2) Should the functions of the IMF be redefined or altered? Today, in determining the optimal degree of supranationality in monetary affairs, both types of questions must be addressed directly. The following discussion will take up each of them in turn.

Organizational Survival

The first question challenges the Fund's central position in the monetary order. Some observers have suggested that some of the Fund's functions might better be transferred to other existing international organizations, such as the Bank for International Settlements (BIS) in Basel or the Organization for Economic Cooperation and Development (OECD) in Paris. Others have suggested that the Fund itself should go, to be replaced by an entirely new (and presumably better designed) international monetary organization. Behind all these suggestions lies a distinct dissatisfaction with the IMF as it has operated in the past. This dissatisfaction is not entirely unjustified, as even defenders of the Fund's record have been prepared to concede.[9] But to react to unsatisfactory performance by gutting an institution hardly seems a constructive alternative, and to jettison the institution altogether is like throwing out the baby with the bathwater. The preferable alternative, I would argue, is to preserve the Fund in its central position in the monetary order—and improve it.

Suggestions for sharing out the functions of the IMF are based on the principle of organizational pluralism. International organizations, it is argued, operate according to "the law of inverse salience": the greater the political prominence of an issue, the less likely it is that states will adhere voluntarily to an organization's decisions. Autonomous institutions can operate effectively only when rules and conventions are universally accepted as legitimate. When issues become prominent they tend to become controversial (that is, "politicized"), and the legitimacy of the rules themselves is thrown into question. Hence, an argument can be made for limiting the scope of an individual organization's domain to a narrow range of issues that are more likely to be susceptible to technical than to broad political treatment. A multiplicity of functionally specific organizations might be able to operate more effectively and with less controversy than could one single institution charged with a very wide range of responsibilities. To be sure, such organizational pluralism might also give rise to administrative messiness and problems of overlaps and gaps in institutional jurisdictions. But as Lawrence Krause and Joseph Nye have pointed out, "organizational neatness is not necessarily a virtue from a political systemic point of view."[10]

On the other hand, neither is decentralization necessarily a virtue—especially if it comes at the expense of the efficiency objective. The key question, in assigning responsibilities to institutions, is the appropriate level of specificity of functions: how finely should the range of issues be sliced? One could reasonably argue that the range of issues under the head "international economic relations" has already been sliced about as finely as it should be. Individual institutions already exist to deal with such problems as trade (the General Agreement on Tariffs and Trade), aid (the World Bank), and the special international economic concerns of less-developed countries (the United Nations Conference on Trade and Development). By assigning principal responsibility for international monetary affairs to one institution (the IMF), governments probably have already gone about as far as they should in the direction of organizational pluralism. Money, after all, is fungible. The broad problems of international monetary relations are best treated holistically. Triffin may be mistaken about the inevitability of a world central bank, but he is certainly correct in detecting a historical tendency toward centralization in international monetary institutions. That is a tendency that accords with the underlying nature of money itself. It is therefore a tendency that should be promoted rather than diluted.

This does not rule out assigning particular subsidiary or supplementary functions to other existing institutions (such as the BIS or OECD) or even to informal groupings of nations (such as the Rambouillet group of six or the Group of Ten). Quite the contrary, in fact. If, for example, only limited numbers of countries are directly affected by an issue, they can probably deal with it most efficiently on their own, in their own chosen forum (as, say, the central banks of the major financial powers deal with short-term exchange-rate problems largely on their own in the BIS), rather than in a larger and more universal setting. Nevertheless, if the broad problems of monetary relations are to be treated holistically, it seems clear that responsibility for all genuinely fundamental decisions should be unified. This argues for continuing to reserve the central position in the monetary order for a single autonomous organization.

Should that organization be the IMF? The reasonable answer is: why not? Suggestions to replace the IMF have little to recommend them, apart from their simplicity. The idea of "starting anew" is superficially appealing but wasteful. Over the years, the Fund has accumulated an enviable stock of experience and information, as well as a highly skilled and competent professional staff, and has become the focal point for the transgovernmental elite network responsible for international monetary policies. These are valuable resources that we would do well not to lose, no matter how disappointing the Fund's performance may have been in other respects. The more efficient course would be to build on the basis of this heritage, rather than reject it. The objective should be reform—to improve IMF performance—not revolution.

In any event, suggestions to replace the IMF are basically unrealistic. They ignore the fact that institutions like the Fund tend to develop their own vested interests, the most basic of which are status and survival. As one source puts it: "What most organizations are after, quite understandably, is prestige and self-preservation."[11] Once established, international organizations rarely (if ever) go out of existence. Invariably, they find and assert some role for themselves, if only because, as Harry Johnson put it (not entirely cynically), "they have too many high priced people working for them not to find something useful to do."[12] Such has been the history, for example, of the BIS, whose raison d'être has changed several times since it was first created as agent for the transfer of German reparations payments during the interwar period.[13] Likewise, such has been the history of the IMF itself since the Bretton Woods system collapsed in 1971. Not only has the Fund managed to survive the disappearance of the very monetary order for which it was designed, but it has actually succeeded in rationalizing an expansion of its activities in the Committee of Twenty and Interim Committee. Any realistic reform of the framework of monetary relations must take cognizance of the Fund's evident determination to remain a going concern.

Organizational Structure

However, if the IMF *is* to retain its central position in the monetary order, cognizance should also be taken of those aspects of its organizational structure that affect the efficiency of its decision making. Any realistic reform ought to aim at ensuring that, whatever functions are eventually assigned to the Fund, it will be capable of performing them effectively.

As originally constituted, the Fund had two essential elements: (1) the *Board of Governors* and *Executive Board*, responsible for broad policy and general Fund operations; and (2) the *Managing Director* and his staff (the secretariat), responsible for conducting the routine business of the Fund on a day-to-day basis. In principle, all ultimate powers of the Fund were vested in the Board of Governors, consisting of one governor from each member country. However, since in practice the Board was ordinarily expected to meet no more than once each year, provision was also made for delegating a variety of its powers to the Executive Board, functioning in continuous session at the Fund's headquarters in Washington. The Executive Board consists of twenty executive directors, five appointed by the five members with the largest quotas in the IMF (currently the United States, Britain, Germany, France, and Japan), and fifteen elected by groups of member countries constituting roughly homogeneous constituencies.[14] The executive directors were given the responsibility of selecting the Managing Director, who in turn was made responsible for appointing and organizing his own professional staff.

Since governors and executive directors exercise their powers as representatives of member countries, they inevitably concern themselves most with national interests that are relatively narrowly defined. Their role is quite different from that of the Managing Director and his staff, whose responsibility is solely to the broader policy interests of the international community. In the ongoing operations of the Fund, therefore, tensions were bound to arise between the Board of Governors and Executive Board on the one hand, and the secretariat on the other. Such tensions were unavoidable, however, and could never be resolved through any sort of legal or institutional reform. They simply reflect the underlying tension between the consensual and conflictual elements inherent in all international monetary relations.

The crucial defect in the organizational structure of the Fund has always been the relationship between the Executive Board and the Board of Governors. Historically, the range of decision-making powers delegated to the executive directors by the governors was limited mainly to general Fund operations and normally excluded broader policy questions. (Only some of these limitations reflected provisions of the Fund Charter itself.) Accordingly, a lacuna has existed in the fundamental policymaking element of the IMF structure. On the one hand, there was the Board of Governors, authorized to set broad policy for monetary relations but meeting too infrequently to be able to exercise effective ongoing management. On the other hand, there was the Executive Board, functioning on a continuing basis but lacking sufficient authority to play an effective management role. In the Second Amendment to the Articles of Agreement (as indicated in Chapter 4), machinery was provided to establish a permanent IMF Council of Governors with precisely this question in mind. The purpose of the Council, in principle, was to fill the gap in order to improve the efficiency of the Fund's policymaking apparatus. In line with the original recommendation of the Committee of Twenty, the Council was supposed to be a "political body" with real decision-making authority. In the words of the Report of the Executive Directors accompanying the Second Amendment, "the Council is conceived of as an organ composed of persons with political responsibility."[15] However, in practice, since the procedures to establish the Council were not expected to be implemented quickly, the lacuna in the Fund's policymaking apparatus appears as wide as ever.

Because of fears of supranationality in the Interim Committee, the idea of an IMF Council had almost failed in the negotiations leading up to Jamaica. Negotiators were concerned that, once established, a permanent Council might become too ambitious and appropriate new responsibilities for itself, moving too far in the direction of a world central bank. Consequently, the real powers of the Council (if any) were left deliberately vague: most of its powers (like those of the Executive Board) are to be delegated to it by the Board of Governors.[16] The Second Amendment merely restates the expressed hope of the Committee of Twenty that the Council "shall supervise the management and adaptation of the international monetary system."[17] The question still remains of just what (if anything) that is to mean in practical terms. If it is to mean anything at all, it ought

to mean that the powers of the Council will be sufficiently well
defined to enable it, if and when it ever comes into existence, to
oversee the monetary order effectively. This, by itself does not mean
increasing the functions of the IMF. All it means is making the
decision-making authority of the Council more explicit, in order to
increase the *efficiency* with which such functions get performed.
The question of what those functions should be still remains to be
discussed.

The Functions of the IMF

In a sense, the three functions assigned to the IMF at Bretton Woods—
regulatory, financial, and consultative—already exhaust the categories
of responsibilities that any international monetary institution might
be expected to assume. A world central bank could not ask for a
more comprehensive set of assignments. The point, however, is not
taxonomy but content. The problem is not to alter the list of
categories but rather to define their substance. If the objective is to
improve IMF performance in order to approach the optimal degree
of supranationality in monetary affairs, the *extent* of Fund responsibilities implied by each of the three categories must be spelled out in
some detail.

The Regulatory Function

The regulatory function of the IMF has always centered on the
mechanism of payments adjustment. Before 1971, this meant
administering the rules of the par-value regime. Today, it means
administering the rules—the code of good conduct—of a regime of
managed floating. The Fund can play an important role, at both
operational and policymaking levels, in ensuring fulfillment of the
four conditions which, I argued in the previous chapter, are essential
to making such a code effective.

At the operational level, the secretariat has the most important role to play. It can monitor adherence to the rules governing direct or indirect manipulations of exchange rates, offer interpretations and clarifications of the rules whenever controversies arise owing to legal ambiguities, and implement specific sanctioning procedures against individual governments whenever violations of the rules are judged to occur. The Managing Director and his staff already have ample means for the required data collection and technical analysis. By applying these means to such routine informational and adjudicatory tasks, they can do much to keep the code of good conduct from being either abused or ignored.

At the broader policymaking level, the Council of Governors could play an important role by providing a mechanism for review of the multilateral structure of exchange rates, for judging when violations of the rules do in fact occur, and for resolving policy conflicts and inconsistencies when and if they arise. The secretariat, by definition, can normally provide services of only a relatively technical sort. The Council of Governors, on the other hand, being composed of representatives of national constituencies, would be well suited to play a more overtly political role in the payments adjustment process.

A more active IMF role in reviewing the structure of exchange rates is particularly desirable in order to avoid any drift back toward the rigidity characteristic of the par-value regime. Under the rules of the Bretton Woods system, the Fund could not play an active role in this area. Formally, all decisions to alter par values had to be proposed by governments: all the Fund could do after "consultation" was "concur or object."[18] Accordingly, there was little the Fund could do in practice (even had it been inclined to do so) to reverse the tendency toward inertia in decision making. A greater power of initiative on the part of the Fund would be a useful stimulant to overcoming the Bretton Woods bias toward rigidity. Some observers have suggested, perhaps optimistically, that this could be done even within some resurrected construct of par values and bands. Fred Hirsch, for example, has proposed giving the Fund authority to set for each country an "equilibrium parity zone," within which governments would be required to set specific par values; by periodically reviewing and altering national parity zones as circumstances warrant, the Fund could "provide stronger and more institutionalized international pressures against exchange rates becoming manifestly out of line."[19] However, if the argument of the previous chapter is correct, the only way that the bias toward rigidity can be fully eliminated is by doing away with the artificial construct of par values altogether, preferably along the lines of the Ethier-Bloomfield reference-rate proposal. If this proposal is adopted, the IMF would seem to be the natural forum in which to conduct the necessary periodic revisions of the structure of reference rates.[20]

Likewise, the Fund would seem to be the natural forum in which to deal with the other fundamental questions concerning the balance-of-payments adjustment process, such as the respective obligations of surplus and deficit countries and the pressures, if any, to be brought to bear on countries in persistent violation of the rules. At this point, however, the regulatory function of the IMF obviously begins to blend into its consultative function, to be discussed below.

The Financial Function

The financial function of the IMF has always centered, of course, on the mechanism of reserve supply. Before the 1968 agreement establishing Special Drawing Rights, this meant supplying supplementary liquidity through the Fund system of national quotas. Today it means, even more importantly, administering allocations and use of SDRs. Through this role, the Fund is ideally placed to contribute to a "better international management of global liquidity" (to quote once again from the *Outline of Reform* of the Committee of Twenty and the Second Amendment to the Articles of Agreement).

A central role for the IMF in the international management of global liquidity has long been urged by figures both inside and outside government.[21] In fact, the variety of proposals put forward toward this end, before the 1968 agreement, was truly enormous. Some observers, like Triffin, argued for total internationalization of all national monetary reserves, transferring all existing gold and foreign-exchange reserves to the Fund in exchange for a newly created international fiduciary asset. Others argued, less ambitiously, for a new form of reserve asset that would merely *supplement* rather than *replace* existing national monetary reserves. Some of these authors would have had the Fund issue a new reserve asset to countries in exchange for a part of their existing reserve holdings;[22] others would have issued the new asset to countries in exchange for deposits of their own national currencies;[23] others would have issued it in exchange for securities created to raise long-term capital for financing investments in less-developed countries;[24] and still others would have issued it in exchange for purchases of selected storable primary commodities.[25] During the 1960s, the business of designing a new international fiduciary asset was a real growth industry.

Yet when the agreement to establish SDRs was finally reached in 1968, it turned out, strikingly, to be fundamentally unlike any of the plans that had been proposed during the previous decade. The crucial difference was that it did not provide either credits from or claims against the IMF as an issuing agency. All previous plans had focused on a "central debtor" whose liabilities were to be the reserve assets of national central banks. But under the SDR agreement there are no liabilities of the issuing agency: countries holding SDRs do not collect from or draw on the IMF. SDRs are simply a draft, a form of fiduciary unit that can be transferred between central banks under agreed conditions in exchange for convertible foreign exchange. They are acceptable to central banks not because of any obligation or liability assumed by the IMF, but simply by virtue of the international agreement underlying their establishment and use. In the long view of economic history, this was a development of enormous significance. As Fritz Machlup wrote at the time:

> The liquidation of the fiction of the central debtor of money in circulation is a genuine breakthrough in monetary thinking. In the nation, no recipient, holder, or spender of money ever thinks of the existence of a legal debtor who issued the money and continues to "owe" something to the holder. The only thing in the mind of the recipient and holder of money is its transferability to and acceptability by others. The holder of money does not expect to "collect" from the issuing agency, but only to pass on the

money to those who have something to sell. The holder of special drawing rights, likewise, will not collect from or draw on the Fund or its Special Drawing Account. Instead, the participating country will pass its SDR's on to other participants in payment for convertible currencies. In other words, the SDR's are international money accepted by the participating monetary authorities in payment for various convertible national currencies. Since only the acceptability of SDR's has to be secured, and is in fact secured by the obligations undertaken by the participants, there is no need for any obligation or liability to be assumed by the agency that issues or allocates them.[26]

Machlup went on to explain why all previous plans had retained the fiction of the central debtor—the "myth of backing," as he called it:

> Not that any reputable economist of our time has believed the old myth; but they were convinced that all bankers and other practical men of the world of finance believed in the myth and could not possibly be "enlightened." Thus, the academic economists had not dared to recommend schemes that would do away with the trappings of backing. Now the forward-looking experts of the Fund and the negotiating governments have proved that their reputation for backwardness in economic thinking had been undeserved.[27]

Why were the experts of the Fund and the negotiating governments so forward-looking? Certainly it was not because they believed in the inevitability of any trend toward a world central bank. Rather, it was because they recognized that the myth of backing inhibited increases of global liquidity *on a net basis*. If the creation of money, domestic or international, requires simultaneous acquisition of credits from or claims against the money's issuer, the growth of assets is simply matched by a growth of liabilities. No *net* increase of the money stock can occur unless the issuer ensures that the offsetting liabilities will remain long-term and illiquid. Moreover, assets that are created by granting loans can also be destroyed by repayment of loans: if repayments exceed new borrowings, the stock of money will actually be reduced. The only certain way to increase money supply, therefore, is to sever the connection with "backing." This was long ago accomplished at the domestic level, as Machlup noted, where money is ordinarily accepted as a claim on real resources without being a legal claim on anybody. At the international level, only gold had previously circulated formally as "nondebt money." For the experts of the Fund and the negotiating governments, it seemed clear that if international liquidity was to be increased on a net basis, SDRs too would have to circulate as nondebt money. Hence, the decision was made to allocate SDRs gratis rather than require governments to surrender assets for them or consider them as debts to be repaid. In this respect at least, SDRs fully deserve the title given them by the newspapers—"paper gold."

In other respects, however, the title is less well deserved— particularly with regard to the regulations governing allocations, cancellations, and use. These are by no means simple.[28] SDR allocations, for example, can only be made when a weighted majority of 85 percent of the participating membership of the Fund, voting in the Board of Governors, decides that SDRs are needed to supplement the existing global reserve supply. Conversely, cancellations may be approved if a majority decides that the existing reserve supply is excessive. In principle, decisions are taken for "basic periods" of five years (even though, as mentioned before, the initial 1969 decision to allocate SDRs was made for only three years). The SDR agreement was intended to deal only with long-term trends in the need for reserves (trend liquidity), not with short-term problems of macroeconomic management (crisis liquidity). Allocations or cancellations are made in annual installments and are distributed roughly in proportion to each member's quota in the Fund. No decision on allocations or cancellations may be taken without a proposal by the Managing Director and a concurring vote by the Executive Board.

Once allocated, SDRs are held in a Special Drawing Rights Department in the Fund, to be transferred between central banks in exchange for convertible currencies when and if the occasion arises. But as indicated in Chapter 4, under the terms of the original 1968 agreement, tight restrictions were instituted to control their use. A member had to demonstrate to the IMF a genuine balance-of-payments need before it could exchange its SDRs for foreign exchange. In turn, the IMF had to designate the countires with whom authorized SDR transactions could be conducted. A country receiving SDRs was obligated to accept them up to a maximum of 200 percent of its initial allocation (i.e., to a maximum holding in the Special Drawing Rights Department equal to three times its initial allocation). A country using SDRs was obligated to reconstitute its minimum holding within each basic period such that net use did not exceed 70 percent of its net cumulative allocation. (In other words, over each basic period it had to carry an average minimum balance of 30 percent of its net cumulative allocation.) Minor exceptions were permitted, but not normally without the concurrence of the Fund.

Because of the complexity of all these regulations, the scope for the use of SDRs is still, on the whole, much more narrowly defined than that of other existing reserve assets. The Committee of Twenty succeeded in making the SDR more attractive as an asset to hold; the Interim Committee confirmed the SDR's growing importance as numeraire of the monetary order[29] and also went some way toward reducing the complexity of the regulations affecting SDR use. But there is still much room for improving the attributes of the SDR as a reserve asset.

To what extent should the attributes of the SDR be improved? Some observers have suggested that the SDR should be raised to the very center of the international monetary order, eliminating all other reserve assets altogether and establishing in lieu of the present mixed monetary standard a pure "SDR standard."[30] However, this approach would imply a much greater degree of supranationality in monetary affairs than most governments can reasonably be expected to accept. The logic of a pure SDR standard in essence is exactly the same as that of a world central bank: it promises to promote the efficiency objective through rational control of a homogeneous reserve supply. It suffers, therefore, from the same critical fallacy: it expects governments to put themselves willingly in a position where their national monetary policies could be effectively disciplined. Governments might conceivably be prepared to accept an elevation of the SDR to a position of parity in relation to other existing assets; they may even countenance making it the "principal reserve asset" of the monetary order. But so long as they remain politically sovereign, they are unlikely to make themselves totally dependent on this (or any other) single source of liquidity. Diversity of reserve composition is viewed as a guarantee of policy autonomy.

A pure SDR standard, therefore, is out of the question. Elevation of the relative status of the SDR, on the other hand, is not. In fact, putting the SDR on a par with other existing reserve assets would seem to be highly desirable in view of the interest of governments in preserving diversity of reserve composition. This suggests that a case can be made, on not very controversial grounds, for further simplifying the regulations governing SDR use. For example, now that Special Drawing Rights have been generally accepted by monetary authorities, there seems little reason to retain legal limits on acceptance obligations. Likewise, now that governments have come to view their SDRs as full-bodied reserve assets comparable to more traditional reserve media, there seems little reason to continue insisting on reconstitution obligations. Residual requirements to demonstrate balance-of-payments need and to obtain Fund designations for authorized transactions could also reasonably be abolished.

On somewhat more controversial grounds, a case can also be made for adding greater flexibility to the regulations governing allocations and cancellations of SDRs. Even if Special Drawing Rights are not intended to deal with short-term problems of macroeconomic management, it can be argued that basic periods of three to five years (with annual installments) are simply too long a time to cope adequately with changing economic circumstances. The Fund would seem to be the natural forum for trying to exert more effective control over the supply and rate of growth of world reserves in the shorter as well as the longer term. However, at this point the financial function obviously begins to blend into the consultative function. Both adjustment and liquidity problems meet under this heading.

The Consultative Function

The consultative function of the IMF has long spanned both adjustment and liquidity problems. In fact, over the years, governments have found the Fund a convenient place to consult across the full range of issues affecting international monetary relations. I suggested in Chapter 3 that the creation of a permanent institutional forum for collective monetary management was potentially the most significant of all the achievements of Bretton Woods. Following collapse of the Bretton Woods system in 1971, the worth of the Fund in this respect was clearly demonstrated anew. That the element of cooperation in monetary affairs could hold firm and the conflictual element be suppressed was due in no small measure to the availability of established lines of communication through the Fund. Likewise, that a controlled process of reform could be quickly initiated and carried forward was due in no small measure to the inherited experience of consultation and negotiation in the Fund. Today, the IMF role as a consultative forum is fully accepted by all nations. The Fund, as I said, has become the focal point for the transgovernmental elite network responsible for international monetary policies.

The consultative function of the Fund is essential to both its regulatory and its financial functions. Clearly, enforcement of a code of good conduct and management of global liquidity both require more than purely technical decisions. Fundamental questions are involved, as I have indicated—questions concerning *inter alia* the respective adjustment obligations of surplus and deficit countries, the pressures (if any) to be brought to bear on countries in persistent imbalance, and the supply and growth rate of world reserves. Such questions are highly charged politically. Indeed, they are the very stuff of which policy conflict is made. At issue is the distribution of economic welfare, national prestige, and decision-making authority. If the argument in this chapter regarding a world central bank is correct, such questions are certainly too highly controversial to be the exclusive responsibility of an international secretariat. That would be viewed by governments as too great an infringement on their formal political sovereignty. Yet answers to the questions must be found. If the Fund is to play any useful role at all in either the adjustment process or the management of global liquidity, it must facilitate the collective search for these answers. That is why its consultative function is so essential.

In the first place, by acting as a forum for international consultation and cooperation, the Fund can help ensure that the right questions will be asked. And second, by including all countries, directly or indirectly, in the consultation process, it can help to ensure that the agreed-upon answers will be respected (i.e., accepted as legitimate). I emphasized in the last chapter that if the "rules of the game" are to be accepted as legitimate, they must not leave scope for the self-interested exercise of state power. The point of this chapter is that by transferring certain functions to the Fund and agreeing collectively to adhere to its decisions, governments jointly limit the scope for such self-interested action. They thereby enhance the sense of legitimacy in monetary affairs without imposing an unacceptably high degree of supranationality. As Joseph Nye has written:

> To envisage international organizations as incipient world governments having supranational authority above states is to focus on a small (and frequently inaccurate) aspect of their political roles. More important is the way they affect the political process. . . . The political importance of international organizations, particularly on interdependence issues, is less in their power *above* states than in their role in coordinating bits and pieces of power *across* states.[31]

The appropriate instrument for this role would be the Fund's Council of Governors. Indeed, here is where the Council could come fully into its own. The main advantage of the Council is precisely that it would not have supranational authority above states. It would impose no special element of supranationality on sovereign governments, over and above that to which they are already committed by their collective adherence to Fund decisions. It is intended to be a representative body, not an autonomous organ; its rulings and recommendations would reflect a consensus of all its principal members, not a view imposed from above. Consequently, governments could more easily accede to its judgments than they could to those of an independent and discretionary institution.

However, the Council alone would not be a sufficient instrument for this role. Effectiveness in the consultation process demands more than merely institutionalizing the collective search for answers. It also demands an expert international secretariat which can enhance the probability that the outcome of the search will be successful. This is where the Managing Director and his staff come into their own. National representatives have only a limited concern for the broader policy interests of the international community; their first responsibility is to defend the narrower interests of their own constituencies. And where these interests seem better served by disagreement than by agreement, the national representatives will do little to contribute to a successful outcome. In other words, their commitment to the consultation process is a contingent one. The commitment of the secretariat, by contrast, is total. By definition, its principal interest is to suppress the conflictual element in monetary relations and reduce policy inconsistencies among states. In practice, therefore, it is ideally suited to promote agreement on adjustment and liquidity issues. Toward this end, the Managing Director and his staff can fulfill three important tasks.

First comes the task of data collection and technical analysis emphasized earlier. Such work, though largely routine, is nonetheless crucial if the consultation process is to be informed. Discussions must not become bogged down merely because of false or misleading arguments.

Second comes the task of "steering." I have said that the Fund's consultative function can help ensure that the right questions will be asked. This function—in effect, setting the agenda for deliberations— means much more than just selecting proposals to be discussed. It means spotting new problems, or problems with long lead times, and stimulating work on them before they become critical or unmanageable. It also means taking an active role in controlling and directing the outcome of deliberations, by adapting and reformulating proposals to facilitate final agreement. The secretariat is particularly well placed for such an "honest broker" role. From its more disinterested perspective, it can better judge what outcomes may be acceptable as well as viable, and can synthesize and mold proposals and engage in informal lobbying and coalition-building to reach those outcomes. The steering task must be performed subtly, if the secretariat is not to antagonize sovereign governments. But if it is pursued actively and innovatively, it can go a long way toward ensuring that sound answers will be found.[32]

Finally, there is the task of ensuring that the answers will be respected. In effect, this requires that the secretariat become a "defender of minority interests." I have emphasized that the main advantage of the Council of Governors is that its rulings and recommendations would reflect a consensus of views of all its principal members. But this consensus must not reflect merely the existing distribution of power in international monetary relations. If it did, it could result in such asymmetry of rights and obligations that weaker states, feeling discriminated against, would refuse to accept Council decisions as legitimate. The secretariat can play a valuable role in securing general consent to agreed outcomes by representing and promoting the interests of the less powerful (as, for instance, it represented and promoted the interests of LDCs in the G-10 negotiations leading to the creation of Special Drawing Rights). This task too must be performed subtly, if the secretariat is not to antagonize the strong[33] or compromise its other responsibilities.

Of course, there are limits to what even the most ingenious and dedicated professional staff can do. The secretariat certainly can do much to refine issues, shape discussions, and eliminate needless frictions. But, in the end, it can do nothing at all to eliminate the fundamental conflicts of interest that exist between states. Ultimately, these can be resolved only if governments share a presumption that agreement is desirable—that is, only if there is (to use the fashionable phrase) sufficient "political will." As Edward Bernstein has written, "Ultimately, the role of the Fund will depend on what its members want it to be."[34] The IMF's consultative function is designed to encourage the development of the necessary political will. But it cannot guarantee it. Nothing can.

Conclusions

The defect of supranationality as an organizing principle is that, like automaticity, it expects too much and delivers too little. Like the gold standard or absolute exchange-rate flexibility, a world central

bank would demand more of politically sovereign states than governments can realistically be expected to surrender. Consequently, like
such fully automatic monetary orders, the supranational approach
could never deliver as much in terms of economic welfare as its
advocates would have us believe. This too is not a viable option.

Just as in the last chapter the real problem was to find some compromise that would approach an optimal degree of exchange-rate
flexibility, the problem here is to find the optimal degree of supranationality in monetary affairs—that is, the optimal range of functions for an international monetary institution. The preferred alternative, I have argued, is to preserve the International Monetary Fund
in its central position in the monetary order, but to improve its performance by increasing the efficiency of its decision making and by
extending its traditional functions of regulation, finance, and consultation. In a well-organized monetary order, this too would be an
essential ingredient.

Chapter 7

Hegemony

Hegemony as an organizing principle for the monetary order means a regime organized around a single country with broadly acknowledged responsibilities and privileges as leader. The leader must have sufficient structure power to be able to determine and maintain the framework of rules and conventions governing international monetary relations. The framework itself must have sufficient clarity to distinguish the rights and obligations of the leader from those normally applying to other countries. The principal right of the hegemonic power is to be formally freed from all balance-of-payments constraints. The rationale for hegemony as an organizing principle is that it thus reduces the risk of policy conflict between states through the willingness of the hegemonic power to play the passive, nth-country role in the adjustment process: with only $n - 1$ countries setting independent external financial targets, the redundancy problem is avoided and consistency in monetary relations can be ensured. Meanwhile, the hegemonic power takes responsibility for management of the monetary order as a whole. That is its principal obligation. In contemporary circumstances, the only state conceivably capable of playing such a leadership role in monetary affairs is still the United States. At the extreme, therefore, one can imagine a monetary order based exclusively on the dollar—a pure dollar standard. This chapter discusses the case for a pure dollar standard, and then considers some possible compromise arrangements embodying more limited roles for the United States and the dollar in monetary affairs.

A Pure Dollar Standard

Advocacy of a pure dollar standard began relatively late. Unlike the gold-standard model, the case for a dollar standard had no well-accepted myth of a Golden Age to hearken back to. Unlike the idea of a world central bank, it had no "inevitable" trends of historical evolution to appeal to. And unlike the case for flexible exchange rates, it had no famous article to help it achieve intellectual respectability—at least not until 1966, when a major statement advocating a dollar standard was published by three eminent American economists, Emile Despres, Charles Kindleberger, and Walter Salant.[1] Subsequently, the case for a dollar standard attracted widespread attention and was argued by a variety of observers, including the original trio themselves.

For example, Despres in 1966 advocated a dollar standard in testimony before the U.S. Congress: "The central postulate underlying this proposal is that the dollar is not only 'as good as gold' but is, fundamentally, much better than gold. . . . The dollar is not merely a national currency; it is, indeed, the predominant international currency."[2] In 1967, Kindleberger argued that "a return to gold as advocated by the French, the adoption of a new international currency proposed by Triffin, or of a new international asset to supplement gold and dollars, under consideration by the Group of Ten, would each be contrived, artificial, and less efficient than the dollar standard."[3] And in 1969 another American economist, Ronald McKinnon, wrote that "a dollar standard can be . . . a most efficient practical instrument for providing badly needed international money."[4] In the opinion of many observers, events since August 1971 have only served to confirm the validity of these various propositions.

The Case

The key requirement for the dollar standard is general acceptance of the hegemonic position of the United States. Monetary reserves would consist of dollars alone, and the United States would be explicitly acknowledged as money manager of the world. America would assume formal responsibility for the trio of managerial roles played informally earlier in the postwar period (and by Britain in the nineteenth century): maintaining a relatively open market for goods, providing contracyclical foreign long-term lending, and acting as lender of last resort in times of exchange crisis. The Federal Reserve would assume all responsibility for the functions that might otherwise be assigned to a world central bank. Global stability would be ensured by the willingness of the United States to abjure any external financial target of its own in favor of taking responsibility for operation of the monetary order itself. The consensual and conflictual elements in monetary relations would be accommodated through America's willingness to practice a policy of "benign neglect" in the payments adjustment process.

Payments passivity on the part of the United States is regarded by advocates of the dollar standard as the most practical way to minimize the risk of policy conflict among states (and thereby promote the consistency objective). In McKinnon's words: "A benign policy that allows foreign central banks to peg freely to the center country's stable currency is likely to be the simplest *consistent* system that can be devised in a world of separate political jurisdictions."[5] At the same time, such passivity is regarded as the most practical way to maximize global economic welfare (and thus promote the efficiency objective as well). Given the size and strength of the American economy and the dominant U.S. position in international financial markets, conditions inside the United States inevitably have a considerable influence on the pace of economic developments elsewhere, an influence that few (if any) other countries can either escape or reciprocate. The case for a dollar standard tries to make a virtue of this deep and pervasive asymmetry in the structure of the world economy. By formally freeing the United States from all balance-of-payments constraints, it raises the probability that America can successfully stabilize its own domestic economy. This in turn raises the probability that economic conditions elsewhere can be successfully stabilized as well. As Robert Mundell has written:

> The advantage of turning the U.S. economy into a bastion of stability is so great, not just for the U.S., but for the whole world,

that any international monetary system making it possible,
including even ... a dollar standard ... must be a welcome
possibility.[6]

Like the world central bank approach, a dollar standard is an
"integrationist" solution to the problem of monetary organization
insofar as it concentrates the power to guide world monetary policy
in the hands of a single hegemonic authority. Yet at the same time
it is also a "disintegrationist" solution insofar as it allows other
governments to continue setting independent external financial targets. In effect, it seeks to revive, in more formal terms, the informal
implicit bargain of the earlier postwar period. Other governments
would be free to use the system to promote their own economic
prosperity. The United States would be free to concentrate on pursuit of its own policy priorities. The bargain would presumably be
acceptable to the United States because it legitimizes American
policy autonomy. It would presumably be acceptable to others
because it promises to promote both the consistency and efficiency
objectives.

In principle, a dollar standard, like a world central bank, is compatible with a variety of alternative mechanisms of balance-of-
payments adjustments, other than rigidly fixed or absolutely flexible
exchange rates. (If rates are rigidly fixed, the dollar loses its unique-
ness as a fiduciary reserve asset, since all national currencies become
equally acceptable as international money. If rates are absolutely
flexible, no stockpile of reserves at all is required.) As in the world
central bank approach, the critical element is the pure fiduciary
standard, which makes the supply and rate of growth of world
reserves solely a function of America's balance-of-payments position.
So long as America itself plays a passive role in the adjustment
process, consistency in monetary relations can be ensured within any
type of exchange-rate regime between the two polar alternatives,
whether it be some resurrected construct of par values and bands or
a regime of managed floating.

For example, in a par-value regime such as existed before 1971,
where external financial targets normally take the form of some level

and/or rate of change of reserves, consistency is ensured by America's willingness to accept the residual net deficit or surplus in its balance of payments. Conversely, in a regime of managed floating, where external financial targets normally take the form of some level and/or rate of change of exchange rates, consistency is ensured by America's willingness to accept the residual net appreciation or depreciation of its exchange rate. The point is not the adjustment mechanism but the policy attitude of the United States. So long as American passivity in the adjustment process is maintained, leaving only $n - 1$ independent external targets, the redundancy problem is resolved within any type of exchange-rate regime.

The logic of the case for a dollar standard, like that for a world central bank, is drawn essentially from economic history. As mentioned in Chapter 3, over the course of the last century there have been only two successful monetary orders—and each was organized around a single hegemonic country. In the opinion of dollar-standard enthusiasts, this suggests that hegemony is the *only* organizing principle that could ever work successfully. "The main lesson," says Kindleberger, is "that for the world economy to be stabilized, there has to be a stabilizer, one stabilizer."[7] And he concludes:

> Leadership is a word with negative connotations in the 1970s when participation in decision-making is regarded as more aesthetic. Much of the overtones of *der Führer* and *il Duce* remain. But if leadership is thought of as the provision of the public good of responsibility, rather than exploitation of followers or the private good of prestige, it remains a positive idea.[8]

Kindleberger's conclusion focuses attention directly on the two assumptions that are key to the whole dollar-standard case. First, hegemonic leadership must be "responsible"—that is, the economic policy of the leader must truly be stabilizing, imparting neither inflationary nor recessionary impulses to the rest of the world. Otherwise, the efficiency objective will not be promoted. Second, hegemonic leadership must be thought of as nonexploitative—that is, it must be accepted as legitimate, generating neither resentment nor policy conflict over the distribution of economic welfare or other political values to the rest of the world. Otherwise, the consistency objective will not be promoted. Ever since the case for a dollar standard first started attracting attention a decade ago, criticism has centered on these two assumptions. Today, what seems clear is that neither assumption is at all justified.

The Responsibility Assumption

The importance of the responsibility assumption to the dollar-standard case has been well understood by most observers. Writing in 1970, Lawrence Krause posed this question: "If the United States is the central country in the dollar standard, what is its proper balance-of-payments policy stance for preserving the system?"[9] He answered:

> The United States should pursue a passive policy. By this I mean policy makers should refuse to take any measures in response to the usual signals of trouble from the balance-of-payments accounts. . . . A passive balance-of-payments strategy would involve only adaptive policies of the financing variety. . . . A passive balance-of-payments strategy means that in the event of large official settlement deficits—and likewise of large surpluses—the United States would refrain from any policy action.[10]

Others writing at about the same time came to much the same conclusion, calling variously for a "policy of benign neglect,"[11] an "inner-directed" payments policy,[12] and an "abolition of any conscious target in international payments."[13] However, none of these sources regards payments passivity as the equivalent of license. Quite the contrary, they all insist that such a policy carries a concomitant responsibility for stability of the monetary order as a whole. "Neglect of the balance of payments does *not* imply neglect of either the interests of the U.S. or of those of our trading partners."[14] Though formally freed of balance-of-payments constraints, the United States would still be obliged to manage its domestic policies with the needs of the rest of the world in mind. It would have to avoid the extremes of inflation or recession; its economic performance would have to be reasonably predictable. In short, it would have to behave "responsibly." As McKinnon put it, the United States would have an increased obligation to maintain stable internal policies. It would be the balance wheel of the world economy. As such, maintenance of stability in the prices of tradable goods is highly important, as is the avoidance of cyclical fluctuations in income and employment.[15]

Being the balance wheel does not mean imposing a single policy on all other countries. Rather, it means providing a fixed point in the monetary order around which other governments can organize their own policy priorities. Stable economic performance inside the United States—in particular, stable price performance[16]—gives others a useful standard of reference by which to manage their own economic affairs. A dollar standard would not force all governments to march together in lockstep. Governments prepared to tolerate a higher rate of inflation at home for the sake of promoting fuller employment could allow their reserves to decline or their exchange rates to fall vis-à-vis the dollar; governments preferring a trade-off in favor of relatively greater price stability could, conversely, allow their reserves to rise or their exchange rates to appreciate. Divergent policymaking in individual national economies is entirely compatible with hegemony as an organizing principle.

The key question is whether hegemony would prove a stabilizing balance wheel. What assurance is there that the United States would in fact behave responsibly? The answer is—no assurance at all. The United States may find itself with an increased obligation to maintain stable internal policies in a formal dollar standard. But there is no parallel increase of certainty that such an obligation would actually be honored. The dollar standard formally removes all external discipline on American policy autonomy. Many advocates see this as an advantage. Precisely because the United States would no longer have to concern itself with problems of external balance, the American government would enjoy an extra degree of freedom in the formulation of domestic macroeconomic policy. The probability that internal balance could be successfully maintained would thereby be increased. But the removal of all external discipline on the United States could also be seen as a disadvantage for the outside world if, for example, the American government were to become more receptive to domestic inflationary pressures. The responsibility assumption cannot really be justified.

That is not to argue that American policy would necessarily become irresponsible—only that there is no certainty that it would *not* become irresponsible. The problem with the dollar standard is not that it is inherently unstable, but rather that it is not necessarily stable. Given the absence of any formal international deterrent, the possibility always exists that sooner or later, accidentally or deliberately, the United States may take advantage of its special position to initiate policies that would tend to destabilize the world economy—as occurred after 1965, for example. Power corrupts. As David Calleo writes, "It is unlikely that monetary hegemony will not eventually be abused."[17] The threat of irresponsibility at the center haunts the case for a dollar standard.

The threat is conceded by most advocates. Writes McKinnon: "Clearly, a 'pure' key-currency system is not well designed to deal with instability in the key-currency country itself, although it can handle considerable upheaval elsewhere."[18] Writes Kindleberger: "Benevolent despotism . . . is the best form of government. . . . The difficulty . . . is to keep it benevolent."[19] Perhaps the only way to cope with the threat, some advocates suggest, is to increase the role of foreign governments in the decision-making process within the United States. Others should be given the right to state what American policies they believe would best serve the needs of the world community; the United States would be required to take the advice of foreign governments into account in managing its own economic affairs. Kindleberger once proposed that non-Americans be formally represented as voting participants in the internal deliberations of the Federal Reserve System.[20] Mundell has proposed the creation of an international consultative committee, operating either through the Group of Ten or the IMF, to determine and administer Federal Reserve Policy.[21]

However, all such proposals risk undermining the fundamental rationale on which the dollar standard is ostensibly based. The bargain is presumed to be acceptable to the United States because it legitimizes American policy autonomy. Why then should America sacrifice the end (policy autonomy) merely in order to save the means (the dollar standard)? Mundell insists that "the U.S. can and probably would find it in its own interest to submit to discipline intelligently administered."[22] But that is doubtful: even if "intelligently administered" (whatever that means), external discipline runs counter to the most basic vested interest of the United States, which is freedom from external constraint. America might be willing to take responsibility for operation of the monetary order itself; it might even be prepared to consult with other governments in various international forums, as it does now. But it is not likely to accept a formal dollar standard if that means a loss of fundamental policy autonomy. Advocates cannot have it both ways, giving with one hand while taking with the other. The very essence of the dollar standard is hegemonic leadership. If one advocates a dollar standard, one must also acknowledge the consequences of hegemonic leadership. One of those consequences is the ever-present threat of irresponsibility.

The Legitimacy Assumption

But that is not the only consequence. Even if hegemonic leadership is not irresponsible, it can give rise to feelings of discrimination and exploitation. A dollar standard does not have to be unstable to generate conflict over the distribution of economic welfare or other political values. The legitimacy assumption of the dollar-standard case is perhaps even less easy to justify than the responsibility assumption. The potential for policy conflict, like the threat of irresponsibility at the center, is built into the very design of such a monetary order. This point too is conceded by most advocates of the approach. Again in the words of McKinnon: "The resulting asymmetry in world monetary arrangements will always be politically objectionable to many."[23]

Some who find the asymmetry objectionable do so on straightforward ideological grounds. This is especially true of Marxist and radical writers, for whom the dollar standard is simply one more manifestation of capitalist exploitation, reflecting "the power of American imperialism within the international capitalist system."[24]

Indeed, establishment of a formal dollar standard, it is argued, would actually operate to perpetuate capitalist exploitation, since it "orders intercapitalist relations and suppresses conflict. . . . Without a dominant power the exchange relations of the capitalist world are basically unstable and break out in destructive, competitive rivalries."[25] However, ideology is not the only basis for resentment of a dollar standard. Even non-Marxists and nonradicals find manifold grounds for objecting to the resulting asymmetry in world monetary arrangements.

In the first place, the asymmetry has evident implications for the distribution of political status in the international community. The United States would gain enormous prestige from being explicitly acknowledged as money manager of the world; other countries and their currencies would be relegated, conversely, to positions of distinct inferiority. For many foreign governments, this is not a matter of particularly great moment. As indicated in Chapter 4, even state actors as large as Germany or Japan remain relatively unconcerned about prestige in monetary relations. For a few, however, prestige is a rather more important policy objective. This is especially true of France, where nationalistic resentment of monetary dominance by Anglo-Saxons has a very long and well-recorded history.[26] Today, the objections of many influential Frenchmen to the case for a dollar standard can be clearly traced to this one overriding concern.[27]

Second, the asymmetry has evident implications for the distribution of the privilege or burden of governmental decision making in the international community. The United States would formally be accorded freedom of action in both domestic and foreign policy; other countries, in the event of international disequilibrium, would be obliged to bear principal responsibility for taking action to initiate the adjustment process. This may be resented by foreign governments despite the fact that there is no direct correlation between the distribution of adjustment responsibilities and the allocation of adjustment costs. In the words of one British observer: "Benign neglect is a luxury for the United States that others can only envy. . . . It is not clear on what grounds of equity this privilege is claimed."[28] The "exorbitant privilege" is especially objectionable to others if it encourages the American government to pursue policies abroad that they consider abhorrent, such as the U.S. involvement in Vietnam.

Finally, the asymmetry has evident implications for the distribution of economic welfare in the international community. This concerns both the real costs of the adjustment process and the net seigniorage gains associated with the creation and issue of international reserves. On the one hand, the United States would be in a favorable position to reduce its own adjustment vulnerability significantly, since as money manager of the world it would enjoy considerably enhanced power to transfer the burden of adjustment costs to others. On the other hand, America would be in a favorable position to enhance its own share of the net seigniorage benefit significantly, since with competition from alternative reserve sources eliminated, America could considerably lower the interest rates paid on foreign-held dollar liabilities. Other countries cannot really be blamed for resenting the fact that their share of the welfare pie would have to be correspondingly reduced.

Critics of the dollar standard do not find it surprising that virtually all advocates of the approach are American. Why should Americans (or anyone else, for that matter) be as sensitive to the interests of foreign countries as they are to those of their own? Most Americans are inclined to underestimate the importance others attach to such matters as the distribution of economic welfare or other political values; they are also inclined to overestimate their own indifference to these very same concerns.[29] In fact, owing to the dollar's long dominance in international monetary affairs, many Americans merely assume that the interests of the global economy must be coincident, if not identical, with those of the United States, and that therefore the needs of other countries would be best served by a monetary standard that best serves American needs. Prolonged experience of hegemony tends to create an "imperial bias" in policy recommendations.[30] Advocates of the dollar standard simply cannot understand why foreigners would object to a monetary order that promises to promote both the consistency and efficiency objectives. As Susan Strange has written:

Americans cannot help feeling that everybody *ought* to share their enthusiasm for maintaining and improving the present international monetary system and organizations such as the International Monetary Fund on their terms. . . . Their monetary role naturally inclines them to the opinion that anyone who does not fully support their cause is somehow morally delinquent or mentally defective.[31]

Critics also do not find it surprising that advocacy of a pure dollar standard really began to spread only when the dollar-exchange standard itself began to weaken. In fact, the approach can be viewed as an essentially defensive reaction to the unraveling of the postwar bargain, just as official U.S. reform proposals after 1971 could be viewed as an essentially defensive reaction against any loss of inherited privilege. In the early postwar years, the hegemony built into the Bretton Woods system was tolerated by other countries precisely because the asymmetry between them and the United States was so great: they had little choice but to accept America's leadership position as legitimate. As I emphasized in Chapter 3, the key to the arrangement was a political relationship of American dominance and foreign dependence. By the middle of the 1960s, however, that relationship was changing dramatically. America's rule-making capacity was in evident decline. Foreign economies were no longer so weak and uncompetitive as they had been immediately after the war, and foreign governments, especially in Europe and Japan, were no longer so satisfied to accept a political role subordinate to that of the United States. The legitimacy of the dollar's hegemony, therefore, came under increasing challenge. At the practical level, response to the challenge took the form of the various ad hoc measures initiated to shore up the position of the dollar. At the intellectual level, one response took the form of the case for a pure dollar standard—a plea to establish formally what had previously existed only informally. According to advocates of this approach, all that was needed by way of monetary reform was a clearer comprehension of how the Bretton Woods system really worked. In Kindleberger's words: "The dollar-exchange standard would be a good international monetary system if it were understood."[32]

But good for whom? Even if the dollar standard were to promote global economic welfare, foreigners would not be blamed for being concerned about the distributional implications of asymmetry. The political and economic conditions that made dollar hegemony acceptable—or tolerable—in the early postwar years currently no longer exist. Leadership depends on the consent of the led. Today, the governments of Europe and Japan no longer feel anything like the same sense of dependence on the goodwill of the United States. As I pointed out in Chapter 4, these countries presently are determined that their enhanced relative position in the world be reflected in the structure of the monetary order as well. Establishment of a new and formal dollar hegemony would inevitably be regarded by them as illegitimate and exploitative; policy conflict over distributional issues would almost certainly erupt. In contemporary circumstances, the case for a pure dollar standard is really no more than an anachronism. However relevant it may have been to an earlier era, it is just not a viable policy option today.

Does this mean that there can be no asymmetry at all in global monetary arrangements? Must a monetary order, to be viable, be perfectly symmetrical? Not at all. As in the previous two chapters, the choice is not limited just to the extremes. International political relationships today may not be quite so asymmetrical as they were three decades ago. But neither have they become entirely symmetrical. In Chapter 5, I criticized the case for a gold standard on the grounds that, *inter alia*, it denied the real-world asymmetry of politically sovereign states. Any realistic monetary reform must make allowance for the existence—and persistence—of such political asymmetry. This is not a matter of an optimal degree of asymmetry. Rather, the problem is to find the optimal degree of *accommodation* of asymmetry—in short, a way to live with politics. To be effective, a monetary order must first of all be capable of establishing and maintaining harmony with the political order.

The Issue of Asymmetry

Like the searches for the optimal degree of exchange-rate flexibility and supranationality, the search for the optimal degree of accommodation of asymmetry is not new. Indeed it was, as I have said, one of the main preoccupations of the negotiators in the Committee of Twenty. Under the Bretton Woods system, pronounced assymmetries had grown out of the reserve-currency and intervention-currency roles of the dollar. In the Committee's deliberations, the United States proposed to correct for these asymmetries by imposing rigidly symmetrical adjustment obligations on all countries; European governments countered by demanding rigidly symmetrical convertibility obligations for all countries. With the wisdom of hindsight we can see now that both sides, in effect, were trying to push the pendulum too far. Proposals such as these were bound to fail. They were doomed both by the general lessons of monetary history and by the specific circumstances of the dollar in the 1970s.

The Lessons of History

At the conclusion of Chapter 3, I noted that at the structure-level of analysis, where rules and conventions are established, politics inherently dominates. The underlying shape of incentives and constraints inevitably reflects the prevailing pattern of interstate relations. Since historically the political order has always been characterized by conditions of asymmetry and hierarchy, it follows that the monetary order too will normally tend to display such features. In this issue-area, as in others, perfect symmetry is a will-o-the-wisp, an "illusion."[33] As Kindleberger says: "Symmetry is not the way of the world."[34] Structure power is not distributed evenly. All currencies may be formally equal, as the products of politically sovereign states, but some currencies, in good Orwellian fashion, tend to be quite a bit more equal than others. Stratification, not parity, is the general rule. Hegemony is an ever-present reality.

Stratification, however, is no simple matter. It is a caricature to think of hegemony in terms of one single country dominating and setting the rules for a homogeneous collection of powerless smaller states. In reality, the hierarchical networks of monetary relations have always tended to be rather complex and heterogeneous, even labyrinthian—layers within layers overlapping layers. Alongside global hegemonics have existed regional hegemonies; within individual hegemonies there have been differing degrees of dominance and dependence; and for many dependent countries, dominance has tended to come from more than one direction simultaneously. The asymmetry of the monetary order, like that of the political order, has always been multidimensional rather than unidimensional.

For example, even at the height of British domination of the classical gold standard, there were multiple dimensions to international monetary relations. Sterling itself was like the core of series of concentric circles, the nearest circle comprising Britain's colonies and other dependent territories, the second circle consisting of the self-governing dominions of the British Empire, and the third circle including other sovereign states closely linked to the British through historic ties of trade and finance.[35] At its outer limits, sterling's world overlapped other regional hegemonies based on such currencies as the franc, the mark, and (later) the dollar. In the 1920s, as I have indicated, competition from some of these rival currencies became more than the weakened pound could bear. As a result, the interwar experiment failed and separate regional hegemonies coalesced into rival currency blocs.

Likewise, even during the heyday of the dollar after World War II, the degree of dominance by the United States varied from currency to currency, and important regional hegemonies persisted in the form of the sterling area and French franc zone. And more recently a new regional hegemony has emerged in the form of the European "snake"—really nothing more than a local Deutsche mark zone. The tendency back toward currency blocs since the start of generalized floating in 1973 confirms the complex nature of stratification in the world monetary order.[36]

These developments also confirm the *dynamic* nature of stratification in the monetary order. Hegemony is not only not simple: it is also not static. As Peter Kenen says, "Times change and so do the sizes of nations."[37] Networks of relations undergo alterations reflecting transformations of the political order. In the real world, allocative behavior in the economic process has always tended to alter the prevailing pattern of interstate relations, by modifying the distribution of structure power. Consequently, the monetary order has always tended to mutate as a result of its own impact on the evolution of the monetary system. As I also noted at the conclusion of Chapter 3, at the process-level of analysis, which focuses on the effects of marginal changes within a given structural framework of relations, economics inherently dominates. The point bears repeating: the monetary system is a living thing. Asymmetry must be regarded as a variable, not a parameter.

George Santayana said that those who ignore history are condemned to repeat it. In the case of international monetary relations, the lessons of history are clear. If the monetary order is to establish and maintain harmony with the political order, it must accommodate not only the complexity but also the mutability of international monetary stratification. It must be sufficiently flexible to live with inequality in the distribution of monetary power; it must also (restating the final conclusion of Chapter 3) have the capacity to adapt to evolutionary changes in the distribution of monetary power. Proposals to impose rigidly symmetrical adjustment or convertibility obligations on all countries ignore these lessons of history. They are, therefore, both unrealistic and inutile as practical guides to policy.

The Circumstances of the Dollar

In any event, such proposals ignore the specific circumstances of the dollar in the 1970s. In the first flush of the collapse of the Bretton Woods system, many observers concluded that the day of the dollar was over. "The dollar as an international money has been tarnished," wrote Robert Aliber in 1973.[38] Wrote Kindleberger a year later:

> The dollar is finished.... The conditions under which the dollar would come back into international use are so many and varied that it is unlikely that they will be achieved within a decade or two.[39]

Such judgments, however, appear to have been premature. In fact, international use of the dollar increased rather than decreased after the transition to generalized floating in 1971-1973. Only in its role as de facto numeraire of the monetary order was there any significant erosion of the dollar's preeminence, owing to the reforms promoting the SDR in all official exchange-rate quotations. In all other international monetary roles—as vehicle currency for private trade and investment and as reserve and intervention currency for central banks—the dollar actually grew in quantitative importance, as Tables 7-1 and 7-2 demonstrate. The best available indicator of the dollar's use at the level of private international transactions is the volume of dollar-denominated liabilities in the Eurocurrency market. Table 7-1 shows that world Eurodollar deposits more than tripled between 1970 and 1975. The best available indicator of the dollar's use at the level of official international transactions is the volume of dollar-denominated assets in central-bank reserves. Table 7-2 shows that the foreign-exchange component of reserves, which according to the IMF is "mainly denominated in U.S. dollars,"[40] almost quadrupled between 1970 and 1975.

In percentage terms, to be sure, the dollar's position slipped somewhat after 1970. At the private level, the dollar share of the Eurocurrency market dropped from 80 percent in 1970 (and a steady 82-84 percent during 1964-1969) to a range nearer 70 percent in 1973-1974. At the official level, available evidence suggests that there was a drop in the dollar share of foreign-exchange reserves as well. (In both cases, the principal gainer was the Deutsche mark.) But this appears to have been largely a transitional phenomenon reflecting portfolio adjustment by private and official dollar holders to the higher level of uncertainty in exchange markets.[41] Indeed, in view of the volatility of fluctuations between the dollar and other major currencies after exchange rates began to float, it is not at all surprising that dollar users would seek to diversify their portfolios in order to cover themselves against the new higher degree of exchange risk. By the end of 1975, however, the process of diversification seems to have come to an end (see Table 7-1), leaving the dollar still in a predominant position vis-à-vis all other currencies. Likewise, after a brief period of experimentation in multicurrency intervention by some European governments in 1972-1973, use of the dollar as intervention currency seems also to have universally recovered. According to one well-placed source writing in 1975, "there has been little, if any, decline in the asymmetry of intervention arrangements in the world."[42]

TABLE 7-1

Eurocurrency Deposits, 1970-1975

(in billions of U.S. dollars)

		OF WHICH: DOLLAR DEPOSITS	
	TOTAL DEPOSITS[a]	AMOUNT	PERCENTAGE OF TOTAL
1970	75.3	58.7	80.0
1971	97.7	70.8	72.5
1972	131.9	96.7	73.3
1973	192.1	131.4	68.4
1974	220.8	156.4	70.8
1975	258.7	189.5	73.3

[a]Gross liabilities reported by banks in eight European countries accounting for approximately three-quarters of total activity in the global Eurocurrency market.

Source: Bank for International Settlements.

The reason for the dollar's continued predominance among currencies is quite simple. It is, as Richard Cooper says, simply that "there is at present no clear, feasible alternative."[43] No other currency can offer anything like the same international attractiveness either as medium of exchange or store of value. Because of the great volume of America's trade and investment transactions with the rest of the world, the exchange market for the dollar is far and away the largest for any currency. This means that the dollar is the most "exchange-convenient" of all currencies.[44] That is to say, it is both the most marketable, in the sense that it can be converted into other currencies at very low cost, and the most reversible, in the sense that at any point of time there tends to be a very small difference between its buying and selling prices. At the same time, because of the great depth, breadth, and resiliency of America's domestic financial markets, the dollar is also far and away the most "capital-certain" of all currencies.[45] This means that it is the most liquid, in the sense that possible capital losses are minimized if dollar assets must be sold off at short notice. Little has happened in recent years to tarnish the

TABLE 7-2

International Monetary Reserves, 1970-1975

(in billions of U.S. dollars)

| | | OF WHICH: FOREIGN EXCHANGE | |
	TOTAL RESERVES	AMOUNT	PERCENTAGE OF TOTAL
1970	93.2	45.4	48.7
1971	131.5	79.3	60.3
1972	159.1	104.1	65.4
1973	183.7	122.7	66.8
1974	220.7	155.5	70.5
1975	227.9	161.3	70.8

Source: International Monetary Fund.

luster of the dollar in either of these respects.

Nor has anything happened to alter what one source calls the "security area properties"[46] of the dollar. In the short run, currencies such as the mark or the yen may offer some competition to the dollar as international money. But in the longer run, social, political, and even military-defense factors weigh heavily in America's favor. In the words of one French observer:

> Of course, the mark and the yen can show greater stability than the dollar over the short term. But what conclusions would be drawn from a comparison extending over two, three, or five decades? How many countries can show greater stability than the United States in their currency (and in their political institutions) over a long period? One only has to ask this question to place in perspective the possibility of competition between the dollar, on the one hand, and the mark or the yen on the other.[47]

These facts make a mockery of proposals to impose rigid symmetry on currency relationships. In fact, there is no escaping the asymmetrical position of the dollar in monetary affairs. That asymmetry is an ineluctable fact and could be suppressed only at great risk to both the efficiency and consistency objectives of the monetary order.

Asymmetry of the dollar promotes the efficiency objective by offering international transactors the advantages of integrated markets and a unified medium of exchange, unit of account, and store of value, thereby reducing total transactions costs. These advantages would be lost if rigid symmetry were imposed on the dollar to eliminate all its international monetary roles.[48] This would certainly be true at the level of private international transactions; it would also be true at the official level. To eliminate the dollar's intervention-currency role, governments would have to choose among (a) intervention in a nonnational money, (b) a clearing union, or (c) multicurrency intervention. The first of these, however, has always been rejected on political grounds; and neither the second nor the third would be as attractive on efficiency grounds as continuing reliance on a single currency like the dollar. To eliminate the dollar's reserve-currency role would require not only consolidation of all outstanding official dollar liabilities but also, in order to prevent future reserve accumulations, a "tight" settlement system of obligatory conversions of all new official dollar liabilities. But this would be unattractive because it would deny central banks access to highly efficient financial markets outside their own borders, thus reducing their ability to manage their asset portfolios effectively.

Asymmetry of the dollar promotes the consistency objective by encouraging the United States to take a responsible attitude toward the operation of the monetary order. True, even under the best of circumstances the threat of American irresponsibility must be acknowledged, as I have argued. But that threat is even more likely to become a reality if an attempt is made to impose rigid symmetry on the dollar. Because of its continuing size and strength, America can always refuse to play by the new rules. As Mundell points out, "it will not retrench or be disciplined if its vital interests are at stake because it always has the option of abandoning the order."[49] Harry Johnson likened the problem to that of "belling the cat":

> The problem that arose in Aesop's well-known fable was the technical difficulty for the mice, having decided that the ideal solution for their cat problem was to bell the cat, of determining precisely how to do it. The present problem of the international

monetary system, as currently conceived, is far more difficult: assume that the cat can only be belled by its own consent, but it is willing to be belled because it is tired of standing on guard over its master's household and would like to move freely among the mice in order to enjoy the mice's privilege of raiding the kitchen without worrying about the effects on the household's fortunes. The cat knows, and the smarter mice also know, that the cat can accept the bell but can scratch it off at any time it wishes to and revert to being a lethal cat. The technical problem then is to work out conditions of belling the cat such that the cat will stay happy with the arrangement and not scratch off the bell. . . .

The problem is that if you turn a cat into an actual mouse you lose his muscle-power; but if you turn the cat into a pseudo-mouse, he may revert at any moment to being a cat again, and eat you up.[50]

Suppose, for example, that the United States were actually to accept a "tight" settlement system. What would be done about the contingency of conversion of private dollar balance? Eliminating all such balances would be possible only at considerable cost to the efficiency of private international transactions and financial markets. On the other hand, if private balances were not eliminated, they could pose a serious threat to U.S. reserves, to the extent that conversions into other currencies put new dollars into the hands of central banks. Unless special provisions were made to accommodate this contingency, America could find the resulting pressures intolerable. If it did, it could simply revert to inconvertibility: the cat could stop playing pseudo-mouse. The choice, therefore, is clear. In the words of Richard Cooper:

It comes down to this: either the United States is put on a short tether, like other countries, or it is not. If the tether imposed by convertibility of the dollar into other reserve assets is too short, it will be intolerable for the United States. . . . But if the tether is long enough to cover this possibility, it inevitably confers on the United States a special position in the international financial system. . . .

These [considerations] thus suggest that the deep asymmetries intrinsic in a market-clearing system will have to be recognized explicitly, and accommodated.[51]

Accommodating Asymmetry

To argue that the deep asymmetries in monetary affairs will have to
be recognized explicitly and accommodated is not to revert to
advocacy of a pure dollar standard. It is, rather, to argue for an
understanding of both the general lessons of monetary history and
the specific circumstances of the dollar in the 1970s. The lessons of
history suggest that the United States—and some other countries as
well—are bound to continue playing a special role in the monetary
order. The specific circumstances of the dollar suggest that the dollar—
and some other currencies as well—are bound to continue playing a
special role in the mechanism of liquidity creation.

The Role of Special Countries

Many observers find it paradoxical that international use of the
dollar has increased in recent years, even as the political and economic
conditions that made postwar dollar hegemony possible are supposed to have ceased to exist. Perhaps, they suggest, conditions have
not really changed so much. Perhaps dollar hegemony has not really
disappeared. Fred Bergsten wrote in 1972 that the events of the
previous year had represented "the inauguration of the pure dollar
standard."[52] There are many who still agree with that early
interpretation.

Consider, for example, the mechanism of liquidity creation. More
than 85 percent of the increase in central-bank reserves between
1970 and 1975 was in the form of foreign exchange, and most of
that consisted of dollar-denominated assets, despite the suspension
of official gold convertibility of the dollar. Gold itself is now supposedly being phased out of the monetary order, and no new SDRs
have been created since 1972. The centerpiece of the monetary
order clearly has become the dollar—even more so than in the years
before 1971, when the dollar was not yet formally inconvertible.
For all intents and purposes, the international liquidity mechanism
today closely resembles the pure fiduciary standard called for in
the case for a dollar standard.

Likewise, the payments adjustment process today closely resembles the solution called for by the case for a dollar standard. The policy attitude of the United States since the transition to generalized floating has been precisely the passive one required to resolve the global redundancy problem. The American government since 1973 has shown remarkably little interest in setting any particular target for its exchange rate, thus freeing other governments to pursue their own external financial objectives through direct or indirect intervention in the exchange market. The residual net appreciations and depreciations of the dollar have been more or less willingly accepted. To be sure, exchange-rate movements since 1973 have not been exactly smooth. But neither has there been any serious outbreak of policy conflict among states in the payments adjustment process. Principal responsibility for this apparently goes to the benign-neglect policy of the United States.

The facts therefore seem clear. Yet they hardly justify the interpretation that dollar hegemony persists. Hegemony requires sufficient structure power to determine the framework of rules and conventions governing monetary relations. This the United States no longer has, despite the fact that it remains the paramount state actor in international affairs. Asymmetries in the political order have plainly narrowed, even if America is still the world's strongest country. Other governments have plainly grown less dependent on the United States, even if they are still sensitive and vulnerable to the impacts of American policy. America retains the power to disrupt. Like Samson, it can still bring the temple crashing down if it wishes; its veto power remains. But America has lost the power to govern. At this juncture of history, it can no longer organize the monetary order unilaterally; its rule-making capacity is gone. As I said in Chapter 4, even though it remains *primus inter pares*, the United States is no longer *primus motor*. Joseph Nye explains why:

> To understand what is changing, we must distinguish power over others from power over outcomes or over the system as a whole. What we are experiencing as we enter our third century is not so much an erosion of power resources compared to those of other countries (although there has been some), but an erosion

of our power to control outcomes in the international system as a whole. The main reason is that the system itself has become more complex. There are more issues, more actors, and less hierarchy. We still have leverage over others, but we have far less leverage over the whole system. . . .

America remains powerful, but without a hegemonic capability.[53]

Thus, conditions *have* changed. Dollar hegemony *has* disappeared. To view the events after 1971 as inaugurating a pure dollar standard is really quite naïve. At best we might call present arrangements, following Aliber, a "limping dollar standard."[54] In monetary relations today, America continues to play a special role, but it is clearly no longer dominant. Marina Whitman calls it "leadership without hegemony."[55]

That special role must be accommodated. In the design of the monetary order, America's power to disrupt must be contained. This can only be done by differentiating the rights and obligations of the United States from those of other countries. In the payments adjustment process, America's basic interest in policy autonomy must to some extent be respected; in the management of international liquidity, America's privilege of liability-financing must to some extent be safeguarded. Concessions to the United States cannot be *too* asymmetric: this would simply revive the threat of conflict over the distribution of economic welfare and other political values. But some degree of asymmetry there must be, if America is to have an incentive to take a constructive rather than destructive attitude on monetary issues. The possibility exists, of course, that as a consequence some other countries may begin to feel discriminated against. But if the differentiation of rights and obligations is carefully defined within an agreed code of good conduct (see Chapter 5 and below), and if the interests of less powerful nations are fully represented in monetary negotiations and the management of monetary institutions (see Chapters 6 and 8), the resulting adjustment and liquidity mechanisms should be capable of winning effective legitimacy. In any event, America too has to regard the monetary order as legitimate. It is just as important that the cat not feel discriminated against as the mouse. That is what accommodating asymmetry in monetary relations is all about.

If the asymmetry in monetary relations is to be *optimally* accommodated, all—not just some—of the lessons of monetary history must be kept in mind. That means acknowledging not just the special role of the United States but the full complexity and mutability of international monetary stratification. The power to disrupt is not an American monopoly. Other key states (e.g., Germany, Japan, the OPEC group) also play special roles in the monetary order. Their importance must also be respected and accommodated by a differentiation of rights and obligations. To some degree, this is already done through the weighted voting procedures of the IMF and through the constituency composition of its Executive Board. The problem is to extend such differentiation to the whole range of issues that must be covered in the international consultation process, but without sacrificing the degree of flexibility needed to adapt to evolutionary changes in the distribution of monetary power. At this point the problem really starts to become one of negotiating procedures among governments. Further discussion, therefore, must be postponed until the next chapter. The remainder of this chapter will concentrate on the problem of accommodating liquidity relationships among currencies.

The Role of Special Currencies

I said that since 1971 the dollar has become, more than ever, the centerpiece of the monetary order. At the same time, some other currencies also have become (or remained) important constituents of the reserves of individual countries—the Deutsche mark in particular, but also the yen, pound, and French franc. What can be done about accommodating the special role of the dollar and these other national reserve currencies in the mechanism of liquidity creation?

One possibility would be to eliminate entirely the foreign-exchange component of international reserves, via either a pure gold standard or a pure SDR standard. Both of these approaches, however, have been dismissed in previous chapters. Another possibility would be to eliminate all minor national reserve currencies in favor of a pure dollar standard; but that approach has also been dismissed. In fact, no single-money system seems capable of offering a viable reform option. As I argued in Chapter 6, governments are loath to put themselves in a position where their national monetary policies could be effectively disciplined. Diversity of reserve composition is viewed as a guarantee of policy autonomy. Consequently, even if some single-money system were to be regarded as attractive on other grounds, it would be rejected on these grounds, as constituting too great a threat to formal political sovereignty. The presence of a multiplicity of national currencies alongside SDRs (and gold?) in international reserves must be accepted as an inevitability.[56]

Effectively, therefore, we arrive at a multiple-reserve-currency standard—a standard employing several different national currencies (plus SDRs), all convertible into one another but none convertible into gold. By process of elimination, this appears to be the most feasible mechanism for the creation of international liquidity. It is the option we must learn to live with.

Few observers have ever actually advocated a multiple-reserve-currency standard as a preferred reform option.[57] Most sources have been inclined to stress the disadvantages rather than the advantages of a multiplicity of national currencies in international reserves. Bergsten's argument is typical:

> The multiple reserve currency system [is] the worst possible approach to reform. The existence of so many competing assets, convertible into each other, is virtually certain to produce frequent "runs." ... The growth of the international use of each currency would be totally unregulated. ... In short, a multiple reserve currency system would replicate all the problems of the past "gold exchange standard" several times over.[58]

It profits little, however, to denounce what is unavoidable. A multiple-reserve-currency standard may be the worst possible approach to reform—except (like democracy) for all the others. The more practical strategy is to accept reality and try to deal with it; that is, to try to design a set of rules and conventions that will permit a multiple-reserve-currency standard to function efficiently and avoid conflict. What is needed, in effect, is a second "code of good conduct" to operate alongside the code for managed floating discussed in Chapter 5. Bergsten's remarks rightly focus on the two main issues that such a code must deal with: the danger of "runs" (the Gresham's Law problem) and the lack of control over reserve supply. What can be done about the possibility of destabilizing shifts among alternative reserve assets in a multiple-reserve-currency standard? And how can the supply and rate of growth of global liquidity be brought under effective international control?

In the context of the pre-1971 gold-exchange standard, some observers proposed to answer these questions by requiring governments either to hold or to use their various reserve assets in certain fixed proportions.[59] In principle, this was intended both to cope with the Gresham's Law problem and to bring the overall stock of currency reserves under some sort of effective control. In practice, however, because of bureaucratic inertia, such an approach would undoubtedly be much too rigid to adapt satisfactorily to the mutability of international monetary stratification. Like the Scylla of excessive detail in a code for managed floating, it could render the monetary order incapable of coping with changes in the monetary system. Likewise, it could also provoke opposition or noncompliance from governments, if they feel that their policy autonomy is unduly threatened.

A preferable approach would make use of the distinction between "thou-shalt" and "thou-shalt-not" rules. Rules requiring governments to hold or use reserve assets in fixed proportions are, like the intervention rules of the old par-value regime, of the "thou-shalt" type, requiring a positive decision to do something. An effective code for a multiple-reserve-currency standard, like the Ethier-Bloomfield reference-rate proposal for exchange rates, should instead rely on rules of the "thou-shalt-not" type, in order to maximize adaptability to change and minimize the danger of noncompliance. Such a code could be based on a reference-rate proposal for *reserves*. It would consist of two rules, both analogous to the rules of the reference-rate proposal for exchange rates:

(1)   No country shall take any action to increase its net reserve liabilities (if it is a reserve center) or its net reserve assets (if it is a nonreserve center) at a rate of change exceeding its reference rate of change, or to decrease them at a rate of

change below its reference rate of change, by more than a
certain fixed percentage.

(2) The structure of reference rates of change for both reserve
centers and nonreserve centers shall be revised at periodic
intervals through a defined international procedure.

The key rule is the first. Just as the first rule of the reference-rate
proposal for exchange rates turns the basic idea of the par-value
regime inside out, the first rule of the reference-rate proposal for
reserves turns the basic idea of an objective reserve-indicator structure
inside out. In the Committee of Twenty the United States argued for
a reserve-indicator structure to act as an automatic trigger for a
"tight" adjustment process. Other governments, objecting that this
would be too inflexible as well as a potential infringement on their
national sovereignty, threatened noncompliance. The first rule of the
reference-rate proposal for reserves is intended to dissolve such
objections by placing compliance on a "thou-shalt-not" rather than
a "thou-shalt" basis. Reserve centers are not required to deflate or
depreciate, for example, if their reserve liabilities are growing too
rapidly; nonreserve centers are not required to inflate or appreciate
if the increase of their reserve assets is excessive. The only obligation on governments is to avoid actions that will aggravate any such
trends. This parallels the obligation to avoid "dirty" floating under
the reference-rate proposal for exchange rates. In fact, the two
proposals complement one another. The first rule minimizes the risk
of policy conflict among states by putting a damper on large-scale
changes of reserve stocks stemming from discriminatory behavior by
either reserve centers or reserve holders.

Because of the complementarity of the two proposals, the proposal for reserves is cast in terms of *rates of change* rather than *levels*.
A rule cast in terms of levels of reserves would marry a flow control
to a stock target. But as Peter Kenen has pointed out, such a union is
almost always apt to be unstable. "The exchange rate can regulate the
balance of payments—the rate of change of reserves. It cannot
regulate the level of reserves. . . . A reserve-level rule cannot stabilize
the stock of reserves without destabilizing the exchange rate."[60] A

reserve-rate rule is stable because it matches a flow control to a flow target.

The second rule of the reference-rate proposal for reserves deals directly with the two issues noted above. Periodic revisions of the structure of reference rates of change can exert some effective international control over the supply and rate of growth of global liquidity as a whole; they can also help to cope with the Gresham's Law problem by facilitating adjustment of the relative supplies of different reserve currencies to correspond with the asset preferences of reserve holders. The natural forum for these periodic revisions would, once again, seem to be the IMF. The Fund could also provide a mechanism for resolving policy conflicts and inconsistencies when and if they arise.

The reference-rate proposal for reserves constitutes the *minimum* element of an effective code for a multiple-reserve-currency standard. Without these two rules, it is difficult to imagine how the standard could always be relied upon to function efficiently and avoid conflict. On the other hand, even with these rules it is possible to imagine inefficiency or conflict arising. The proposal alone will not fully promote the efficiency and consistency objectives. For that, two *supplementary* elements would also be desirable: one to deal with the role of SDRs and gold in a multiple-reserve-currency standard, the other to deal with the role of the private international financial structure.

SDRs and gold. To deal with the role of SDRs and gold in a multiple-reserve-currency standard, it would be desirable to revive the idea, discussed in the Committee of Twenty, of an IMF substitution account.[61] The account would be created specifically to give governments a onetime opportunity to fund some or all of their monetary gold holdings, at an agreed price, in exchange for SDRs. Although the SDRs would be created especially for this purpose, they would in every other respect be exactly equivalent to existing SDRs; in particular, like existing SDRs they would be free of the "myth of backing." Accordingly, over the longer term all of the gold acquired by the substitution account could eventually be sold off in the private market for the benefit of the IMF Trust Fund.

At one and the same time, this proposal would accomplish three objectives. It would facilitate a genuine phasing-out of the reserve role of gold, encourage a buildup of the monetary role of the SDR, and promote a greater flow of resources to less-developed countries.

Reasons for phasing out the "barbarous relic" of gold have already been enumerated in detail in Chapter 5. As I indicated in Chapter 4, the main problem is to ensure that a coalition of rich and poor countries and gold producers does not come together to remonetize gold at a new informal floor price or price range. A one-time offer to fund gold reserves in a substitution account could split off rich countries from the potential coalition by offering them the advantage of immediate capital certainty. It could split off the poor countries by offering them a much larger Trust Fund. Only gold producers would be left with a continuing incentive to support the free-market price—and this would be difficult in the face of the prospective sales from the substitution account. The attractiveness of gold as a usable liquid asset would therefore be significantly reduced. Certainly central banks could continue to hold some gold as a secondary reserve asset, if they so desired (just as even now they can hold other marketable commodities or shares of stock, if they wish, as a kind of "war chest" for emergencies). But the proposal would make it much more difficult for gold ever again to play an important role as a primary reserve asset.

Meanwhile, the role of the SDR would be enhanced by the expansion of its supply through the substitution account. With a larger number of SDRs in circulation, greater control could be exerted over the supply and rate of growth of liquidity in the longer term, and short-term problems of macroeconomic management could be dealt with more effectively. Reserve supply could be contracted or expanded whenever necessary. Of course, the SDR would still only be a supplement to national currencies in the monetary standard, but as the component of reserves most directly subject to conscious international control, it would be strategically placed to improve overall liquidity management. In this sense, it could truly become the "principal reserve asset" of the monetary order.

Finally, by affording an expansion of the IMF Trust Fund, the substitution account would help promote the flow of resources to less-developed countries. This, in turn, should help assuage the dissatisfaction that many poor countries now feel toward the prevailing distribution of the benefits of liquidity creation, and also make LDCs more amenable to a differentiation of rights and obligations in a multiple-reserve-currency standard in favor of such countries as the United States.

The private financial structure. To deal with the role of the private international financial structure, it would be desirable to strengthen existing governmental defenses against possible strains in money and capital markets. At one level, this means defusing the danger of shorter-term financial crises. At a second level, it means eliminating the "Euro-gap" in the longer-term management of international liquidity.

The first level corresponds to the crisis-liquidity function of central banks. As indicated in Chapter 4, governments undertook a number of significant actions in 1974 and 1975 in response to the problem of fragility in the international financial structure. These actions included moderate supervision and regulation of private financial practices, partial responsibility for recycling petrodollars, and informal moves to ensure the existence of a lender of last resort for financially pressed banks. Today what is needed is to ensure that these actions will in fact suffice to cope with the problem. In particular, what is needed is firm assurance that the lender-of-last-resort function will be adequately performed. A multiple-reserve-currency standard is especially vulnerable to speculative shifts of funds by private individuals and institutions—the private confidence problem. That vulnerability can be reduced if central banks formally commit themselves to arrangements for recycling liquid capital movements when and if the need arises. The private confidence problem should not be allowed to jeopardize the stability of the monetary order as a whole.

The second level corresponds to the trend-liquidity function of central banks. The carousel effect of recycling central-bank deposits through the Eurocurrency market was explained in Chapter 4. The only existing restraint on the carousel is the 1971 agreement of the central banks of the Group of Ten to refrain from further Eurocurrency deposits. However, events since 1971, and especially the energy crisis, have demonstrated just how ineffective that restraint really is. In 1974 and 1975, at a time when the "basic balance" of the United States was in cumulative deficit by only $9.3 billion ($10.9 billion on an official settlement basis), dollar deposits in the Euro-currency market increased by $58.1 billion (see Table 7-1). The difference consisted of the surpluses of oil-producing countries that were poured into the Eurocurrency market and re-lent to oil consumers, accounting for the large net increase of global liquidity recorded in Table 7-2.[62] Under the circumstances, the growth of currency reserve balances was undoubtedly beneficial: had consumers not been able to borrow to finance their huge oil deficits, they would have been forced to deflate their economies much more than they actually did. But circumstances may not always be quite so appropriate. At other times, the "Euro-gap" could become a source of great instability in international monetary relations. To eliminate it, governments should agree to limit *all* reserve placements in the Eurocurrency market. Otherwise, the availability of payments financing and supply and growth rate of global liquidity will not be brought under effective international control.

Of course, not even then can we be sure that the monetary order will function efficiently and avoid conflict. Not too much can be claimed for either this or the other two elements of the code for a multiple-reserve-currency standard. The same qualifications apply here as were attached to the recommendations of Chapters 5 and 6. A well-designed code can only increase the probability that a multiple-reserve-currency standard will promote the efficiency and consistency objectives. But it cannot guarantee it. As I said before, nothing can do that.

Conclusions

The defect of hegemony as an organizing principle is the same as that of automaticity and supranationality: it expects too much and delivers too little. Hegemonic leadership can never be relied upon to be as stabilizing as the case for a pure dollar standard required; nor, in contemporary circumstances, can other governments realistically be expected to be as tolerant of American hegemonic leadership as they were in decades past. Neither the responsibility assumption nor the legitimacy assumption is at all justified. Consequently, like fully automatic or supranational monetary orders, a dollar standard could never deliver as much in terms of economic welfare as its advocates would have us believe. In fact, it promotes neither the consistency nor the efficiency objective. It too is not a viable option.

As in the previous two chapters, the real problem is to find some compromise that will approach an optimal degree of accommodation of asymmetry. That requires a differentiation of the rights and obligations of certain special countries like the United States. It also calls for a multiple-reserve-currency standard featuring certain special currencies like the dollar. To function efficiently and avoid conflict, such a standard should be based on a "code of good conduct" comprising three important elements. This would be a third essential ingredient of a well-organized monetary order.

Chapter 8

Negotiation

Negotiation as an organizing principle for the monetary order means a regime of shared responsibility and decision making. The rationale for negotiation is that it reduces the risk of policy conflict between states by increasing collective participation in the management of monetary relations. Governments collectively act as a surrogate for a regime based on either automatic rules, a world central bank, or a single hegemonic leader. The more fully participatory ("pluralistic") a monetary order is, the more likely it is to satisfy the consistency objective. At the extreme, one can imagine a monetary order based exclusively on an ad hoc process of multilateral bargaining among the widest possible number of countries. This chapter discusses the case for negotiation as an organizing principle, and then considers some possible compromise arrangements embodying less exclusive reliance on ad hoc bargaining procedures.

The Case for Negotiation

The case for negotiation rests largely on an oral rather than a written tradition.[1] There are few contributions to the academic literature extolling the virtues of negotiation as a "first-best" organizing principle for the monetary order.[2] Professional scholars have devoted much energy to analysis of bargaining processes in international

monetary relations, but little to advocacy.[3] The main advocates of
the negotiation approach to monetary reform are to be found instead
among the ranks of national and international civil servants—
individuals whose credentials are more practical than academic, and
whose modes of communication are more often private than public.
But this is hardly a reflection on the case itself. Quite the opposite,
in fact. An approach that is so favored by so many practitioners
must have at least something to recommend it (unless we cynically
assume that the sole motive of practitioners is to preserve their own
prerogatives). This option too deserves to be considered seriously on
its merits.

The key requirement for negotiation as an organizing principle is
individual adherence to decisions collectively arrived at. Negotiation
makes explicit the game-theoretic nature of monetary relations and
formally acknowledges the mixed motives of all the players. The
element of competition is openly affirmed in the reliance on bargaining to determine outcomes of the monetary game. The element of
cooperation is openly affirmed in the presumed willingness of governments to accept agreed outcomes for the sake of realizing the game's
potential for joint gain. Negotiation takes as its point of departure
the axiom that every monetary order must inherently be partly consensual and partly conflictual, and tries to turn that fact to advantage.
Like the case for a pure dollar standard, the case for negotiation tries
to make a virtue of reality, by establishing formally what hitherto
has existed only informally.

The reality here is the oligopolistic struggle between states. The
basic characteristics of oligopoly, according to economic theory, are
interdependence and uncertainty. Competitors are sufficiently few
in number so that the behavior of any one has an appreciable effect
on at least some of its rivals; in turn, actions and reactions of rivals
cannot be predicted with certainty. The results are interdependence
of decision making and a preoccupation with problems of strategy.
These define the essence of the international money game. The case
for negotiation simply assumes that the essence of the monetary
game cannot be altered. It tries, therefore, not to suppress the obligop-
olistic struggle between states but, pragmatically, to accommodate it.

Negotiation is compatible with almost any conceivable combination of adjustment and liquidity mechanisms (other than the polar alternatives discussed in previous chapters: a reconstructed gold standard, freely floating exchange rates, a world central bank, or a pure dollar standard). The critical element of the structural framework of relations is the bargaining process itself. Governments are expected to commit themselves in advance to arrangements for mutual surveillance and frequent consultation on the full range of issues affecting international monetary relations, though this commitment does not bind them to outcomes of the bargaining process with which they happen to disagree. Rather, potential conflicts or inconsistencies of policy are expected to be resolved in advance through exchanges of views and through the give-and-take of multilateral discussions. The constraint on formal political sovereignty, therefore, is minimal: the commitment is merely to talk, not to act. "Willingness to *discuss* anything but no prior commitment to *do* anything," is the way one source describes it.[4] But precisely because the constraint is so limited, advocates argue, the bargaining process should be able to reach mutually satisfactory decisions on such fundamental questions as the respective obligations of surplus and deficit countries and the supply and growth rate of world reserves, and governments thus should be willing to adhere voluntarily to all such decisions. These are the two central conditions of the negotiation approach. Assuming they are in fact fulfilled, the efficiency and consistency objectives can both be promoted within any combination of adjustment and liquidity mechanisms.

The efficiency objective is ostensibly promoted because negotiation is expected to enhance the *predictability* of the policies of the countries involved. One inherent feature of oligopoly is a tendency toward cyclical rather than direct approaches to equilibrium. In the absence of consultation and coordination, competitors are driven to experiment with a variety of alternative policies, on a trial-and-error basis, until they finally happen onto an outcome that is more or less satisfactory to all concerned. The advantage of a multilateral bargaining process is that it can cut down on the costly practice of trial and error by increasing the amount of information available to decision makers. In the course of negotiations, governments can develop an awareness of the interests and needs of foreign countries and an understanding of other national policy priorities and constraints. In turn, this will ease the task of framing their own external financial targets. The more that rival actions and reactions can be predicted, the more likely it is that policy objectives can be approached directly rather than cyclically—and the more likely it is that economic welfare can genuinely be increased. Real resources will not have to be wasted because of unanticipated repercussions abroad generated by policy actions taken at home.

The consistency objective is ostensibly promoted because negotiation also is expected to enhance the *flexibility* of the policies of the countries involved. Another inherent feature of oligopoly is a tendency toward discontinuity rather than continuity of change. Once a mutually satisfactory outcome is reached, competitors are also driven to resist any substantial alteration for as long a time as possible, because of the costs of trial and error. As a result, when change finally does occur, it frequently tends to be associated with considerable systemic upheaval. Pressures build up like tensions along a fault line, then release with the force of an earthquake. Periods of relative calm alternate with periods of acute policy conflict. The advantage of a multilateral bargaining process in this respect is that it can cut down on the risk of policy conflict (though not necessarily eliminate it) by increasing the scope for more frequent marginal modifications by decision makers. In the course of negotiations, governments can accommodate systemic changes continually, as they occur, rather than through crisis. It is not necessary to live through a 1931 or a 1971 in order to achieve a change in the rules and conventions governing monetary relations.

Advocates of negotiation do not deny that other organizing principles may be neater and cleaner—that is, more intellectually elegant. An ad hoc bargaining process is obviously a much "messier" solution to the world's problems than a regime of automatic rules, a world central bank, or a pure dollar standard: its outcomes are far less determinate. However, it is precisely for that reason, advocates argue, that negotiation really is the more desirable option. More determinate solutions are also more rigid: they are less capable of ensuring continuing compatibility of the monetary order and the monetary system through time. The virtue of negotiation is that it is indeed capable of accommodating the full complexity and mutability of international monetary stratification. It makes use of the general lessons of monetary history. What it may lack in textbook attractiveness, its advocates argue, it more than makes up for in operational effectiveness.

It is not difficult to understand why this approach is favored by so many practitioners. It combines all the virtues that such people find most appealing—pragmatism, realism, practicality, flexibility. In their view, arguments for alternative approaches are merely idle academic exercises. The real world is a negotiated world: practical problem solving in monetary affairs has always relied most heavily on formal or informal discussions within transgovernmental elite networks. Especially since the breakdown of the Bretton Woods system, the monetary order has been crucially dependent on such discussions to avoid policy conflict and function efficiently. Advocates of negotiation do not find it at all surprising that the conflictual element in monetary affairs could be suppressed after 1971 and the element of cooperation be held firm. As I suggested in Chapter 6, much of the credit for this clearly goes to the availability of established lines of communication between governments and the inherited experience of frequent multilateral consultations. The case for negotiation was put to the test—and passed.

However, as any student (or professor) can testify, there are ways—and ways—of passing. That negotiation successfully prevented governments from replicating the experience of the interwar period cannot be denied. But that is hardly a sufficient ground for awarding this approach the highest grades. One only has to recall the failure of the Committee of Twenty or the questions left unanswered after Jamaica to recognize how limited its success really was. In fact, the case for negotiation leaves much to be desired. Like the cases for any of the alternative organizing principles already discussed, negotiation can also be criticized with sound reason. It too has serious defects.

The defects of negotiation as an organizing principle are the converse of its virtues. A certain amount of "messiness" may be a good thing, but one can have too much of a good thing. A structural framework of relations that is too ambiguous or indeterminate is bound to generate feelings of resentment and discrimination. As I argued in Chapter 5, a monetary order that leaves too much scope for the self-interested exercise of state power is not likely to be broadly accepted as legitimate; and a monetary order that is not broadly accepted as legitimate is not likely to avoid policy conflict for long. Exclusive reliance on an ad hoc bargaining process certainly steers clear of the Scylla of excessive detail, but it does so by veering too far instead toward the Charybdis of vague generality. As a result, it is hardly likely to be as effective in promoting the efficiency and consistency objectives as its advocates tend to claim. Decisions or outcomes in the monetary game will not be easily arrived at, nor will they be readily accepted. The two central conditions of the negotiation approach will not necessarily be fulfilled.

On the other hand, as previous chapters have made plain, some degree of reliance on negotiation is manifestly necessary if the monetary order is to perform its central functions. Supervision of the adjustment process and management of global liquidity both call for more than purely technical decisions. Consultation among governments clearly is essential if the fundamental (and controversial) questions affecting welfare, prestige, and autonomy in monetary relations are to be resolved efficiently without provoking policy conflict. Once again, therefore, the problem reduces to one of optimization—in this case, optimization of the bargaining process. The problem is to maximize the advantages of negotiation as an organizing principle while minimizing its disadvantages. The bargaining process itself must be organized.

Organizing the Bargaining Process

To organize the bargaining process, three questions must be answered satisfactorily: (1) Among what countries will negotiations be conducted? (2) In what institutional forum will they take place?

(3) According to what criteria will outcomes be decided? For convenience, these may be referred to as the questions of who, where, and how.

The Question of Who

Advocates of negotiation tend to be rather vague about the countries expected to be involved. The opportunity for broad participation is regarded as one of the virtues of the approach. All countries are affected by monetary decisions. Therefore, the greater the number of countries that can be directly involved in the decision-making process, the more likely it is that the monetary order will win effective legitimacy. But advocates do not make clear just how large they think that number ought to be.

At one extreme, it could be argued that *all* countries ought to be directly involved, from the biggest to the smallest. Such an argument stresses the narrowing of asymmetries in the monetary order discussed in the last chapter (once again, trying to make a virtue of reality). The United States has lost the power to organize the monetary order unilaterally; other countries (or groups of countries) have gained additional leverage in monetary affairs. The result is that states now find themselves caught in the same "stalemate system"[5] that stymied the Interim Committee. The international hierarchy presently is characterized by a more balanced capacity for mutual harm. Many more governments now have the ability to disrupt the existing order, if they so choose, through the self-interested exercise of state power. What stability prevails in monetary relations today derives more from mutual deterrence than from mutual trust. The advantage of including all countries directly in the bargaining process is that it increases the probability that negotiated outcomes will be voluntarily accepted. Governments are more likely to be persuaded to behave in a mutually consistent manner, and not to attempt to use their available leverage for temporary gain at each other's expense, if they all have an integral role in the multilateral bargaining process. Universal participation would provide them all with an incentive to avoid destabilizing behavior.

The value of the incentive varies inversely with the size and power of each country. Bigger and more powerful countries need little incentive to avoid destabilizing behavior. Their ability to disrupt is too evident: their own interests are too closely identified with the stability of the overall order for them to act "irresponsibly." Smaller and less powerful countries, on the other hand, need a correspondingly greater incentive to act "responsibly," since the identification of their individual interests with broader systemic concerns is relatively less clear.[6] One of the few luxuries afforded smaller countries in an international hierarchy is the privilege to pursue narrow national priorities without regard for the stability of the system as a whole. Since maverick behavior does little damage to the game's joint gain, small countries enjoy greater scope to act as "free riders." These short-run maximizers in the oligopolistic struggle can exploit the benefits of cooperative outcomes while avoiding the costs. Such behavior need not threaten the stability of the overall order unduly if it is indulged in only sporadically or by just a few small countries. But it could be more threatening if indulged in by a greater number of countries, and it may be very threatening indeed if indulged in systematically by countries further up on the scale of size and power. Charles Kindleberger has written of the danger posed by "near-great powers" that "have the power to hurt the system . . . but are tempted to pursue national goals which diverge from the interest of the system."[7] The object of including all countries in the bargaining process would be to suppress that temptation in favor of voluntary acceptance of negotiated outcomes, and thus win effective legitimacy for the monetary order.

However, a critical trade-off exists between the need to win effective legitimacy and the need to reach effective decisions.[8] Broadened participation may make outcomes easier to accept, but it also is likely to make them more difficult to arrive at. Multilateral negotiations, it is true, are sometimes facilitated by raising the number of negotiators. Bargaining becomes more fluid as the potential for shifting alliances and coalitions in alternative issue-areas is increased. But beyond a certain "critical mass," this gain tends quickly to yield to the disadvantages of sheer congestion. Negotia-

tions are characterized by a kind of Malthusian law: above some relatively small number of participants, the complexity of the bargaining
process increases geometrically (owing to the multiplication of bilateral relationships) as the number itself rises arithmetically. Participants
in the Committee of Twenty have eloquently testified how much
more difficult it was to reach agreement among a full two score of
delegations—including both developed and less-developed countries—
than it had been in the smaller and more homogeneous Group of
Ten.[9] Indeed, it was precisely because very similar difficulties were
encountered in the Interim Committee that some of the most important items on the agenda finally had to be resolved in the less crowded
setting of Rambouillet. Plainly, not all countries can be directly
represented in the bargaining process. Some sort of delegation of
authority is required. That is the crux of the matter. The question
is: how can the delegation of authority actually be accomplished?

Some observers have suggested that it might best be accomplished
by formally assigning major responsibility for monetary rule making
and management to a restricted number of leading countries. Fred
Bergsten, for instance, has argued that authority for all major decisions should be assigned to just two countries, the United States and
Germany, the "only two economic superpowers in the world today."
The Bretton Woods hegemony of the dollar would be replaced by a
dollar-mark "bigemony."[10] Ronald McKinnon, in a retreat from
advocacy of a pure dollar standard, has urged inauguration of a
triumvirate, to include Japan as well, in a "new Tripartite Agreement."[11] And other sources have also stressed the special role that
certain key advanced states ought to play as "steerers" or "pace-
setters" of the monetary order.[12] The idea is that the leading
countries—whether a pair, a trio, or "a few"—should collectively
negotiate among themselves to resolve critical monetary issues as
they arise. The states with the greatest power should be given the
greatest authority.

This, however, merely pushes the pendulum back in the opposite
direction. From the point of view of smaller and less powerful
countries, this is not participation but paternalism. The trade-off
implied by a "key-country" approach is far too favorable to the
strong: it withdraws the advantage that broadened participation is

initially supposed to offer. Smaller states question whether bigger states would really be serious about taking their special interests into account. Key countries might merely "give an appearance" of listening to their views without actually being influenced by them. Decisions reached by such an approach, therefore, are particularly apt to be challenged by the unrepresented. Outcomes might be easier to arrive at, but they would be more difficult to accept.

One way to overcome this disadvantage might be to organize the monetary order into several distinct regional groupings, formalizing the de facto tendency toward currency blocs that became evident after 1973. In the words of one observer: "Once progress is made towards solving the *internal* problems of regional monetary areas, the task of regulating monetary relations *among* areas . . . will be greatly simplified."[13] This possibility has been envisaged by a number of writers.[14] Some see two great regional groupings emerging, one centered on the United States and one on the European Community; others imagine more complex arrangements involving larger numbers of key countries. All anticipate that monetary relations would be organized in a kind of "two-tier" fashion. Each key country would take care to consult vertically with members of its own bloc while negotiating horizontally with the other "steerers" of the monetary order. Smaller countries would not be represented directly in the bargaining process, but their views and interests would have an indirect effect on final outcomes. The benefit of participation would be gained without losing the advantage of small numbers.

However, this approach too is likely to be resisted by less powerful countries, and for much the same reason. Formalization of currency blocs means de jure establishment of multiple currency hegemonies on a regional scale. To be effective, such regional hegemonies must satisfy the same two assumptions as a global hegemony —the responsibility assumption and the legitimacy assumption. In fact, though, it is no easier to justify these assumptions at the regional level than it is at the world level. There is no assurance at all that the economic policy of the bloc leader would be truly stabilizing; nor is it likely that other members would always be content with the distributional implications of bloc organization. In any event, many smaller states would undoubtedly resent being forced to restrict their main financial ties to a single key country. I have already mentioned the feelings of dissatisfaction that were generated after 1973, especially among LDCs, by the necessity to peg to a single major currency. Most governments consider it in their interest to diversify foreign monetary links as much as possible.

The bloc approach is also unattractive for a second reason. If less powerful countries do not resist it, the approach may indeed gain the benefit of participation without losing the advantage of small numbers, but the cost could nevertheless be high. The principal virtue of negotiation is supposed to be its capacity to accommodate the full complexity and mutability of monetary stratification. Formalization of currency blocs would make such accommodation difficult, if not impossible. As was indicated in Chapter 5, it is extremely difficult to identify the appropriate domain of a currency area. The real world just does not divide into nice neat regional hegemonies, as the experience of the European "snake" amply testifies. Would the European Community constitute a single monetary grouping in a world of formal blocs, or would France and Britain persist as independent monetary powers alongside Germany? If the latter, in whose bloc would be found countries such as Italy, Belgium, or the Netherlands—or Switzerland, Sweden, or Spain? What of Australia and New Zealand, each caught between fading ties with sterling and growing links with both the U.S. dollar and the Japanese yen? What of South Africa or Saudi Arabia? The bloc approach tends to be unidimensional, whereas the reality of monetary relations is multidimensional. Because of bureaucratic inertia, the bloc approach would also tend to be relatively inflexible, whereas the need of the monetary order is for adaptability to change. This is hardly the most effective way to delegate authority in the bargaining process.

Probably the most effective way to delegate bargaining authority would be to make use of—and build on—the weighted-voting and constituency-representation procedures of the IMF. This approach offers several advantages.

First, it already exists. Procedures of weighted voting and constituency representation have been tested for over three decades in the Board of Governors and Executive Board, as well as more recently in the Committee of Twenty and Interim Committee. They have worked tolerably well, and their legitimacy has been universally accepted. They are integral to the proposed new IMF Council of Governors.

Second, the approach is multidimensional. The Fund's procedures acknowledge the complexity of international monetary stratification. Weighted voting automatically differentiates the rights and obligations of bigger countries from those of smaller countries; the assignment of five seats in the Executive Board and Council of Governors directly to members with the largest quotas automatically accommodates the special role played by the biggest of the big. Yet, at the same time, even the smallest of the small are protected: first, by the IMF secretariat acting as "defender of minority interests"; and second, insofar as amendments of the Fund Charter are concerned, by the provision in IMF rules requiring acceptance not only by a weighted majority of 85 percent of the total voting power but also by 60 percent of the total membership.[15] These features avoid the paternalism of the key-country approach. Small countries have an opportunity to share in the reality, not just the symbols, of collective monetary management. The sense of participation is genuine.

Finally, the approach is adaptable. The Fund's procedures also acknowledge the mutability of monetary stratification. Periodic reviews of Fund quotas ensure that voting weights can be systematically altered to keep pace with changes in the global distribution of monetary power (as, for example, the increased power of OPEC countries after 1973 was recognized in the quota increase agreed at Jamaica). Likewise, the constituency composition of the Executive Board and Council of Governors can be periodically reviewed and revised to take account of shifts in the international hierarchy. If some small countries feel that they are not being consulted adequately by their constituency representative, they can always shift to another constituency or demand a new representative. They are not frozen into a rigid structure of formal currency blocs.

Of course, no one would argue that the Fund's procedures are perfect. As always in human affairs, improvements are possible. For instance, the 60 percent acceptance provision for amendments could be extended to encompass other issues as well. Greater flexibility could perhaps be built into the procedure by differentiating less important decisions requiring a lower percentage of acceptance from more important decisions requiring correspondingly higher percentages. And similarly, some streamlining of the bargaining process itself would be possible to minimize the kinds of congestion difficulties encountered in the Committee of Twenty and Interim Committee. But such changes are really beside the point. The main point is that the Fund procedures do offer a reasonable answer to the question of who. Negotiation as an organizing principle requires identification of a group of countries both ready and able to negotiate. The Fund's organizational structure satisfies that requirement.

The Question of Where

The Fund's organizational structure also satisfies the requirement for an institutional forum. In fact, the question of where was already answered in Chapter 6. The IMF is clearly the most appropriate place for governments to consult on the full range of monetary issues. Other institutions, such as the BIS or OECD, can still play a supplementary or subsidiary role for certain negotiating purposes, as they have in the past. But the central role should continue to be played by the IMF. Only the IMF can offer reasonable certainty that outcomes of the bargaining process not only can be arrived at relatively efficiently but also will be adhered to voluntarily and universally.

The Question of How

The question of how was answered in Chapters 5 and 7. Advocates of negotiation stress the disadvantages of detailed criteria for determining outcomes of the bargaining process. A priori rules or guidelines do not automatically solve problems, they argue: no government can put unlimited faith in the prior commitments of other governments. Practical men prefer the broadest possible latitude for reaching decisions on an ad hoc basis. A world of no rules, however, is not pluralistic but anarchic—precisely what is meant by a free-for-all regime. That option was rejected in the Introduction. An ad hoc bargaining process, devoid of any foundation of agreed rules or conventions, is likely to be inefficient and will almost certainly generate or exacerbate policy conflicts among states. As I have said, the structural framework of relations cannot be too ambiguous or indeterminate. Some basis for harmony is essential if the principle of negotiation is to win effective legitimacy.

That basis for harmony can be provided by the two "codes of good conduct" outlined in Chapters 5 and 7. For issues relating to the adjustment process in a regime of floating exchange rates, negotiation can be based on the reference-rate proposal for exchange rates; for issues relating to the management of global liquidity in a multiple-reserve-currency standard, negotiation can be based on the parallel reference-rate proposal for reserves. By consulting and exchanging views regularly, governments can test mutual compliance with the two codes and can resolve policy conflicts and inconsistencies when and if they arise. By reviewing and revising the structures of reference rates for exchange rates and reserves periodically, they can also anticipate and avoid many such conflicts and inconsistencies even before they have a chance to arise. The value of the two codes is that they restrict the scope for self-interested exercise of state power in the bargaining process. Accordingly, they increase the probability that the two central conditions of the negotiation approach will in fact be fulfilled.

Conclusions

Negotiation shares the same defect as the three other organizing principles previously discussed: it expects too much and delivers too little. Exclusive reliance on an ad hoc bargaining process demands more mutual trust from governments than they can realistically be expected to feel. Consequently, negotiation is less likely to promote the efficiency and consistency objectives than its advocates would have us believe. Here too the real problem is to find some compromise that would permit an optimization of the bargaining process. That requires finding satisfactory answers to the three questions of who, where, and how. The most satisfactory answers, I have argued, are to be found in the organizational structure of the IMF and in the two codes of good conduct outlined in previous chapters. A bargaining process designed along these lines would be a fourth essential ingredient of a well-organized monetary order.

Chapter 9

Conclusions

The time has now come for summing up. Our discussion has been concerned with the problem of how to organize the international monetary order. International monetary relations have been viewed informally as a mixed-motive game incorporating elements of both cooperation and competition. The problem has been to find some structural framework of relations that would successfully accommodate and balance these two elements—and thus promote both the efficiency and consistency objectives. Four alternative organizing principles have been examined: automaticity, supranationality, hegemony, and negotiation. Each of these has been advocated seriously at one time or another by a variety of respected sources. The conclusion of this discussion, however, is that no one of them alone could ever offer a truly viable option. No one principle properly satisfies both objectives entirely on its own.

The defect common to all four alternatives is their intellectual extremism. Because each one represents a limiting case, they are really useful only at a relatively high level of abstraction. Their value lies mainly in helping to define the substantive issues on which a compromise must eventually turn. In the real world, compromise is inevitable because of the multiplicity of values to be allocated. Each polar alternative impinges on at least some vital interests of politically sovereign states. It is essential to disaggregate the four alternatives and then mix their ingredients if the framework of relations is not to collapse under the threat of policy conflict. A viable monetary order must necessarily be a hybrid of purer forms. That is the way the world has always been—and the way it always will be.

Our discussion has identified four essential ingredients of a well-organized monetary order. These are (1) a regime of managed floating, (2) an improved International Monetary Fund, (3) a multiple-reserve-currency standard, and (4) an optimized bargaining process. I have said that there are really just two central issues in organizing any international monetary order, one involving the mechanism of balance-of-payments adjustment, the other the mechanism for creating international liquidity. The four ingredients that I recommend here combine to offer viable solutions to both these central issues.

Principal responsibility for maintaining or restoring equilibrium in international payments would rest with the exchange-rate regime, freed of any artificial construct of par values and bands. "Dirty" floating and inertia in decision making would both be minimized, and the advantages of flexibility and prospects for winning effective legitimacy would both be maximized, by a code of good conduct based on the reference-rate proposal for exchange rates. The rules of the code would be sufficiently flexible to enable governments to choose from among a wide variety of specific arrangements to guide their individual currencies, thus allowing for both the geographic and the temporal dimensions of exchange-rate optimality. Principal responsibility for supervising the adjustment process would rest with the proposed Council of Governors of the IMF, thus simultaneously accommodating the special role played by bigger countries and protecting the rights and interests of smaller countries. The Fund forum would provide a mechanism for reviewing the multilateral structure of exchange rates and for periodically revising the structure of reference rates, as well as for judging the respective adjustment obligations of surplus and deficit countries and for determining the pressures (if any) to be brought to bear on countries in persistent imbalance. Ultimately, all policy conflicts and inconsistencies would be resolved through a multilateral bargaining process based on the Fund's multidimensional and adaptable organizational structure.

Principal responsibility for providing international monetary reserves would rest with the multiple-reserve-currency standard, comprising both national reserve currencies and Special Drawing Rights. The role of gold as a primary reserve asset would be phased out completely, and the role of the SDR deliberately enhanced, by creation of an IMF substitution account. Both the Gresham's Law problem and the supply and rate of growth of reserves as a whole would be brought under more effective international control by a code of good conduct based on the reference-rate proposal for reserves and by restrictions on central-bank reserve placements in the Eurocurrency market. Principal responsibility for managing global liquidity (as for supervising the adjustment process) would rest with the proposed IMF Council of Governors. The Fund forum would provide a mechanism for periodic revisions of the structure of reference rates for reserves, for controlling the overall issuance of SDRs, and for supervising the private international financial structure.

Together, these ingredients effectively define a complete new constitution for the monetary system. Their intention, in effect, is to answer the questions left unanswered after Jamaica. Organizing the monetary order means specifying which instruments of national policy may be used and which targets of policy may be regarded as legitimate. The structural framework recommended here would do precisely that, partly by adopting what already exists in the real world and partly by adapting it. Two criteria of judgment are employed, one economic, the other political. The problem is treated explicitly as one of *joint* maximization of the two objectives of efficiency and consistency. The combination of recommendations that emerges illustrates well both the potentialities and the limits of monetary reform.

These recommendations are not above criticism, of course. On the one hand, some observers might criticize them for attempting to do too much. In effect, the approach calls for a comprehensive American-style approach to constitution writing, somewhat akin to the exercise at Bretton Woods a third of a century ago. Many experts today consider that a piecemeal English-style approach would be rather more appropriate in the context of our present "stalemate system." Peter Kenen, for example, stressing the "very special circumstances that allowed the writing of a monetary constitution in 1944," has argued that "economic and political conditions [today] deprive the international rule-making process of the ingredient that made it work in 1944."[1] In a similar vein, Richard Cooper has written that "in the international monetary sphere, an English-style constitution, built up through a series of acceptable practices, may be both easier to attain and even superior in content to a fully negotiated American-style constitution."[2] Such attitudes, however, seem far too sanguine. In principle, they can be justified only if states can always be relied upon to hold firm to the element of cooperation in monetary relations, even in the absence of a fully accepted legal and conventional framework. In practice, states cannot always be relied upon so confidently. The evident strength of the consensual element in monetary affairs after 1971, for instance, could really prove to be a depleting asset, a transitional legacy of Bretton Woods soon to atrophy if not reinforced by a firm set of controls on national behavior. As John Williamson has cautioned, "current diplomatic tranquility is bought at the cost of possible tension in the future. Without a set of rules governing national behavior in the international arena, there is an ever-present possibility that inevitable differences in national interests will provoke international conflict."[3] An American-style approach to constitution writing, therefore, does not seem overly ambitious. It seems merely prudent.

On the other hand, the approach might be criticized for attempting to do too little—in effect, for leaving too many gaps and ambiguities in the rules and conventions governing the financial conduct of nations. Neither a managed float nor a multiple-reserve-currency standard, after all, is a very elegant monetary mechanism; the reliance of both on a multilateral bargaining process, albeit in the IMF, is admittedly a "messy" solution to the global reform problem. But a messy solution need not be an unstable one. In fact, indeterminacy can be a real strength, insofar as it ensures a sufficient degree of flexibility in the monetary order to accommodate the full complexity and mutability of monetary stratification and the endogenous and purposive role of state actors. No viable monetary order can be as "integrationist" as, say, a gold standard or a world central bank. To endure, every monetary order must be at least a little bit "disintegrationist." As Fred Hirsch says, "Keeping a little apart can at times be the best way of keeping together."[4] Governments always demand a certain margin or leeway for discretionary behavior, a certain number of "safety valves" to permit occasional "cheating" when vital national objectives are at stake. That is only realistic. The trick is to ensure that such cheating will be limited in both frequency and scope—in other words, that the ambiguity in the monetary order will be controlled so that the most important links between national economies will be preserved. Kenen calls this "optimum disintegration."[5] That optimum is what these recommendations attempt to achieve.

If any general lesson emerges from this long discussion, it is that in an imperfect world there are no perfect solutions. The potential for improvement exists—but it is finite, not infinite. Aspiration must be tempered by humility. The monetary order can be better organized; both efficiency and consistency can be promoted. But nothing can ensure for all time that monetary relations will always remain stable and free of policy conflict. So long as there are politically sovereign states and formally independent national currencies, there will be international monetary problems. All we can really hope to do is to minimize the probability that such problems will occur and to restrict the extent of their damage when they do. We can never hope to eliminate them completely.

Notes

Introduction

1. See Robert A. Mundell, "The Future of the International Financial System," in A. L. K. Acheson, J. F. Chant, and M. F. J. Prachowny, eds., *Bretton Woods Revisited* (Toronto: University of Toronto Press, 1972), p. 92; and Richard N. Cooper, "Prolegomena to the Choice of an International Monetary System," *International Organization*, 29 (Winter 1975): 64. The terms "order" and "system" as employed in the text are Mundell's. Cooper prefers the term "regime" to "order."

2. Mundell, "International Financial System," p. 92.

3. Ibid.

4. There are, of course, costs as well as benefits associated with relations of trade and investment. For a discussion, see Benjamin J. Cohen, *The Question of Imperialism* (New York: Basic Books, 1973), chaps. 5, 6.

5. Robert Z. Aliber, *Monetary Reform and World Inflation*, Washington Papers, vol. 1 (Beverly Hills and London: Sage Publications, 1973), p. 43.

6. Harry G. Johnson, *The Problem of International Monetary Reform*, Stamp Memorial Lecture, 1973 (London: Athlone Press, 1974), p. 6.

7. Ibid.

8. Sidney E. Rolfe and James L. Burtle, *The Great Wheel: The World Monetary System—A Reinterpretation* (London: Macmillan, 1974), p. xi.

9. Susan Strange, *Sterling and British Policy* (London: Oxford University Press, 1971), pp. 2-3. See also her "International Economics and International Relations: A Case of Mutual Neglect," *International Affairs*, 46 (April 1970): 304-315.

10. The few exceptions to this rule—economists or political scientists writing on monetary reform who have genuinely tried to bridge the analytical gap between their separate disciplines—stand out in the literature. See, e.g., Aliber, *Monetary Reform*; Cooper, "Prolegomena"; Henry G. Aubrey, "The Political Economy of International Monetary Reform," *Social Research* 33 (Summer 1966): 218-254; Eugene A. Birnbaum, *Gold and the International Monetary System: An Orderly Reform*, Essays in International Finance, no. 66 (Princeton: International Finance Section, 1968); Stephen D. Cohen, *International Monetary Reform, 1964-69: The Political Dimension* (New York: Praeger, 1970); Charles P. Kindleberger, *Power and Money* (New York:

Basic Books, 1970), chaps. 13-14; Harry G. Johnson, "Political Economy Aspects of International Monetary Reform," *Journal of International Economics* 2, no. 4 (1972): 401-423; Anthony Lanyi, "Political Aspects of Exchange-Rate Systems," in Richard L. Merritt, ed., *Communication in International Politics* (Urbana: University of Illinois Press, 1972), chap. 18; David P. Calleo and Benjamin M. Rowland, *America and the World Political Economy* (Bloomington and London: Indiana University Press, 1973); and C. Fred Bergsten, *The Dilemmas of the Dollar* (New York: Council on Foreign Relations, 1975).

Of course, radical and marxist writers have always tried to bridge the gap between economics and politics—on this subject, as on others. See, e.g., Harry Magdoff, *The Age of Imperialism* (New York: Monthly Review Press, 1969); Michael Hudson, *Super Imperialism: The Economic Strategy of American Empire* (New York: Holt, 1972); and Ernest Mandel, *Decline of the Dollar: A Marxist View of the Monetary Crisis* (New York: Monad Press, 1972).

11. Lawrence B. Krause and Joseph S. Nye, "Reflections on the Economics and Politics of International Economic Organizations," *International Organization* 29 (Winter 1975): 323.

12. Robert O. Keohane and Joseph S. Nye, "World Politics and the International Economic System," in C. Fred Bergsten, ed., *The Future of the International Economic Order: An Agenda for Research* (Lexington, Mass.: D. C. Heath, 1973), p. 115. See also David H. Blake and Robert S. Walters, *The Politics of Global Economic Relations* (Englewood Cliffs, N.J.: Prentice-Hall 1976), esp. chaps. 1 and 9.

13. Wilbur F. Monroe, *International Monetary Reconstruction* (Lexington, Mass.: D. C. Heath, 1974), p. 5.

14. Cooper, "Prolegomena," 64.

15. Ibid., 65.

Chapter 1

1. Sir Ralph Hawtrey, *Currency and Credit*, 3rd ed. (New York: Longmans, Green, 1928), p. 1.

2. E. Victor Morgan, *A History of Money* (Baltimore: Penguin Books, 1965), p. 11.

3. Boris P. Pesek and Thomas R. Saving, *Money, Wealth and Economic Theory* (New York: Macmillan, 1967), p. 47.

4. Thomas D. Willett and Edward Tower, "Currency Areas and Exchange-Rate Flexibility," *Weltwirtschaftliches Archiv* 105, Heft 1 (1970): 49.

5. Charles P. Kindleberger, "The Benefits of International Money," *Journal of International Economics* 2, no. 4 (1972): 442. See also Edward Tower and Thomas D. Willett, *The Theory of Optimum Currency Areas and Exchange-Rate Flexibility*, Special Papers in Economics, no. 11 (Princeton: International Finance Section, 1976), chap. 2.

6. The discussion of the foreign-exchange market here is necessarily brief.

For a more detailed discussion see, e.g., Benjamin J. Cohen, *Balance-of-Payments Policy* (Baltimore and London: Penguin Books, 1969), chap. 2.

7. Again, the discussion here is brief. For a more detailed discussion of the several meanings of the term "balance of payments," see ibid., chap. 1.

8. Unilateral transfers comprise personal and institutional remittances and official pensions, reparations, and grants. These also appear on both sides of the balance of payments despite the fact that they are actually one-sided transactions lacking a quid pro quo. The quid pro quo is supplied in the form of a "dummy" entry indicating the character of the gift, which is placed on the side of the account opposite to the entry for the item given or received.

9. For more on Special Drawing Rights and the International Monetary Fund, see below, Chapters 3, 4, and 6.

10. Here and in the remainder of this volume, except where otherwise indicated, imports are interpreted to include unilateral transfers abroad: like purchases of goods and services, these confer purchasing power on foreigners. By the same token, exports are understood to include unilateral transfers received.

11. There are exceptions, of course, such as movements of goods which correspond to a "unilateral transfer in kind" or foreign investments involving the shipment abroad of domestic plant and equipment. These are accommodating transactions, too. But these exceptions do not figure prominently in the balance of payments and, for our purposes, may be ignored.

12. See Cohen, *Balance-of-Payments Policy*, pp. 42-49.

13. In fact, the coverage of the market balance does not quite match up to that of the accounting balance. Discrepancies between the two, however, do not substantially alter the argument in the text. See ibid., pp. 53-54.

14. This is, of course, a very simple description of a very complex process. For a more detailed discussion see, e.g., Charles P. Kindleberger *International Economics*, 5th ed. (Homewood, Ill.: Richard D. Irwin, 1973), chaps. 19-22. The two mechanisms work in reverse for a surplus in the balance of payments.

15. "Reallocation of resources" should be understood to mean not only switches from one type of employment to another but also switches to or from a state of unemployment.

16. The effectiveness of expenditure-switching policies is not unlimited. Over the long term, the influence of relative price changes on the allocation of total spending will be offset by the impact on aggregate demand of changes in the real value of money balances. This is the lesson of the recently developed "monetary" approach to macroeconomic theory. See below, chapter 5. This suggests that the dichotomy between expenditure-changing and expenditure-switching policies is most appropriate for relatively short time periods.

17. Some writers have argued that because the resource reallocations generated by restrictions, subsidies, or exchange control are not the same as the automatic market response, these alternatives cannot be considered genuine balance-of-payments adjustment policies. But such arguments commit the fallacy of "disguised politics"; they embody an illegitimate value judgment. See below, as well as Cohen, *Balance-of-Payments Policy*, pp. 89-104.

18. This trichotomy goes back to the deliberations of a celebrated international study group of 32 economists in 1964. See Fritz Machlup and Burton G. Malkiel, eds., *International Monetary Arrangements: The Problem of Choice* (Princeton: International Finance Section, 1964).

19. See Benjamin J. Cohen, *Adjustment Costs and the Distribution of New*

Reserves, Studies in International Finance, no. 18 (Princeton: International Finance Section, 1966).

20. It should be noted that "real domestic absorption" is understood here to include not only expenditures on real goods and services (the usual definition of the term) but also autonomous investments in assets. Hence, an excess of absorption over income is the analytical equivalent of a deficit of accommodating receipts (i.e., a loss of net foreign liquidity).

21. Economists have been very slow in developing techniques to measure the economic costs of balance-of-payments adjustment. Indeed, the theory of adjustment costs itself is still in its infancy. See Benjamin J. Cohen, "International Reserves and Liquidity," in Peter B. Kenen, ed., *International Trade and Finance: Frontiers for Research* (New York and Cambridge: Cambridge University Press, 1975), p. 423.

22. This, of course, is why some writers have argued that these are not genuine adjustment policies. See note 16.

23. See, e.g., Jagdish N. Bhagwati, *Trade, Tariffs and Growth* (London: Weidenfeld and Nicolson, 1969).

24. Tibor Scitovsky, "Alternative Methods of Restoring Balance", in W. Fellner et al., *Maintaining and Restoring Balance in International Payments* (Princeton: Princeton University Press, 1966), pp. 198-199.

25. This suggests that analysis ought really to be framed in terms of the *optimal* degree of exchange-rate flexibility. For more discussion see below, Chapter 5.

26. See Jan Tinbergen, *On the Theory of Economic Policy* (Amsterdam: North-Holland Publishing Co., 1952).

27. See Robert A. Mundell, *International Economics* (New York: Macmillan, 1968), chaps. 11, 16-18.

28. The term *international liquidity* should not be confused with the net foreign liquidity of a country, which is a much broader concept encompassing the full array of international means of payment owned by or available to the country's residents as well as to the government.

29. See, e.g., Benjamin J. Cohen, *The Future of Sterling as an International Currency* (London: Macmillan, 1971), pp. 13-23.

30. Peter B. Kenen, "Financing and Adjustment: The Carrot and the Stick," in Fellner et al., *International Payments*, p. 152.

31. See Cohen, "International Reserves and Liquidity," in ibid., pp. 413-435.

32. The law is named after Sir Thomas Gresham (1519-1579), a leading Elizabethan businessman and financial adviser to Queen Elizabeth I. Gresham was concerned with the problem of how to keep both gold and silver coins in circulation in a bimetallic monetary system. His law referred to the popular proclivity of many people to hoard coins whose bullion content was rising in value relative to their nominal face value.

33. See Cohen, "International Reserves and Liquidity," in Fellner et al., *International Payments*, pp. 435-440.

Chapter 2

1. Pierre-Paul Schweitzer, "Political Aspects of Managing the International Monetary System," *International Affairs* 52 (April 1976): 208.

2. Thomas Balogh, *Fact and Fancy in International Economic Relations* (Oxford: Pergamon Press, 1973), p. 16.

3. Lawrence B. Krause and Joseph S. Nye, "Reflections on the Economics and Politics of International Economic Organizations," *International Organization* 29 (Winter 1975): 324, 328. The term "endogenous" means inside or integral to the model or system. The opposite is "exogenous," meaning outside or independent of the model or system.

4. Robert O. Keohane and Joseph S. Nye, "World Politics and the International Economic System," in C. Fred Bergsten, ed., *The Future of the International Economic Order: An Agenda for Research* (Lexington, Mass.: D. C. Heath, 1973), p. 162.

5. This is the so-called "realist" paradigm of international relations. The classic source is Hans J. Morgenthau, *Politics Among Nations: The Struggle for Peace and Power*, 4th ed., rev. (New York: Knopf, 1967).

6. See, e.g., Benjamin J. Cohen, *The Question of Imperialism* (New York: Basic Books, 1973), chaps. 2, 4, 7.

7. An extreme exponent of this pluralist point of view is Anthony Downs, who argues that all state actions (not only foreign policies) are motivated exclusively by a desire to maximize votes; policies are merely a means toward this end. It therefore follows, assuming rationality on the part of decision makers, that governmental policy will never represent anything more than the largest possible coalition of particular interests. See his *An Economic Theory of Democracy* (New York: Harper and Row, 1957).

8. See, e.g., Peter J. Katzenstein, "International Politics and Domestic Structures: Foreign Economic Policies of Advanced Industrial States," *International Organization* 30 (Winter 1976): 1-45. In addition to the usual private interest groups (business, labor, farmers, etc.), domestic power relationships should be understood to include elements of the public bureaucratic structure, which frequently take on the character of interest groups in their own right. Indeed, one extreme view of state action runs exclusively in terms of interdepartmental struggles for administrative predominance within the national government (the state itself being viewed largely in terms of bureaucratic structures). This is the so-called "bureaucratic-politics" paradigm of international relations, which assumes that because state action bears the traces of such interdepartmental struggles and contradictions, it will almost inevitably appear haphazard if not irrational. See, e.g., Graham T. Allison, *Essence of Decision: Explaining the Cuban Missile Crisis* (Boston: Little, Brown, 1971).

9. Joseph S. Nye and Robert O. Keohane, "Transnational Relations and World Politics: An Introduction," in Keohane and Nye, eds., *Transnational Relations and World Politics* (Cambridge, Mass.: Harvard University Press, 1972), p. ix.

10. Keohane and Nye, "World Politics and the International Economic System," in Bergsten, *Future*, p. 129. For some useful essays on the importance of transnational relations in this and other international issue-areas, see Keohane and Nye, eds., *Transnational Relations and World Politics*.

11. Richard N. Cooper, "Prolegomena to the Choice of an International Monetary System," *International Organization* 29 (Winter 1975): 69-84.

12. Ibid., 75.

13. John von Neumann and Oskar Morgenstern, *The Theory of Games and Economic Behavior* (Princeton: Princeton University Press, 1953). For a clear and concise introduction to what game theory is all about, see Morton D. Davis, *Game Theory* (New York: Basic Books, 1970).

14. Von Neumann and Morgenstern, *Theory of Games*, p. 540.

15. Only a few economists have made this point explicitly. See, e.g., Cooper, "Prolegomena"; Balogh, *Fact and Fancy*; Anthony Lanyi, "Political Aspects of Exchange-Rate Systems," in Richard L. Merritt, ed., *Communication in International Politics* (Urbana: University of Illinois Press, 1972), chap. 18; Lawrence H. Officer and Thomas D. Willett, "The Interaction of Adjustment and Gold-Conversion Policies in a Reserve-Currency System," *Western Economic Journal* 8 (March 1970): 47-60; and two articles by Koichi Hamada, "Alternative Exchange Rate Systems and the Interdependence of Monetary Policies," in Robert Z. Aliber, ed., *National Monetary Policies and the International Financial System* (Chicago: University of Chicago Press, 1974), esp. pp. 29-31; and "A Strategic Analysis of Monetary Interdependence," *Journal of Political Economy* 84 (August 1976): pp. 677-700.

16. Krause and Nye, "Reflections," p. 332.

17. Cooper, "Prolegomena," p. 84.

18. See Cohen, *Question of Imperialism*, pp. 237-241.

19. C. Fred Bergsten, Robert O. Keohane, and Joseph S. Nye, "International Economics and International Politics: A Framework for Analysis," *International Organization* 29 (Winter 1975): 24.

20. But cf. William D. Grampp, "International Politics and Dollar Policy," *Challenge*, February 1965, pp. 20-23; Benjamin J. Cohen, *Adjustment Costs and the Distribution of New Reserves*, Studies in International Finance, no. 18 (Princeton: International Finance Section, 1966), pp. 11ff; Eugene A. Birnbaum, *Gold and the International Monetary System: An Orderly Reform*, Essays in International Finance, no. 66 (Princeton: International Finance Section, 1968), pp. 2-6; Henry G. Aubrey, *Behind the Veil of International Money*, Essays in International Finance, no. 71 (Princeton: International Finance Section, 1969), pp. 8-10; Stephen D. Cohen, *International Monetary Reform, 1964-69: The Political Dimension* (New York: Praeger, 1970); and C. Fred Bergsten, *The Dilemmas of the Dollar* (New York: Council on Foreign Relations, 1975), pp. 28-45.

Cf. also the radical and marxist writers cited in the Introduction, note 10.

21. See, e.g., James G. Marsh, "The Power of Power," in David Easton, ed., *Varieties of Political Theory* (Englewood Cliffs, N.J.: Prentice-Hall, 1966), pp. 39-70; Jeffrey Hart, "Three Approaches to the Measurement of Power in International Relations," *International Organization* 30 (Spring 1976): 289-305; and Susan Strange, "What Is Economic Power, and Who Has It?", *International Journal* 30 (Spring 1975): 207-224.

22. Keohane and Nye, "World Politics and the International Economic System," in Bergsten, *Future*, p. 122. See also their *Power and Interdependence: World Politics in Transition* (Boston: Little, Brown, 1977), chap 1.

23. Albert O. Hirschman, *National Power and the Structure of Foreign Trade* (Berkeley: University of California Press, 1945), p. 16.

24. Keohane and Nye, "World Politics and the International Economic System," in Bergsten, *Future*, p. 124.

25. Ibid., p. 117.

26. See Cohen, *Adjustment Costs*, p. 11; and John Williamson, *The Choice of a Pivot for Parities*, Essays in International Finance, no. 90 (Princeton: International Finance Section, 1971), pp. 11-13.

27. See, e.g., James Tobin, "Adjustment Responsibilities of Surplus and Deficit Countries," in W. Fellner et al., *Maintaining and Restoring Balance in International Payments* (Princeton: Princeton University Press, 1966), chap. 16; J. Marcus Fleming, *Guidelines for Balance-of-Payments Adjustment Under the Par-Value System*, Essays in International Finance, no. 67 (Princeton: International Finance Section, 1968); Raymond F. Mikesell and Henry N. Goldstein, *Rules for a Floating-Rate Regime*, Essays in International Finance, no. 109 (Princeton: International Finance Section, 1975); and Wilfred Ethier and Arthur I. Bloomfield, *Managing the Managed Float*, Essays in International Finance, no. 112 (Princeton: International Finance Section, 1975).

28. H. Peter Gray, *An Aggregate Theory of International Payments Adjustment* (London: Macmillan, 1974), p. 190.

29. Robert Z. Aliber, *Choices for the Dollar*, Planning Pamphlet no. 127 (Washington, D.C.: National Planning Association, 1969), p. 11.

30. Cooper, "Prolegomena," p. 92.

31. See Emil-Maria Claassen, "Demand for International Reserves and the Optimum Mix and Speed of Adjustment Policies," *American Economic Review* 65 (June 1975): 447.

32. Anthony Lanyi, *The Case for Floating Exchange Rates Reconsidered*, Essays in International Finance, no. 72 (Princeton: International Finance Section, 1969), p. 23. See also Benjamin J. Cohen, *Balance-of-Payments Policy* (Baltimore and London: Penguin Books, 1969), pp. 119-121.

33. See Cohen, *Adjustment Costs*.

34. In technical terms, monopoly power in world markets implies a relatively low price elasticity of demand for the country's exports and a relatively high price elasticity of supply; monopsony power, a relatively high demand elasticity for the country's imports and a relatively low supply elasticity. The ideal condition from the national point of view is a combination of high demand and supply elasticities at home and low elasticities abroad. Economic theory teaches that *ceteris paribus* high price elasticities of demand for exports and imports ensure that an expenditure-switching policy such as devaluation will improve a deficit country's balance of payments. (Formally, this is known as the Marshall-Lerner condition.) But if the product of demand elasticities exceeds the product of supply elasticities, the devaluing country's terms of trade will improve as well, and at least some of the continuing cost of adjustment will be transferred to surplus countries. See, e.g., Charles P. Kindleberger, *International Economics*, 5th ed. (Homewood, Ill.: Richard D. Irwin, 1973), chap. 19 and Appendix G.

35. See, e.g., Robert Triffin, *Our International Monetary System: Yesterday, Today, and Tomorrow* (New York: Random House, 1968), chap. 1; and Peter B. Kenen, *British Monetary Policy and the Balance of Payments, 1951-1957* (Cambridge, Mass.: Harvard University Press, 1960), pp. 56-63. But for some qualifications, see A. G. Ford, "Bank Rate, The British Balance of Payments, and the Burdens of Adjustment, 1870-1914," *Oxford Economic Papers* 16 (March 1964): 24-39. Ford points out that insofar as deflation did occur in the periphery, demand for British exports was also reduced; accordingly, at least some resource unemployment was experienced in the United Kingdom as well.

36. For a more detailed analysis of this phenomenon, see Benjamin J. Cohen, "Mixing Oil and Money," in J. C. Hurewitz, ed., *Oil, the Arab-Israel Dispute, and the Industrial World: Horizons of Crisis* (Boulder, Colo.: Westview Press, 1976), pp. 195-211.

37. The costs of information gathering and decision making, and the duration of temporary unemployment of productive resources, are a direct function of the degree of mobility and flexibility in goods and factor markets. The greater the imperfections of competitive conditions in a national economy, the greater will be frictional changeover costs, regardless of the choice of particular adjustment policies.

38. See, e.g., Tibor Scitovsky, *Requirements of an International Reserve System*, Essays in International Finance, no. 49 (Princeton: International Finance Section, 1965).

39. Jacques L'Huillier, "Some Misconceptions on the Sharing of the Burden of Adjustment between Deficit and Surplus Countries," in Michael B. Connolly and Alexander K. Swoboda, eds., *International Trade and Money* (London: George Allen and Unwin, 1973), pp. 203-204.

40. Herbert Stein, "The Evolving International Monetary System and Domestic Economic Policy," *American Economic Review* 55 (May 1965): 204.

41. The conventional economics literature offers few clues concerning this question. In fact, to my knowledge only two serious discussions of the issue have so far appeared in print. One, by Robert Mundell, suggests that the distribution of transitional adjustment costs depends on the size of the countries involved (specifically, on the size of their respective money supplies). The other, by myself, suggests that it is necessary to decompose the ambiguous concept of size into more specific structural attributes of national economies, such as diversification of production, degree of industrialization, international investment status, and secular growth rate. See Robert A. Mundell, *International Economics* (New York: Macmillan, 1968), chap. 13; and Cohen, *Adjustment Costs.*

42. See Herbert G. Grubel, "The Distribution of Seigniorage from International Liquidity Creation," and Harry G. Johnson, "A Note on Seigniorage and the Social Saving from Substituting Credit for Commodity Money," in Robert A. Mundell and Alexander K. Swoboda, eds., *Monetary Problems of the International Economy* (Chicago: University of Chicago Press, 1969), pp. 269-282, 323-329; and Benjamin J. Cohen, "International Reserves and Liquidity," in Peter B. Kenen, ed., *International Trade and Finance: Frontiers for Research* (New York and Cambridge: Cambridge University Press, 1975), pp. 441-445.

43. For citations, see below, chapters 5-8.

44. Cooper, "Prolegomena," pp. 69-70.

45. See, e.g., E. M. Harmon, *Commodity Reserve Currency* (New York: Columbia University Press, 1959); and two articles by Albert G. Hart, "The Case For and Against an International Commodity Reserve Currency," *Oxford Economic Papers* 18 (July 1966): 237-241, and "The Case as of 1976 for International Commodity-Reserve Currency," *Weltwirtschaftliches Archiv* 112, Heft 1 (1976): 1-32. A commodity-reserve-currency standard would employ a reserve asset issued by a duly constituted international agency, as required by the liquidity needs of the monetary order, in exchange for

primary commodities acquired in world markets. These commodities would then be stored as backing for the reserve asset. Producers of the primary commodities would benefit in two ways: first, from the effective price support of their exports; and second, from the additional command over real resources embodied in the reserve assets they receive in payment.

46. Fritz Machlup, "The Cloakroom Rule of International Reserves," *Quarterly Journal of Economics* 79 (August 1965): 353-355.

47. Alexander K. Swoboda, *The Euro-Dollar Market: An Interpretation*, Essays in International Finance, no. 64 (Princeton: International Finance Section, 1968), p. 12. In fact, no national banking system has such monopolies, owing to the existence of the Eurocurrency and worldwide foreign-exchange markets. Thus, at least some transactions in the national currency, though certainly not all, are likely to take place outside the frontiers of the reserve center, and the private seigniorage gains of the financial sector will be correspondingly reduced. See ibid., pp. 17-19.

48. The key assumption of this method is that IMF quotas do in fact reflect each country's average long-term demand for reserves, so that on average and over the long term, cumulative allocations of SDRs will actually be held rather than used to acquire or lend resources through the monetary system. (That is, there will be no permanent unrequited redistribution of wealth internationally.) Empirical evidence suggests, however, that IMF quotas may in fact underestimate the average long-term demand for reserves of less-developed countries and correspondingly overestimate that of advanced countries, in which case the method of allocating SDRs in proportion to quotas may actually shift resources internationally from the poor to the rich. See Robert G. Hawkins and C. Rangarajan, "On the Distribution of New International Reserves," *Journal of Finance* 25 (June 1970): 881-891.

49. See Y. S. Park, *The Link Between Special Drawing Rights and Development Finance*, Essays in International Finance, no. 100 (Princeton: International Finance Section, 1973); and Geoffrey Maynard, "Special Drawing Rights and Development Aid," *Journal of Development Studies* 9 (July 1973): 518-543.

50. See, e.g., Robert Z. Aliber, "The Costs and Benefits of the U.S. Role as a Reserve Currency Country," *Quarterly Journal of Economics* 78 (August 1964): 442-456; Herbert G. Grubel, "The Benefits and Costs of Being the World Banker," *National Banking Review* 2 (December 1964): 189-212; John R. Karlik, "The Costs and Benefits of Being a Reserve Currency Country: A Theoretical Approach Applied to the United States," in Peter B. Kenen and Roger Lawrence, eds., *The Open Economy: Essays on International Trade and Finance* (New York: Columbia University Press, 1968); Benjamin J. Cohen, *The Future of Sterling as an International Currency* (London: Macmillan, 1971) chap. 5; and Bergsten, *Dilemmas of the Dollar*, chap. 7.

51. In the case of a secondary reserve center such as the United Kingdom, which was confronted by conditions approximating perfect competition and free entry, it appears that virtually all of the net seigniorage benefit was redistributed to overseas sterling holders. See Benjamin J. Cohen, "The Seigniorage Gain of an International Currency: An Empirical Test," *Quarterly Journal of Economics* 85 (August 1971): 494-507.

52. Aubrey, *Behind the Veil*, p. 9.

53. See Mundell, *International Economics*, pp. 195-198.

Chapter 3

1. The historical treatment of the classical gold standard in this section is necessarily cursory. For a fuller exposition, see, e.g., Leland B. Yeager, *International Monetary Relations* (New York: Harper and Row, 1966), chap. 14.

2. Carlo M. Cipolla, *Money, Prices, and Civilization in the Mediterranean World: Fifth to Seventeenth Century* (Princeton: Princeton University Press, 1956), chap. 2.

3. See Arthur I. Bloomfield, *Short-Term Capital Movements Under the Pre-1914 Gold Standard*, Studies in International Finance, no. 11 (Princeton: International Finance Section, 1963), pp. 7-19; and Peter H. Lindert, *Key Currencies and Gold, 1900-1913*, Studies in International Finance, no. 24 (Princeton: International Finance Section, 1969), pp. 9-16. Bloomfield's ("almost complete") figures of official foreign-exchange holdings show a total of $963 million at the end of 1913, up from $60-70 million in 1880 and $130-150 million in 1899. Lindert's figures ("at least 90 percent of the world total") show a total of $1,132 million at the end of 1913. The resulting ratios of gold to foreign-exchange reserves of 5:1 (Bloomfield) or 4:1 (Lindert) are much higher than the ratio of roughly 1:1 effective at the height of the Bretton Woods era.

4. Arthur I. Bloomfield, *Monetary Policy under the International Gold Standard, 1880-1914* (New York: Federal Reserve Bank of New York, 1959).

5. A central bank's deposit-reserve ratio (i.e., the fraction of the domestic banking system's deposit liabilities backed by cash reserves held with the central bank) is the inverse of the so-called *deposit-creation multiplier*, which identifies the extent to which the domestic money supply may, in principle, be changed by a change in the level of central bank reserves. If the deposit-reserve ratio is 50 percent, a one-unit change of central-bank reserves may lead to a full two-unit change of the domestic money supply (the deposit-creation-multiplier is 2); if the reserve ratio is 5 percent, the domestic money supply could in principle change by as much as 20 units (the multiplier is 20).

6. Robert Triffin, *Our International Monetary System: Yesterday, Today, and Tomorrow* (New York: Random House, 1968), chap. 1. The terms-of-trade changes to which Triffin refers were the mechanism by which core countries like Britain managed to transfer most of the continuing cost of adjustment to the periphery, as explained above in Chapter 2.

7. Ibid., p. 9.

8. Ibid., p. 13.

9. See Benjamin J. Cohen, *The Future of Sterling as an International Currency* (London: Macmillan, 1971), pp. 58-63.

10. See, e.g., David Williams, "The Evolution of the Sterling System," in C. R. Whittlesey and J. S. G. Wilson, eds., *Essays in Money and Banking* (Oxford: Oxford University Press, 1968,) pp. 266-297; and Harold van Buren Cleveland, "The International Monetary System in the Interwar Period," in Benjamin M. Rowland, ed., *Balance of Power or Hegemony: The Interwar Monetary System* (New York: New York University Press, 1976), pp. 18-22.

11. See Charles P. Kindleberger, *The World in Depression, 1929-1939* (Berkeley and Los Angeles: University of California Press, 1973), p. 292.

12. Yeager, *International Monetary Relations*, p. 261*n*; italics in the original.

13. Fred Hirsch, *Money International* (London: Penguin, 1967), p. 28.

14. See, e.g., Cleveland, "International Monetary System," in Rowland, *Balance of Power*, pp. 23-27; and, in the same volume, David P. Calleo, "The Historiography of the Interwar Period: Reconsiderations," pp. 237-246.

15. Marcello de Cecco, *Money and Empire: The International Gold Standard, 1890-1914* (Oxford: Basil Blackwell, 1974), p. 128.

16. The classic sources on the financial history of the interwar period are W. A. Brown, *The International Gold Standard Reinterpreted, 1914-1934*, 2 vols. (New York: National Bureau of Economic Research, 1940); and League of Nations, *International Currency Experience* (1944). See also Yeager, *International Monetary Relations*, chaps. 15-17.

17. Currency Resolution of the Genoa Conference, as quoted in League of Nations, *International Currency Experience*, p. 28.

18. Ibid. As another economy measure, central banks were also urged to withdraw gold coins from circulation.

19. The word "experiment" is Brown's. See Brown, *Gold Standard*, 2: 731. For a discussion of the participating nations, see ibid., 2: 732-734.

20. This is the customary interpretation of events after 1931. But for a contrary view, arguing that the depreciations of the period were not competitive, see Sidney E. Rolfe and James L. Burtle, *The Great Wheel: The World Monetary System—A Reinterpretation* (London: Macmillan, 1974), part 1.

21. Because the Tripartite Agreement contained an escape clause permitting revocation of obligations on one day's notice, it quickly became known as the "twenty-four-hour" gold standard.

22. League of Nations, *International Currency Experience*, p. 105.

23. Kindleberger, *World in Depression*, pp. 298, 299, and 301.

24. "The system as a whole was compromised by the special difficulties due to the undervaluation of the French franc, the repatriation of private French funds and the desire of the French authorities to return to a fully metallic standard" (League of Nations, *International Currency Experience*, p. 217).

25. Brown, *Gold Standard*, 2: 769.

26. Comprehensive histories of the wartime discussions and Bretton Woods Conference can be found in International Monetary Fund, *The International Monetary Fund, 1945-1965*, (Washington, D.C.: 1969), vol. 1, part 1; and Richard N. Gardner, *Sterling-Dollar Diplomacy* (Oxford: Clarendon Press, 1956), chaps. 5, 7.

27. For a representative example of the "conventional wisdom" of the day, see League of Nations, *International Currency Experience*, chap. 9 ("Review and Conclusion").

28. Ibid., p. 211.

29. Ibid.

30. Ibid., p. 214.

31. Ibid., p. 218.

32. Even this privilege was restricted after 1934 to central banks only. Since World War II no other currency has any longer been convertible directly into gold. Once exchange control was invented in the 1930s, convertibility generally came to have a different meaning than previously: the privilege of exchanging a currency not for gold but simply for other currencies.

33. Ibid., p. 229.

34. Ibid., p. 220.

35. Ibid., pp. 226-227.

36. Ibid., p. 46.

37. For a history of monetary developments in the first years after the war, see Yeager, *International Monetary Relations*, chaps. 18-25.

38. The expression "benign neglect" did not come into vogue until the late 1960s. See Gottfried Haberler and Thomas D. Willett, *A Strategy for U.S. Balance of Payments Policy* (Washington: American Enterprise Institute, 1971).

39. Marina v. N. Whitman, "The Current and Future Role of the Dollar: How Much Symmetry?" *Brookings Papers on Economic Activity*, no. 3 (1974): 542.

40. Benjamin J. Cohen, "The Revolution in Atlantic Economic Relations: A Bargain Comes Unstuck," in Wolfram Hanrieder, ed., *The United States and Western Europe: Political, Economic and Strategic Perspectives* (Cambridge, Mass.: Winthrop, 1974), pp. 113-120.

41. Marina v. N. Whitman, "Leadership Without Hegemony," *Foreign Policy*, no. 20 (Fall 1975): 140.

42. Once again, the historical treatment here is necessarily cursory. For fuller expositions, see Richard N. Cooper, *The Economics of Interdependence* (New York: McGraw-Hill, 1968), chap. 2; Rolfe and Burtle, *Great Wheel*, chaps. 5-8; C. Fred Bergsten, *The Dilemmas of the Dollar* (New York: Council on Foreign Relations, 1975), pp. 62-95; and Susan Strange, "International Monetary Relations," in Andrew Shonfield, ed., *International Economic Relations of the Western World, 1959-1971, Vol. 2: International Monetary Relations* (London: Oxford University Press, 1976), pp. 18-359.

43. Harold van Buren Cleveland, "How the Dollar Standard Died," in Richard N. Cooper, ed., *A Reordered World: Emerging International Economic Problems* (Washington, D. C.: Potomac Associates, 1973), p. 67.

44. David P. Calleo, "American Foreign Policy and American European Studies: An Imperial Bias?", in Hanrieder, *United States and Western Europe*, p. 62.

45. Rolfe and Burtle, *Great Wheel*, p. 60.

46. Robert Triffin, *Gold and the Dollar Crisis* (New Haven: Yale University Press, 1960). The book first appeared in the form of two long journal articles in 1959.

47. For two views of the SDR negotiations, see Fritz Machlup, *Remaking the International Monetary System* (Baltimore: Johns Hopkins Press, 1968); and Stephen D. Cohen, *International Monetary Reform, 1964-69: The Political Dimension* (New York: Praeger, 1970). For more on the SDR in concept and practice, see below, Chapters 4 and 6.

The Group of Ten first came into existence in 1961 with the General Arrangements to Borrow. In fact, the group included eleven countries, since all of its meetings were attended by Switzerland—a nonmember of the IMF—on an ex officio basis.

48. Eurodollars, for example, are simply dollars deposited in banks located outside of the United States. On the origins and operation of the Eurocurrency market, see, e.g., Jane Sneddon Little, *Euro-Dollars: The Money-Market Gypsies* (New York: Harper and Row, 1975).

49. Robert A. Mundell, "Optimum Currency Areas," *Economic Notes* 3 (September-December 1975): 36.

50. See, e.g., Charles P. Kindleberger, "The International Monetary Politics of a Near-Great Power: Two French Episodes, 1926-1936 and 1960-1970," *Economic Notes* 1 (May-December 1972): 30-41.

51. See, e.g., Fritz Machlup, *Involuntary Foreign Lending* (Stockholm: Almqvist and Wiksell, 1965), pp. 28-38.

52. See, e.g., James S. Duesenberry, "Worldwide Inflation: A Fiscalist View," in David I. Meiselman and Arthur B. Laffer, eds., *The Phenomenon of Worldwide Inflation* (Washington, D.C.: American Enterprise Institute, 1975), pp. 113-124. But for a contrary view, cf. H. Robert Heller, "International Reserves and World-Wide Inflation," *International Monetary Fund Staff Papers* 23 (March 1976): 65-70. Heller argues that it was not the overheating of the American economy but rather a shift by the private sector out of dollars and into other currencies that was mainly responsible for the huge increase of the world's reserve base after 1965. In a statistical sense this was true. But in an analytical sense the argument begs the key question: what caused the shift out of dollars by the private sector? In fact, it was the deterioration of the U.S. balance of payments—and that was due precisely to the overheating of the American economy. Heller's argument mistakes symptom for cause.

53. Robert Gilpin, *U.S. Power and the Multinational Corporation: The Political Economy of Foreign Direct Investment* (New York: Basic Books, 1975), pp. 40-41.

54. Ibid., p. 43.

55. See Robert O. Keohane and Joseph S. Nye, *Power and Interdependence: World Politics in Transition* (Boston: Little, Brown, 1977), esp. chap. 3; and Andrew Shonfield, ed., *International Economic Relations of the Western World, 1959-1971*. Vol. 1: *Politics and Trade* (London: Oxford University Press, 1976), pp. 93-137.

56. Robert Z. Aliber, *Monetary Reform and World Inflation*, The Washington Papers, vol. 1 (Beverly Hills and London: Sage Publications, 1973), p. 63.

Chapter 4

1. For more on the Smithsonian Agreement and its aftermath, see Sidney E. Rolfe and James L. Burtle, *The Great Wheel: The World Monetary System—A Reinterpretation* (London: Macmillan, 1974), chap. 9.

2. Modeling the Committee of Twenty on the Executive Board was acceptable to Third World countries because it gave them assurance of nine seats. It was acceptable to developed countries because they were not outnumbered. For a comprehensive analytic history of the Committee of Twenty, see John Williamson, *The Failure of World Monetary Reform, 1971-74* (London: Thomas Nelson, 1977). See also Benjamin J. Cohen, "Major Issues of World Monetary Reform," in *Trade, Inflation and Ethics: Critical Choices for Americans*, (Lexington, Mass: D.C. Heath, 1976), 5: 47-78.

3. Jeremy Morse, as quoted in *IMF Survey*, April 8, 1974, p. 97.

4. Committee on Reform of the International Monetary System and Related Issues, *International Monetary Reform: Documents of the Committee of Twenty* (Washington, D.C.: International Monetary Fund, 1974).

5. *Outline of Reform*, ¶ 2, in ibid.

6. Ibid., # annex 4.

7. See *IMF Survey*, June 17, 1974, pp. 177, 185.

8. For a discussion of this and alternative valuation techniques, see *Outline of Reform*, annex 9.

9. See *IMF Survey*, January 19, 1976; and International Monetary Fund, *Annual Report 1976* (Washington, D.C., 1976), chap. 3 and appendix III.

10. *Proposed Second Amendment to the Articles of Agreement of the International Monetary Fund: A Report by the Executive Directors* (Washington, D.C.: International Monetary Fund, 1976). Hereafter referred to as *Second Amendment*.

11. See *IMF Survey*, May 3, 1976, p. 129.

12. Ratification of amendments to the Articles of Agreement requires acceptance by three-fifths of the members of the Fund representing four-fifths of the total voting power.

13. Willy de Clercq, "Important Stage in International Monetary History," *NATO Review* 24 (April 1976): 12.

14. William Simon, as quoted in *International Herald Tribune*, January 10, 1976, p. 7.

15. *International Herald Tribune*, January 13, 1976, p. 9.

16. The portion of the profits corresponding to the shares of eligible developing countries in total Fund quotas was to be transferred directly to these countries.

17. Tom de Vries, "Jamaica, or the Non-Reform of the International Monetary System," *Foreign Affairs* 54 (April 1976): 603. For a variety of other views on the package, see the eight essays collected in Edward M. Bernstein et al., *Reflections on Jamaica*, Essays in International Finance, no. 115 (Princeton: International Finance Section, 1976).

18. Robert O. Keohane and Joseph S. Nye, "World Politics and the International Economic System," in C. Fred Bergsten, ed., *The Future of the International Economic Order: An Agenda for Research* (Lexington, Mass.: D. C. Heath, 1973), p. 134; and Harold van Buren Cleveland, "Modes of International Economic Organization: A Stalemate System," in David P. Calleo, ed., *Money and the Coming World Order* (New York: New York University Press, 1976), pp. 1-14.

19. Fritz Machlup, "Between Outline and Outcome the Reform was Lost," in Bernstein et al., *Reflections on Jamaica*, p. 30.

20. *Second Amendment*, Article IV (1).

21. See, e.g., Fred Hirsch and David Higham, "Floating Rates—Expectations and Experience," *Three Banks Review*, June 1974, pp. 3-34; and Samuel I. Katz, "'Managed Floating' as an Interim International Exchange Rate Regime, 1973-1975," *The Bulletin* (New York University, Graduate School of Business Administration, Institute of Finance), 1975-3.

22. Declaration of Rambouillet, November 17, 1975, ¶ 12.

23. See *Outline of Reform*, ¶ 4-17 and annexes 1-4.

24. Edward M. Bernstein, "The New International Monetary System," in Bernstein et al., *Reflections on Jamaica*, p. 10. Robert Triffin's comment is more biting: "I find this text more worthy of a slapstick comedy than of a solemn treaty defining a new international monetary system." See Triffin, "Jamaica: 'Major Revision' or Fiasco?", in ibid., p. 47.

25. See *International Herald Tribune*, November 19, 1975, p. 1.

26. Robert V. Roosa, "Some Questions Remaining," in Bernstein et al., *Reflections on Jamaica*, p. 42.

27. Suppose the Deutsche mark moved up against the dollar by 1 percent, while the French franc moved down by 1 percent. In relation to each, the dollar exchange rate had changed by 1 percent; the mark-franc rate, however, had changed by 2 percent.

28. J. Marcus Fleming, "Floating Exchange Rates, Asymmetrical Intervention, and the Management of International Liquidity," *International Monetary Fund Staff Papers* 22 (July 1975): 267.

29. Richard N. Cooper, "Eurodollars, Reserve Dollars and Asymmetries in the International Monetary System," *Journal of International Economics* 2 (September 1972): 325-344.

30. See *Outline of Reform*, ¶ 12 and annex 3.

31. Peter B. Kenen, "After Nairobi—Beware the Rhinopotamus," *Euromoney*, November 1973, p. 19.

32. See Council of Economic Advisers, *Annual Report, 1973*, pp. 160-174; and U.S. Treasury, "U.S. Views on Major Issues of Monetary Reform," press release, August 27, 1973, pp. 3-5.

33. *Outline of Reform*, ¶ 10.

34. See ibid., annex 2.

35. Ibid., ¶ 31.

36. *Second Amendment,* Article XII (1).

37. Article IV (3).

38. Articles VIII (7) and XXII.

39. Articles of Agreement of the International Monetary Fund, Article IV (unamended). The Article went on to read " . . . or in terms of the United States dollar of the weight and fineness in effect on July 1, 1944." This appeared to give the dollar equal status as a numeraire—but appearances can be misleading. All it actually did was give equal status to the *gold value* of the dollar of July 1, 1944—to be precise, to 0.888671 grams of fine gold. In other words, the Article was redundant: par values were to be expressed in terms of gold.

40. The italics identify the key original constraints on SDR use. For more detail, see Chapter 6.

41. *Second Amendment,* Articles XIX (2) and (3).

42. Ibid., ch. Q.

43. See *Outline of Reform*, annex 3.

44. See ibid., annex 7.

45. Machlup. "Between Outline and Outcome," p. 34.

46. See *IMF Survey*, January 19, 1976, p. 19.

47. Ibid.

48. Ibid. One point left unclear was whether this initial two-year period dated from August 1975 (the time of the Washington understanding) or January 1976 (the time of the Jamaica meeting).

49. Technically, central banks were prohibited by the existing IMF Charter from purchasing gold at a price above $42.22 per ounce. To get around this restriction, pending approval and ratification of the amendment abolishing the official gold price, central banks were expected to use the Bank for International Settlements in Basel as an intermediary buying agent. In addition to the Bank of France, the central banks of Belgium and Switzerland were reportedly interested in buying some of the IMF gold. See *International Herald Tribune*, January 13, 1976, p. 9.

50. *The Economist*, January 17, 1976, p. 81. In the opinion of some observers, far from being phased out of the monetary system, gold was merely being phased out of the IMF. See "Gold: The Winter of Our Discontent," *Financial Mail* (South Africa), August 13, 1976 (supp.), p. 26.

51. *Outline of Reform*, annex 7.

52. Henry S. Reuss, "The Golden Rule, IMF Style," *Congressional Record*, September 17, 1975, H. 8776, 8777.

53. *IMF Survey*, January 19, 1976, pp. 23, 24. In addition, of course, LDCs would benefit from their share of the Fund's planned restitution of gold holdings. Witteveen's estimate of the anticipated profit from Fund gold sales was disputed by many informed observers, such as the general manager of the BIS, who argued that in the thin gold market, the prospect of sales of such magnitude was bound to depress price and reduce revenue. (See *International Herald Tribune*, January 7, 1976, p. 7.) This of course added to the incentive of the poor countries to join in a de facto coalition with the rich countries and gold producers to set an informal official floor price or price range for gold transactions in the future. As it turned out, the gold price *was* depressed, from near $140 per ounce in January to a $120-125 range by the time of the first two auction sales in June and July. See *Finance and Development* 13 (September 1976): 2.

54. See, e.g., Edward R. Fried and Charles L. Schultze, eds., *Higher Oil Prices and the World Economy* (Washington, D.C.: Brookings Institution, 1975).

55. For more detail, see Benjamin J. Cohen, "Mixing Oil and Money," in J. C. Hurewitz, ed., *Oil, the Arab-Israel Dispute, and the Industrial World: Horizons of Crisis* (Boulder, Colo.: Westview Press, 1976), pp. 197-198.

56. But cf. John Williamson, "The International Financial System," in Fried and Schultze, *Higher Oil Prices*, pp. 203-208.

57. Again, cf. Williamson, "International Financial System," pp. 215-216.

58. See *IMF Survey*, September 16, 1974, p. 304.

59. All that occurs in the dollar liabilities of the United States is a change of ownership of the original deposit, from the central bank that previously owned it to the Eurocurrency bank in London. The potential deposit-creation multiplier in the Eurocurrency market is very high because reserve requirements in the market are extremely low or nonexistent.

60. See Helmut W. Mayer, *Some Theoretical Problems Relating to the Euro-Dollar Market*, Essays in International Finance, no. 79 (Princeton: International Finance Section, 1970), p. 13. See also Fritz Machlup, "The Magicians and Their Rabbits," *Morgan Guaranty Survey*, May 1971, pp. 3-13.

61. See Jane Sneddon Little, *Euro-Dollars: The Money-Market Gypsies* (New York: Harper and Row, 1975), pp. 198-199.

62. Guido Carli, "Why Banks Are Unpopular," lecture quoted in *IMF Survey*, July 19, 1976, pp. 212-214.

63. Wilbur F. Monroe, *International Monetary Reconstruction* (Lexington, Mass.: D. C. Heath, 1974), p. 81.

64. For a more extensive discussion of the U.S. interest in and attitudes on monetary reform, see C. Fred Bergsten, *The Dilemmas of the Dollar* (New York: Council on Foreign Relations, 1975), chaps. 10-14.

65. See, e.g., Judith L. Kooker, "French Financial Diplomacy: The Interwar Years," in Benjamin M. Rowland, ed., *Balance of Power or Hegemony: The Interwar Monetary System* (New York: New York University Press, 1976), pp. 85-145.

66. See F. Boyer de la Giroday, *Myths and Reality in the Development of International Monetary Affairs*, Essays in International Finance, no. 105 (Princeton: International Finance Section, 1974), p. 16.

67. For more detail on the origins and early experience of the "snake," see Arthur I. Bloomfield, "The Historical Setting," in Lawrence B. Krause and Walter S. Salant, eds., *European Monetary Unification and Its Meaning for the United States* (Washington, D.C.: Brookings Institution, 1973) pp. 1-30.

68. *Report of the Study Group "Economic and Monetary Union 1980"* (Brussels, March 1975), p. 1.

69. See, e.g., Benjamin J. Cohen, "The Euro-Dollar, the Common Market, and Currency Unification," *Journal of Finance* 18 (December 1963): 605-621.

70. *Report of the Study Group "Economic and Monetary Union 1980,"* p. 3.

71. Fred Hirsch, "The Politics of World Money," *The Economist*, August 5, 1972, p. 57.

72. Geoffrey Maynard and Graham Bird, "International Monetary Issues and the Developing Countries: A Survey," *World Development* 3 (September 1975): 610.

73. *Group of Ten, Report of Deputies*, July 1966, ¶ 60.

Chapter 5

1. Paul Einzig, *The Destiny of Gold* (London: Macmillan, 1972), pp. 1, 7-8.

2. Ian Shannon, *Gold and the American Balance of Payments* (Chicago: Henry Regnery, 1966), p. 22.

3. Charles de Gaulle, press conference, February 4, 1965. De Gaulle's views on the subject were greatly influenced by the advice he received from the eminent French economist Jacques Rueff, an ardent advocate of the gold standard for more than half a century. For a representative sample of Rueff's views, see Jacques Rueff, "The Rueff Approach," in Randall Hinshaw, ed., *Monetary Reform and the Price of Gold* (Baltimore: Johns Hopkins Press, 1967), pp. 37-46.

For a representative sample of other recent advocates of the gold standard, see the essays collected in Hans F. Sennholz, ed., *Gold Is Money* (Westport, Conn.: Greenwood Press, 1975); and Lewis E. Lehrman, "The Creation of International Monetary Order," in David P. Calleo, ed., *Money and the Coming World Order* (New York: New York University Press, 1976), pp. 71-120. Also, see below, the discussion of the so-called Mundell-Laffer hypothesis.

4. Einzig, *Destiny of Gold*, p. vii.

5. Charles P. Kindleberger, "Lessons of Floating Exchange Rates," paper prepared for the Carnegie-Mellon/Rochester University Monetary Conference, November 1974, mimeographed, p. 26.

6. Fritz Machlup, "International Monetary Systems and the Free Market Economy," in American Enterprise Institute, *International Payments Problems* (Washington, D.C.: American Enterprise Institute, 1966), p. 158.

7. Shannon, *Gold*, p. 22.

8. Don D. Humphrey, "The Case for Gold," in C. Fred Bergsten and William Tyler, eds., *Leading Issues in International Economic Policy: Essays in Honor of George N. Halm* (Lexington, Mass.: D. C. Heath, 1973), p. 88.

9. Robert A. Mundell, "Toward a Better International Monetary System," *Journal of Money, Credit and Banking*, 1 (August 1969): 646.

10. See Benjamin J. Cohen, "International Reserves and Liquidity," in Peter B. Kenen, ed., *International Trade and Finance: Frontiers for Research* (New York and Cambridge: Cambridge University Press, 1975), pp. 425-426.

11. A gold price increase has also been advocated by other writers who are not gold-standard enthusiasts and who are in fact opposed to such an impersonal and fully automatic monetary order. Such writers favor, rather, a *gold-exchange standard* and base their advocacy on the premise that a gold price increase is necessary to make a gold-exchange standard work better. See, e.g., Humphrey, "The Case for Gold," in Bergsten and Tyler, *Leading Issues*; Sir Roy Harrod, *Reforming the World's Money* (London: Macmillan, 1965), chap. 3; Miroslav A. Kriz, *Gold: Barbarous Relic or Useful Instrument?*, Essays in International Finance, no. 60 (Princeton: International Finance Section, 1967); and Milton Gilbert, *The Gold-Dollar System: Conditions of Equilibrium and the Price of Gold*, Essays in International Finance, no. 70 (Princeton: International Finance Section, 1968). See also below, Chapter 7.

12. John Williamson, *The Failure of World Monetary Reform, 1971-74* (London: Thomas Nelson, 1977).

13. Egon Sohmen, *Flexible Exchange Rates*, rev. ed. (Chicago: University of Chicago Press, 1969), p. xii.

14. Harry G. Johnson, "The Case for Flexible Exchange Rates, 1969," in Goerge N. Halm, ed., *Approaches to Greater Flexibility of Exchange Rates: The Bürgenstock Papers* (Princeton: Princeton University Press, 1970), p. 92.

15. Milton Friedman, "The Case for Flexible Exchange Rates," in Friedman, *Essays in Positive Economics* (Chicago: University of Chicago Press, 1953), pp. 157-203.

16. Johnson, "The Case . . . 1969," p. 97.

17. Ibid., p. 109.

18. Robert A. Mundell, "A Plan for a European Currency," in Harry G. Johnson and Alexander G. Swoboda, eds., *The Economics of Common Currencies* (Cambridge, Mass.: Harvard University Press, 1973), p. 149.

19. Vicente Galbis, "Monetary and Exchange Rate Policies in a Small Open Economy," *International Monetary Fund Staff Papers* 22 (July 1975): 329.

20. Charles P. Kindleberger, "The Case for Fixed Exchange Rates," in *The International Adjustment Mechanism* (Boston: Federal Reserve Bank of Boston, 1970), pp. 94, 95.

21. For a useful survey of this topic, see Robert D. McTeer, "Economic Independence and Insulation Through Flexible Exchange Rates," in Nicholas A. Beadles and L. Aubrey Drewry, Jr., eds., *Money, the Market and the State* (Athens, Ga.: University of Georgia Press, 1968), pp. 102-133.

22. Peter B. Kenen, "Flexible Exchange Rates and National Autonomy," *Rivista internazionale di scienze economiche e commerciali* 23, no. 2 (1976): 120.

23. McTeer, "Economic Independence," p. 129; italics in the original.

24. Kindleberger, "Case for Fixed Exchange Rates," p. 95.

25. See, e.g., Samuel I. Katz, "'Imported Inflation' and the Balance of Payments," *The Bulletin* (New York University, Graduate School of Business

Administration, Institute of Finance), nos. 91-92 (October 1973); Organization for Economic Cooperation and Development, "The International Transmission of Inflation," *Economic Outlook* (OECD), no. 13 (July 1973): 81-96; and Gottfried Haberler, "Inflation as a Worldwide Phenomenon—An Overview," in David I. Meiselman and Arthur B. Laffer, eds., *The Phenomenon of Worldwide Inflation* (Washington: American Enterprise Institute, 1975), pp. 13-25.

26. Of course, even with fixed rates, the discipline imposed by fear of reserve losses is incomplete, as noted above. Still, there is nothing in logic (or psychology) to suggest that by removing a deterrent, even an incomplete one, we leave unaffected the behavior supposedly being deterred. At best, we may hope that there will be no significant change of behavior; more realistically, we must assume that behavior will deteriorate to some extent. Fritz Machlup argues that "on theoretical grounds it cannot be established that central bankers would be more inclined to inflate under flexible-rate systems than under fixed-rate systems" (see Machlup, "International Monetary Systems," p. 161). But a fairer presumption would be less sanguine. Only if fear of exchange-rate depreciation is as strong as fear of reserve losses will the discipline on behavior remain the same. But that, in turn, would imply that central banks are prepared to surrender the very policy autonomy that flexibility is intended to provide. It is probably more realistic to assume that, if provided with greater autonomy, central banks will use it.

27. Helen B. Junz and Rudolf R. Rhomberg, "Price Competitiveness in Export Trade Among Industrial Countries," *American Economic Review* 63 (May 1973): 412-418.

28. Kindleberger, "Lessons of Floating Exchange Rates," p. 25. One of the first writers to stress the "ratchet" effect of floating rates was Robert Triffin. See his *Gold and the Dollar Crisis* (New Haven: Yale University Press, 1960), pp. 82-83.

29. OECD, "International Transmission of Inflation," p. 81.

30. See, e.g., Marina v. N. Whitman, "The Payments Adjustment Process and the Exchange Rate Regime: What Have We Learned?", *American Economic Review* 65 (May 1975): 141-144; and Andrew D. Crockett and Morris Goldstein, "Inflation Under Fixed and Flexible Exchange Rates," *International Monetary Fund Staff Papers*, 3 (November 1976): 509-544.

31. Samuel I. Katz, "Exchange-Risk Under Fixed and Flexible Exchange Rates," *The Bulletin* (New York University, Graduate School of Business Administration, Institute of Finance), nos. 83-84 (June 1972), p. 9.

32. Charles P. Kindleberger, "The Benefits of International Money," *Journal of International Economics* 2 (September 1972): 425

33. For more detailed discussion of the forward market, see Benjamin J. Cohen, *Balance-of-Payments Policy* (Baltimore and London: Penguin Books, 1969), chap. 2.

34. A related activity is "hedging," which technically refers to purchases or sales of forward exchange to protect the value of capital assets rather than anticipated receipts or payments. See ibid., pp. 59-60.

35. Johnson, "The Case . . . 1969," p. 101.

36. Anthony Lanyi, *The Case for Floating Exchange Rates Reconsidered*, Essays in International Finance, no. 72 (Princeton: International Finance Section, 1969), p. 16.

37. See Kindleberger, "Case for Fixed Exchange Rates," pp. 102-105; and Katz, *Exchange-Risk*, esp. chap. 2.

38. See Michael G. Duerr, *Protecting Corporate Assets Under Floating Currencies* (New York: The Conference Board, 1975); and H. Fournier and J. E. Wadsworth, eds., *Floating Exchange Rates—The Lessons of Recent Experience* (Leyden: A. W. Sijthoff, 1976), pp. 15-29, 95-103.

39. Johnson, "The Case . . . 1969," p. 99.

40. Friedman, "Flexible Exchange Rates."

41. See, e.g., W. J. Baumol, "Speculation, Profitability and Stability," *Review of Economics and Statistics* 39 (1957): 263-271; Jerome L. Stein, "Destabilizing Speculative Activity Can Be Profitable," *Review of Economics and Statistics* 43 (1961): 301-302; and John Williamson, "Another Case of Profitable Destabilizing Speculation," *Journal of International Economics* 3 (February 1973): 77-83. But cf. Sohmen, *Flexible Exchange Rates*, pp. 59-74.

42. Harry G. Johnson, "Destabilizing Speculation: A General Equilibrium Approach," *Journal of Political Economy* 84 (February 1976): 107.

43. See Whitman, "What Have We Learned?" 137-138; and Ronald I. McKinnon, "Instability in Floating Exchange Rates: A Qualified Monetary Interpretation," paper prepared for the meetings of the Western Economic Association, June 1976, mimeographed.

44. Paul A. Volcker, "Domestic Adjustment to Balance of Payments Disequilibrium: Discussion," *American Economic Review*, 65 (May 1975): 154. Theoretical developments reinforce this concern as well: recent models of exchange-rate determination suggest that overshooting is inherent in the dynamic adjustment process. See, e.g., Rudiger Dornbusch, "Expectations and Exchange Rate Dynamics," *Journal of Political Economy*, 84 (December 1976): 1161-1176.

45. For more detail on the "monetary" approach to the balance of payments, see Jacob A. Frenkel and Harry G. Johnson, eds., *The Monetary Approach to the Balance of Payments* (London: George Allen and Unwin, 1976); and the proceedings of a conference, "Flexible Exchange Rates and Stabilization Policy," *Scandinavian Journal of Economics* 78, no. 2 (1976).

46. See, e.g., Arthur B. Laffer, "Balance of Payments and Exchange Rate Systems," *Financial Analysts Journal*, July/August 1974, pp. 1-10. There is no fully articulated exposition of Mundell's ideas on this subject in print, but only scraps in widely scattered and mostly ephemeral sources. For a review of the Mundel-Laffer view, see Marina v. N. Whitman, "Global Monetarism and the Monetary Approach to the Balance of Payments," *Brookings Papers on Economic Activity*, no. 3 (1975): 491-536.

47. Jude Wanniski, "The Mundell-Laffer Hypothesis—A New View of the World Economy," *Public Interest*, Spring 1975, p. 36.

48. Laffer, "Balance of Payments," pp. 2, 9.

49. Wanniski, "Mundell-Laffer," pp. 51-52.

50. This relationship, which goes under the rubric of the "theory of purchasing power parity," is well established empirically as a secular tendency. See Lawrence H. Officer, "The Purchasing-Power-Parity Theory of Exchange Rates: A Review Article," *International Monetary Fund Staff Papers* 23 (March 1976): 1-60.

51. See Whitman, "What Have We Learned," 138-141; Michael Connolly and Dean Taylor. "Testing the Monetary Approach to Devaluation in Developing Countries," *Journal of Political Economy* 84 (August 1976): 849-859; and Rudiger Dornbusch and Paul Krugman, "Flexible Exchange Rates in the Short Run," *Brookings Papers on Economic Activity*, 3 (1976): 558-568.

52. For a characteristic collection of such proposals, see, e.g., Halm, ed., *Bürgenstock Papers,* pp. 24-30.

53. See Fritz Machlup, "On Terms, Concepts, Theories, and Strategies in the Discussion of Greater Flexibility of Exchange Rates," in ibid., chap. 3; and Machlup, "Exchange-Rate Flexibility," *Banca Nazionale del Lavoro Quarterly Review,* no. 106 (September 1973): 183-205.

54. See also Herbert G. Grubel, "The Case for Optimum Exchange Rate Stability," *Weltwirtschaftliches Archiv* 109, Heft 3 (1973): 351-381; and John H. Makin, "Eurocurrencies and the Evolution of the International Monetary System," in Carl H. Stem, John H. Makin, and Dennis E. Logue, eds., *Euro-currencies and the International Monetary System* (Washington, D.C.: American Enterprise Institute, 1976), pp. 36-45.

55. Development of the modern theory of optimum currency areas originated with a seminal article by Robert Mundell. See Robert A. Mundell, "A Theory of Optimum Currency Areas," *American Economic Review* 51 (September 1961): 657-665. For useful surveys of the theory, see Thomas D. Willett and Edward Tower, "Currency Areas and Exchange-Rate Flexibility," *Weltwirtschaftliches Archiv* 105, Heft 1 (1970): 48-65; Yoshihide Ishiyama, "The Theory of Optimum Currency Areas: A Survey," *International Monetary Fund Staff Papers* 22 (July 1975): 344-383; and Edward Tower and Thomas D. Willett, *The Theory of Optimum Currency Areas and Exchange-Rate Flexibility,* Special Papers in International Economics, no. 11 (Princeton: International Finance Section, 1976).

56. Harry G. Johnson, "The Exchange Rate Question for a United Europe: Internal Flexibility and External Rigidity versus External Flexibility and Internal Rigidity," in Alexander K. Swoboda, ed., *Europe and the Evolution of the International Monetary System* (Leiden: A. W. Sijthoff, 1973), p. 85.

57. Ishiyama, "Theory of Optimum Currency Areas," p. 360.

58. Tower and Willett, *Theory,* p. 51.

59. Robert A. Mundell, "Uncommon Arguments for Common Currencies," in Johnson and Swoboda, eds., *Economics of Common Currencies,* p. 115.

60. Most LDCs simply lack the financial expertise and institutional sophistication required to manage a truly floating exchange rate. See "Developing Countries Faced with New Policy Questions with Rates Floating," *IMF Survey,* February 2, 1976, pp. 35-39. Of 97 LDCs surveyed in this article at the end of 1975, 72 were pegged to a single major currency (52 to the dollar alone), and 20 to some basket of major currencies. Only five were floating freely.

61. Robert A. Mundell, "Optimum Currency Areas," *Economic Notes* 3 (September-December 1975): 43-44.

62. Carlos F. Diaz-Alejandro, *Less Developed Countries and the Post-1971 International Financial System,* Essays in International Finance, no. 108 (Princeton: International Finance Section, 1975), pp. 7-8; italics in the original. A country's effective exchange rate is a weighted average of all of its individual bilateral exchange rates. Changes of the effective exchange rate measure the average change of a country's exchange rate against all foreign currencies. See Rudolf R. Rhomberg, "Indices of Effective Exchange Rates," *International Monetary Fund Staff Papers* 23 (March 1976): 88-112.

63. See above, note 57. For a discussion of some of these arrangements, see Joseph Aschheim and Y. S. Park, *Artificial Currency Units: The Forma-*

tion of Functional Currency Areas, Essays in International Finance, no. 114 (Princeton: International Finance Section, 1976).

64. See, e.g., Alexandre Kafka, "Domestic Adjustment to Balance of Payments Disequilibrium: Discussion," *American Economic Review*, 65 (May 1975): 151-153. But cf. William R. Cline, *International Monetary Reform and the Developing Countries* (Washington, D.C.: Brookings Institution, 1976), chap. 2.

65. Ishiyama, "Theory of Optimum Currency Areas," p. 378.

66. Willett and Tower, "Currency Areas," p. 61. See also Tower and Willett, *Theory*, chap. 7.

67. Conrad J. Oort, *Steps to International Monetary Order* (Washington, D.C.: Per Jacobsson Foundation, 1974), pp. 12-13.

68. Ibid., p. 28.

69. Johnson, "The Case . . . 1969," p. 104. The removal of the one-way option by the move to generalized floating in 1973 helps to explain the subsequent paucity of speculation in the exchange market, as discussed above.

70. Xenophon Zolotas, *Speculocracy and the International Monetary System* (Athens: Bank of Greece, 1969).

71. But cf. Samuel I. Katz, *The Case for the Par-Value System, 1972*, Essays in International Finance, no. 92 (Princeton: International Finance Section, 1972).

72. George N. Halm, *Toward Limited Exchange-Rate Flexibility*, Essays in International Finance, no. 73 (Princeton: International Finance Section, 1969), p. 4; reprinted in Halm, ed., *Bürgenstock Papers*, chap. 1.

73. The name most often associated with the band proposal is George Halm. See, e.g., Halm, *The "Band" Proposal: The Limits of Permissible Exchange Rate Variations*, Special Papers in International Economics, no. 6 (Princeton: International Finance Section, 1965); and ibid.

74. Machlup, "Exchange-Rate Flexibility," 194.

75. *The Role of Exchange Rates in the Adjustment of International Payments: A Report by the Executive Directors* (Washington, D.C.: International Monetary Fund, 1970). Two years later, the attitude of the executive directors on this point was essentially unchanged. See *Reform of the International Monetary System: A Report by the Executive Directors* (Washington, D.C.: International Monetary Fund, 1972). For useful evaluations of these two reports, see George N. Halm, *The International Monetary Fund and Flexibility of Exchange Rates*, Essays in International Finance, no. 83 (Princeton: International Finance Section, 1971); and Halm, "Reforming the Par-Value System," *Weltwirtschaftliches Archiv* 109, Heft 2 (1973): 171-190.

76. See, e.g., George H. Chittenden, "Asymmetrical Widening of the Bands Around Parity," in Halm, ed., *Bürgenstock Papers*, chap. 27.

77. Machlup, "Exchange-Rate Flexibility," 196.

78. The crawling-peg type of proposal also goes under such names as "gliding parity" and "sliding parity." Among its early advocates were James E. Meade, "The International Monetary Mechanism," *Three Banks Review*, September 1964: 3-25; John H. Williamson, *The Crawling Peg*, Essays in International Finance, no. 50 (Princeton: International Finance Section, 1965); and J. Black, "A Proposal for the Reform of Exchange Rates," *Economic Journal* 76 (June 1966): 288-295.

79. But cf. Peter B. Kenen, "Floats, Glides and Indicators: A Comparison of Methods for Changing Exchange Rates," *Journal of International Economics*

5 (May 1975): 107-151; and Donald J. Mathieson, "Is There an Optimal Crawl?" *Journal of International Economics* 6 (May 1976): 183-202.

80. See, e.g., the Bürgenstock Communiqué, issued by a majority of thirty-eight economists attending an international conference on exchange rates in Bürgenstock, Switzerland, in 1969; reprinted in Halm, ed., *Bürgenstock Papers*, pp. vii-viii. For a detailed evaluation of this type of proposal, see Stephen Marris, *The Bürgenstock Communiqué: A Critical Examination of the Case for Limited Flexibility of Exchange Rates*, Essays in International Finance, no. 80 (Princeton: International Finance Section, 1970).

81. Wilfred Ethier and Arthur I. Bloomfield, *Managing the Managed Float*, Essays in International Finance, no. 112 (Princeton: International Finance Section, 1975), p. 8.

82. Alfred Hayes, *Emerging Arrangements in International Payments: Public and Private* (Washington, D.C.: Per Jacobsson Foundation, 1965), p. 5.

83. Lanyi, *Case for Floating Exchange Rates Reconsidered*, p. 24; italics in the original.

84. See Ethier and Bloomfield, *Managing the Managed Float*.

85. Ibid., p. 10.

86. If reference rates are expressed in terms of an effective exchange rates, rather than in terms of a single national currency (such as the dollar), incentives for destabilizing speculation will be even further reduced. Since an effective exchange rate does not translate immediately into market rates for specific currencies, it provides no obvious target for speculators to bet against.

87. Periodic revisions of reference rates could not easily be based on a single objective indicator (such as relative price trends or a moving average of past exchange-rate performance) since any single indicator could be manipulated directly or indirectly by governmental action. A variety of indicators would have to be used in making the requisite judgments. Accordingly, an explicit bargaining process is necessarily implied.

Chapter 6

1. William McChesney Martin, *Toward a World Central Bank?* (Washington, D.C.: Per Jacobsson Foundation, 1970), p. 13.

2. Robert Triffin, *Gold and the Dollar Crisis* (New Haven: Yale University Press, 1960), p. 146. See also his *The World Money Maze: National Currencies in International Payments* (New Haven: Yale University Press, 1966); and *Our International Monetary System: Yesterday, Today, and Tomorrow* (New York: Random House, 1968).

3. To be fair to Triffin, it should be noted that although he advocates this sort of approach to reform, he never explicitly advocates a world central bank as such. What he proposes are simply steps in that direction. Triffin is no political innocent: he is always sufficiently realistic to keep his reform proposals gradualistic and incremental, so that they will be politically convincing and negotiable. But an objective reading of his extensive writings can leave little doubt about the ambitiousness of his ultimate goal. In this sense, it is not unfair to associate his name closely with the case for a world central bank.

4. Triffin, *Our International Monetary System*, pp. 178-179; italics in the original.

5. Erich Fromm, *May Man Prevail?* (New York: Anchor Books, 1961), p. 208, quoted in Triffin, *Our International Monetary System*, p. 75.

6. Ibid., pp. 75-76; italics in the original.

7. Robert O. Keohane, "*International Organization* and the Crisis of Interdependence," *International Organization* 29 (Spring 1975): 363.

8. For a representative sample of such proposals, see below, footnotes 21-25.

9. See, e.g., Edward M. Bernstein, "The Evolution of the International Monetary Fund," A. L. K. Acheson, J. F. Chant, and M. F. J. Prachowny, eds., *Bretton Woods Revisited* (Toronto: University of Toronto Press, 1972), pp. 51-65; and Pierre-Paul Schweitzer, "Political Aspects of Managing the International Monetary System," *International Affairs* 52 (April 1976): 208-218.

10. Lawrence B. Krause and Joseph S. Nye, "Reflection on the Economics and Politics of International Economic Organizations," *International Organization* 29 (Winter 1975): 336.

11. Michele Fratianni and John C. Pattison, "When It Pays to Co-operate," *The Banker* 126 (August 1976): 893.

12. Harry G. Johnson, "A General Commentary," in Acheson, Chant, and Prachowny, *Bretton Woods Revisited*, pp. 131-132.

13. See, e.g., H. H. Schloss, "The Bank for International Settlements," *The Bulletin* (New York University, Graduate School of Business Administration, Institute of Finance), nos. 65-66 (September 1970).

14. Under the original Articles of Agreement, the Fund had to determine the number of elective executive directors. Fifteen came to be traditional. In the Second Amendment to the Articles of Agreement, the number fifteen is incorporated formally. See *Proposed Second Amendment to the Articles of Agreement of the International Monetary Fund: A Report by the Executive Directors* (Washington, D.C.: International Monetary Fund, 1976), Article XII (3). Hereafter referred to as *Second Amendment*.

15. Ibid., Part II, sec. P, ¶ 5.

16. Ibid., Part II, sec. P, ¶ 1, 3, 4.

17. Ibid., schedule D, ¶ 2 (a).

18. In the words of the original IMF Charter: "A change in the par value of a member's currency may be made only on the proposal of the member and only after consultation with the Fund. . . . The Fund may either concur or object" (Articles of Agreement of the International Monetary Fund, Article IV). In practice, because of fears that speculative currency shifts might be provoked by lengthy consultative procedures, governments generally tended simply to alter first and consult later—in effect, merely notifying the Fund of a fait accompli.

19. Fred Hirsch, "The Exchange Rate Regime: An Analysis and a Possible Scheme," *International Monetary Fund Staff Papers* 19 (July 1972): 273. For an interesting variation of Hirsch's proposal, see Henry C. Wallich, *The Monetary Crisis of 1971: The Lessons to Be Learned* (Washington, D.C.: Per Jacobsson Foundation, 1972), pp. 33-40.

20. Ethier and Bloomfield themselves are less insistent about using the IMF forum for this purpose. See Wilfred Ethier and Arthur I. Bloomfield, *Managing the Managed Float*, Essays in International Finance, no. 112 (Princeton: International Finance Section, 1975), p. 15.

21. Among the earliest such figures were Sir Oliver Franks, "Annual Statement to Shareholders of Lloyds Bank" (London, 1958); Sir Maxwell Stamp, "The Fund and the Future," *Lloyds Bank Review*, October 1958; and Triffin, *Gold and the Dollar Crisis*.

22. See, e.g., James W. Angell, "The Organization of the International Monetary System: An Alternative Proposal," *Economic Journal* 71 (December 1961): 691-708.

23. See, e.g., Edward M. Bernstein, "Further Evolution of the International Monetary System," *Moorgate and Wall Street*, Summer 1965, pp. 51-70; and Robert V. Roosa, *Monetary Reform for the World Economy* (New York: Harper and Row, 1965).

24. See, e.g., Sir Maxwell Stamp, "The Stamp Plan—1962 Version," *Moorgate and Wall Street*, Autumn 1962: 5-17.

25. See, e.g., Albert G. Hart, Nicholas Kaldor, and Jan Tinbergen, *The Case for an International Commodity Reserve Currency*, United Nations Conference on Trade and Development, background document, E/conf. 46/P/7 (Geneva 1964). Also, see above, Chapter 2, note 45.

26. Fritz Machlup, *Remaking the International Monetary System* (Baltimore: Johns Hopkins Press, 1968), p. 34.

27. Ibid., p. 65.

28. For detailed explanations, see ibid., esp. chaps. 2-3; and Joseph Gold, *Special Drawing Rights: Character and Use*, 2d ed. (Washington, D.C.: International Monetary Fund, 1970).

29. Following the reforms of the Committee of Twenty and Interim Committee, the SDR replaced the dollar not only in all official exchange-rate quotations but also for a variety of other purposes, such as quotations of worldwide air fares and Suez Canal tolls. In addition, by the end of 1975 the currencies of nine countries were formally pegged to the SDR for intervention purposes. See *IMF Survey*, June 9, 1975, p. 164; and February 2, 1976, p. 35.

30. See, e.g., Fred Hirsch, *An SDR Standard: Impetus, Elements, and Impediments*, Essays in International Finance, no. 99 (Princeton: International Finance Section, 1973).

31. Joseph S. Nye, "Independence and Interdependence," *Foreign Policy*, no. 22 (Spring 1976): 146-147; italics in the original.

32. See Fratianni and Pattison, "When It Pays," 893.

33. The task has not always been performed subtly, and the strong have sometimes been antagonized—as, for example, the United States was antagonized in 1970-1971 when the Managing Director of the Fund, Pierre-Paul Schweitzer, took a strong public stand in favor of the European demand for a devaluation of the dollar. The result was that the United States vetoed Schweitzer's reappointment when his position came up for renewal.

34. Edward M. Bernstein, "The New International Monetary System," in Bernstein et al., *Reflections on Jamaica*, Essays in International Finance, no. 115 (Princeton: International Finance Section, 1976), p. 8.

Chapter 7

1. Emile Despres, Charles P. Kindleberger, and Walter S. Salant, "The Dollar and World Liquidity: A Minority View," *The Economist*, February 5, 1966.

2. Emile Despres, "Statement," in *New Approach to United States International Economic Policy*, Hearings before the Subcommittee on International Exchange and Payments of the Joint Economic Committee of the Congress (Washington, D.C.: 1966), p. 39.

3. Charles P. Kindleberger, *The Politics of International Money and World Language*, Essays in International Finance, no. 61 (Princeton: International Finance Section, 1967), p. 1.

4. Ronald I. McKinnon, *Private and Official International Money: The Case for the Dollar*, Essays in International Finance, no. 74 (Princeton: International Finance Section, 1969), p. 5.

5. Ronald I. McKinnon, *A New Tripartite Monetary Agreement or a Limping Dollar Standard?*, Essays in International Finance, no. 106 (Princeton: International Finance Section, 1974), p. 2; italics in the original.

6. Robert A. Mundell, "Toward a Better International Monetary System," *Journal of Money, Credit and Banking* 1 (August 1969): 644. Mundell's views have changed over the years. In the early 1960s he was an ardent advocate of floating. In the late 1960s he was favorably inclined toward the case for a dollar standard. Today, as indicated in Chapter 5, he has become a convert to the cause of the gold standard.

7. Charles P. Kindleberger, *The World in Depression, 1929-1939* (Berkeley and Los Angeles: University of California Press, 1973), p. 305.

8. Ibid., p. 307; italics in the original.

9. Lawrence B. Krause, "A Passive Balance-of-Payments Strategy for the United States," *Brookings Papers on Economic Activity*, no. 3 (1970): 342.

10. Ibid., 342, 344, 348.

11. Gottfried Haberler and Thomas D. Willett, *A Strategy for U.S. Balance of Payments Policy* (Washington, D.C.: American Enterprise Institute, 1971), p. 15.

12. Mundell, "Toward," 643.

13. McKinnon, *Private and Official International Money*, p. 30.

14. Haberler and Willet, *Strategy*, p. 15; italics in the original.

15. McKinnon, *Private and Official International Money*, p. 30.

16. Stable price performance in this context is defined by Thomas Willett as being equal to the (weighted) average of "desired" rates of inflation in all countries other than the United States. See Thomas D. Willett, "Secular Inflation and the International Monetary System: A Comment," *Journal of Money, Credit and Banking*, 5 (February 1973): 520, note 1.

17. David P. Calleo, "The Decline and Rebuilding of an International Economic System: Some General Considerations," in David P. Calleo, ed., *Money and the Coming World Order* (New York: New York University Press, 1976), p. 50.

18. McKinnon, *New Tripartite Monetary Agreement*, p. 4.

19. Charles P. Kindleberger, "Systems of International Economic Organization," in Calleo, ed., *Money and the Coming World Order*, p. 38.

20. Kindleberger, *Politics of International Money*, pp. 6-7. But cf. "The Euro-Dollar and the Internationalization of United States Monetary Policy," *Banca Nazionale del Lavoro Quarterly Review* 22 (1969): 11-15.

21. See Mundell, "Toward," 643. See also "The Future of the International Financial System," in A. L. K. Acheson, J. F. Chant, and M. F. J. Prachowny, eds., *Bretton Woods Revisited* (Toronto: University of Toronto Press, 1972), p. 100.

22. Ibid.

23. McKinnon, *New Tripartite Monetary Agreement*, p. 2.

24. Ernest Mandel, *Decline of the Dollar: A Marxist View of the Monetary Crisis* (New York: Monad Press, 1972), p. 114.

25. J. B. Crotty and L. A. Rapping, "The 1975 Report of the President's Council of Economic Advisers: A Radical Critique," *American Economic Review* 65 (December 1975): 798-799. Crotty and Rapping are obviously more impressed by the conflictual than the consensual element in international monetary relations.

26. See, e.g., Charles P. Kindleberger, "The International Monetary Politics of a Near-Great Power: Two French Episodes, 1926-1936 and 1960-1970," *Economic Notes* 1 (May-December 1972): 30-41; and Judith L. Kooker, "French Financial Diplomacy: The Interwar Years," in Benjamin M. Rowland, ed., *Balance of Power or Hegemony: The Interwar Monetary System* (New York: New York University Press, 1976), pp. 84-145.

27. See Kindleberger, *Politics of International Money*, p. 2. For a representative example of such French objections, see Michel Debré, "La monnaie du bon plaisir," *Le Monde*, January 28, 1976, p. 1. Robert Mundell has suggested (not convincingly) that such "psychological" objections could perhaps be satisfied by changing the name of the dollar standard to "Jeurodollar standard." See Mundell "Toward," 645.

28. John Williamson, *The Choice of a Pivot for Parities*, Essays in International Finance, no. 90 (Princeton: International Finance Section, 1971), pp. 10, 13-14.

29. An exception is Kindleberger, who writes: "Considerations of prestige partly govern United States policies with regard to international monetary reform. My reason for wanting to keep the dollar-exchange standard is efficiency, but I suspect that many Americans take the same position for reasons of prestige." Kindleberger, *Politics of International Money*, p. 4.

30. See David P. Calleo, "American Foreign Policy and American European Studies: An Imperial Bias?" in Wolfram F. Hanrieder, ed., *The United States and Western Europe: Political, Economic and Strategic Perspectives* (Cambridge, Mass.: Winthrop, 1974), pp. 56-78.

31. Susan Strange, *Sterling and British Policy* (London: Oxford University Press, 1971), p. 39.

32. Kindleberger, *Politics of International Money*, p. 1.

33. F. Boyer de la Giroday, *Myths and Reality in the Development of International Monetary Affairs*, Essays in International Finance, no. 105 (Princeton: International Finance Section, 1974), p. 4.

34. Kindleberger, *World in Depression*, p. 292.

35. See Benjamin J. Cohen, *The Future of Sterling as an International Currency* (London: Macmillan, 1971), pp. 65-68.

36. Susan Strange has tried to capture some of this complexity in what she calls a "political theory of international currencies" (which is not really a theory at all but merely a typology). She distinguishes four different types of international currency: (1) the *Top Currency*—the currency of the predominant state in the international economy (examples: sterling in the nineteenth century, the dollar in the twentieth); (2) *Master Currencies*—currencies that emerge when an imperial power imposes the use of its money on political dependencies (examples: sterling in the sterling area, the franc in the French franc zone); (3) *Negotiated Currencies*—what Master Currencies become when

the dominance of the imperial power begins to weaken, and inducements must be substituted for coercion to encourage holders to continue using them (examples: sterling in the latter stages of the sterling area, the dollar in the 1960s); and (4) *Neutral Currencies*–currencies whose use originates in the strong economic position of the issuing state, not necessarily one of hegemonic leadership but nevertheless inspiring confidence (examples: the Swiss franc, the Deutsche mark, to a lesser extent the yen). See Strange, *Sterling and British Policy*, chap. 1; and "The Politics of International Currencies," *World Politics* 23 (January 1971): 215-231.

37. Peter B. Kenen, "Reforming the Monetary System–You Can't Get There From Here," *Euromoney*, October 1974, p. 22. See also Kindleberger, "Systems," in Calleo, ed., *Money*, p. 31; and Calleo, "The Decline and Rebuilding of an International Economic System," in ibid., p. 49.

38. Robert Z. Aliber, *Monetary Reform and World Inflation*, The Washington Papers, vol. 1 (Beverly Hills and London: Sage Publications, 1973), p. 39.

39. Charles P. Kindleberger, "The Dollar–Yesterday, Today, and Tomorrow," in Jules Backman and Ernest Bloch, eds., *Multinational Corporations, Trade and the Dollar* (New York: New York University Press, 1974), pp. 32, 37. See also his "Systems of International Economic Organization," in Calleo, ed., *Money*, p. 35.

40. International Monetary Fund, *Annual Report 1975* (Washington, 1975), p. 35.

41. See, e.g., Marina v. N. Whitman, "The Current and Future Role of the Dollar: How Much Symmetry?" *Brookings Papers on Economic Activity*, no. 3 (1974): 555-570.

42. J. Marcus Fleming, "Floating Exchange Rates, Asymmetrical Intervention, and the Management of International Liquidity," *International Monetary Fund Staff Papers* 22 (July 1975): 267.

43. Richard N. Cooper, "The Future of the Dollar," in Cooper, ed., *A Reordered World: Emerging International Economic Problems* (Washington, D.C.: Potomac Associates, 1973), p. 76.

44. See Cohen, *Future of Sterling*, p. 27.

45. Ibid.

46. Robert A. Mundell, "The Santa Colomba Conclusions 1975," *Economic Notes* 3 (September-December 1974): 32.

47. Boyer de la Giroday, *Myths and Reality*, pp. 13-14.

48. See, e.g., Richard N. Cooper, "Eurodollars, Reserve Dollars, and Asymmetries in the International Monetary System," *Journal of International Economics* 2 (1972): 325-344.

49. Mundell, "Future of the International Financial System," in Acheson, Chant, and Prachowny, eds., *Bretton Woods*, pp. 99-100.

50. Harry G. Johnson, "Political Economy Aspects of International Monetary Reform," *Journal of International Economics* 2 (1972): 404.

51. Cooper, "Eurodollars," 344.

52. C. Fred Bergsten, *Reforming the Dollar: An International Monetary Policy for the United States* (New York: Council on Foreign Relations, 1972), p. 5. But cf. his *Dilemmas of the Dollar* (New York: Council on Foreign Relations, 1975), pp. 93-95, 399-407.

53. Joseph S. Nye, "Independence and Interdependence," *Foreign Policy*, no. 22 (Spring 1976): 145.

54. Robert Z. Aliber, *National Preferences and the Scope for International Monetary Reform*, Essays in International Finance, no. 101 (Princeton: Inter-

national Finance Section, 1973), p. 9. Aliber probably borrowed this expression from old-fashioned metallic-money discussions, which used the phrase "limping standard" to describe a nominally bimetallic standard in which, for example, the silver component was frozen but the gold component was left free to change.

55. Marina v. N. Whitman, "Leadership Without Hegemony," *Foreign Policy*, no. 20 (Fall 1975): 138-160.

56. The question of gold will be dealt with below.

57. But cf. Friederich Lutz, *The Problem of International Equilibrium* (Amsterdam: North-Holland Publishing Co., 1962); and *The Problem of International Liquidity and the Multiple-Currency Standard*, Essays in International Finance, no. 41 (Princeton: International Finance Section, 1963).

58. Bergsten, *Reforming the Dollar*, pp. 10-11. See also his *Dilemmas of the Dollar*, pp. 482-487.

59. For some discussion, see, e.g., Raymond F. Mikesell, *Financing World Trade: An Appraisal of the International Monetary System and of Proposals for Reform* (New York: Crowell, 1969), pp. 81-82, 86-87.

60. Peter B. Kenen, "Floats, Glides and Indicators: A Comparison of Methods for Changing Exchange Rates," *Journal of International Economics* 5 (May 1975): 128. The U.S. reserve-indicator proposal embodied a reserve-level rule. For similar earlier proposals, see Franco Modigliani and Peter B. Kenen, "A Suggestion for Solving the International Liquidity Problem," *Banca Nazionale del Lavoro Quarterly Review* 19 (1966): 3-17; and Robert Triffin, "International Adjustment: Issues and Options," in Randall Hinshaw, ed., *The Economics of International Adjustment* (Baltimore: John Hopkins Press, 1971), pp. 18-22. For an early version of a reserve-rate rule, see Richard N. Cooper, "Sliding Parities: A Proposal for Presumptive Rules," in George N. Halm, ed., *Approaches to Greater Flexibility of Exchange Rates: The Bürgenstock Papers* (Princeton: Princeton University Press, 1970), pp. 251-259.

61. For two views of this idea, see Edward M. Bernstein, "The New International Monetary System," and Nurul Islam, "Jamaica and the Developing Countries," both in Edward M. Bernstein et al., *Reflections on Jamaica*, Essays in International Finance, no. 115 (Princeton: International Finance Section, 1976), pp. 5, 17.

62. See Weir M. Brown, *World Afloat: National Policies Ruling the Waves*, Essays in International Finance, no. 116 (Princeton: International Finance Section, 1976), pp. 1-7.

Chapter 8

1. The following discussion is based mainly on interviews conducted in Europe and North America while this book was in progress.

2. But cf. the writings of David P. Calleo, e.g., his "American Foreign Policy and American European Studies: An Imperial Bias?" in Wolfram F. Hanrieder, ed., *The United States and Western Europe: Political, Economic and Strategic Perspectives* (Cambridge, Mass.: Winthrop, 1974), pp. 56-78; "The Historiography of the Interwar Period: Reconsiderations," in Benjamin

M. Rowland, ed., *Balance of Power or Hegemony: The Interwar Monetary System* (New York: New York University Press, 1976), pp. 229-260; and "The Decline and Rebuilding of an International Economic System: Some General Considerations," in Calleo, ed., *Money and the Coming World Order* (New York: New York University Press, 1976), pp. 41-69. Calleo is an ardent advocate of a "pluralistic" or "balance-of-power" approach to the organization of international monetary relations. Usually his arguments are posed in contrast to the case for hegemony as an organizing principle.

3. See, e.g., Stephen D. Cohen, *International Monetary Reform, 1964-69: The Political Dimension* (New York: Praeger, 1970); and Robert W. Russell, "Transgovernmental Interaction in the International Monetary System, 1960-1972," *International Organization* 27 (Autumn 1973): 431-464.

4. Miriam Camps, *"First World" Relationships: The Role of the OECD* (Paris and New York: Atlantic Institute for International Affairs and Council on Foreign Relations, 1975), p. 20; italics in the original.

5. Robert O. Keohane and Joseph S. Nye, "World Politics and the International Economic System," in C. Fred Bergsten, ed., *The Future of the International Economic Order: An Agenda for Research* (Lexington, Mass.: D. C. Heath, 1973), p. 134; and Harold van Buren Cleveland, "Modes of International Economic Organization: A Stalemate System," in Calleo, ed., *Money*, pp. 1-14.

6. See Mancur Olson, *The Logic of Collective Action* (Cambridge, Mass.: Harvard University Press, 1965).

7. Charles P. Kindleberger, "The International Monetary Politics of a Near-Great Power: Two French Episodes, 1926-1936 and 1960-1970," *Economic Notes* 1, nos. 2-3 (1972): 31.

8. See, e.g., Richard N. Cooper, "Prolegomena to the Choice of an International Monetary System," *International Organization* 29 (Winter 1975): 93-95.

9. See, e.g., John Williamson, *The Failure of World Monetary Reform, 1971-74* (London: Thomas Nelson, 1977).

10. C. Fred Bergsten, "The United States and Germany: The Imperative of Economic Bigemony," in Bergsten, *Toward a New International Economic Order: Selected Papers of C. Fred Bergsten, 1972-1974* (Lexington, Mass.: D. C. Heath, 1975), chap. 23. The quotation is from p. 333. See also Kiyoshi Kojima, "A Competitive Bipolar Key Currency System," *Hitotsubashi Journal of Economics* 17 (June 1976): 1-8.

11. Ronald I. McKinnon, *A New Tripartite Monetary Agreement or a Limping Dollar Standard?*, Essays in International Finance, no. 106 (Princeton: International Finance Section, 1974).

12. See, e.g., Miriam Camps, *The Management of Interdependence: A Preliminary View* (New York: Council on Foreign Relations, 1974), especially pp. 44-49, 54-55.

13. Giovanni Magnifico, "The European and International Currency Problem," in Harry G. Johnson, ed., *The New Mercantilism* (Oxford: Basil Blackwell, 1974), p. 146; italics in the original.

14. See, e.g., Harold van Buren Cleveland, "How the Dollar Standard Died," in Richard N. Cooper, ed., *A Reordered World: Emerging International Economic Problems* (Washington, D.C.: Potomac Associates, 1973), pp. 65-74; and "Modes of International Economic Organization," in ibid., pp. 1-14. See also David P. Calleo, "The Decline and Rebuilding of an International Economic System," in ibid., pp. 41-69.

15. See *Proposed Second Amendment to the Articles of Agreement of the International Monetary Fund: A Report by the Executive Directors* (Washington, D.C.: International Monetary Fund, 1976), Part II, sec. N, ¶ 4. Under the original Articles of Agreement, the voting requirement for amendments was an 80 percent weighted majority. In three exceptional cases, unanimity has traditionally been required for amendment.

Chapter 9

1. Peter B. Kenen, "Reforming the Monetary System—You Can't Get There from Here," *Euromoney*, October 1974, pp. 21-22.

2. Richard N. Cooper, "Prolegomena to the Choice of an International Monetary System," *International Organization* 29 (Winter 1975): 96. See also Andrew Shonfield, "International Economic Relations of the Western World: An Overall View," in Shonfield, ed., *International Economic Relations of the Western World, 1959-1971*. Vol 1: *Politics and Trade* (London: Oxford University Press, 1976), pp. 130-137.

3. John Williamson, "The Benefits and Costs of an International Monetary System," in Edward M. Bernstein et al., *Reflections on Jamaica*, Essays in International Finance, no. 115 (Princeton: International Finance Section, 1976), p. 56.

4. Fred Hirsch, "Is There a New International Economic Order?", *International Organization* 30 (Summer 1976): 531.

5. Kenen, "Reforming the Monetary System," p. 22.

Index